SOLDIERS' STORIES

A COLLECTION OF WWII MEMOIRS

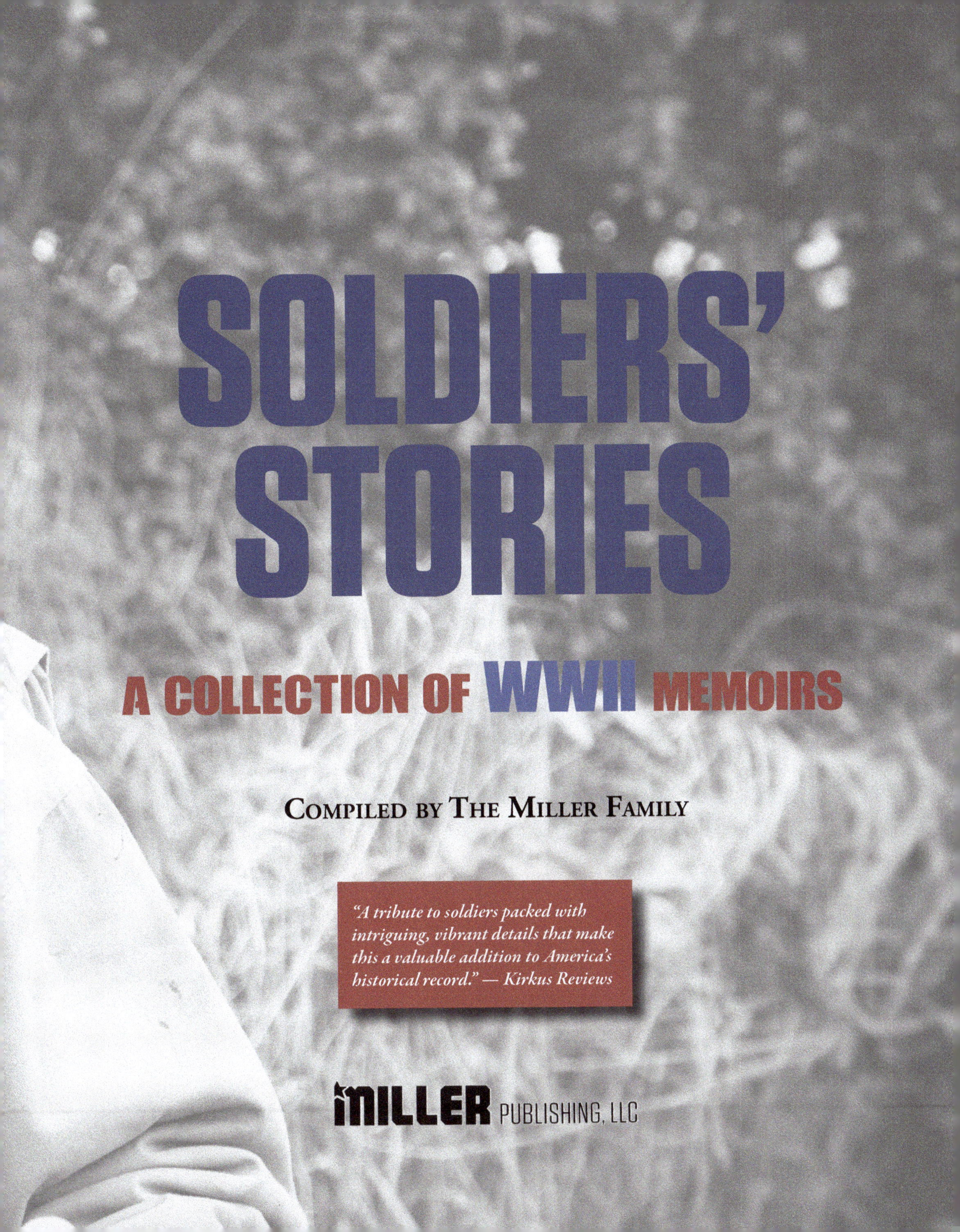

SOLDIERS' STORIES

A COLLECTION OF WWII MEMOIRS

Compiled by The Miller Family

> *"A tribute to soldiers packed with intriguing, vibrant details that make this a valuable addition to America's historical record."* — Kirkus Reviews

MILLER PUBLISHING, LLC

SOLDIERS' STORIES: A Collection of WWII Memoirs

Copyright © 2016 by Miller Publishing, LLC
The Miller Family
With Myra Miller, PhD and Ken Miller, Del Miller, Marshall Miller, Lynette Miller Ballard

All rights reserved.

No part of this book may be reproduced, scanned, transmitted, or distributed in any form by any means, electronic or mechanical, including photocopying, recording, or by any information storage and retrieval system, without specific written permission from the publisher. The scanning, uploading, and distribution of this book via the Internet or via any other means without the permission of the publisher is illegal and punishable by law. Please purchase only authorized electronic editions, and do not participate in or encourage electronic piracy of copyrighted materials.

All stories submitted are memories and recollection of events. No factual research has been done to confirm the validity or accuracy of the stories compiled in this book. Photographs were reprinted with permission by the story submitters and photo credit was given if source was known. All story submitters were given an opportunity to approve their page(s) prior to printing.

For additional copies of the book, go to www.footstepsresearchers.com

Miller Publishing LLC
St. Louis, Missouri
www.footstepsresearchers.com

Library of Congress Number: 2017930350

Editors: Lynette Miller Ballard and Jane Roth

Cover and Book Design: Myra Miller
Cover and Book Illustrations: Ken Miller
Cover Photography: Spoonful of Sugar Photography
Interior Reenactor Photographs: Antony Burch Photography

ISBN: 978-0-9987318-4-1 (hardcover)
ISBN: 978-0-9987318-5-8 (paperback)

First Edition: December 2016
Second Edition: January 2017
Third Edition: February 2018
10 9 8 7 6 5 4 3

Printed in the United States of America

Table of Contents

Introduction, Coming Home	vii
The Book	viii
Acknowledgements	xi
James R. Hickey	1
George R. Young	2
Arlie Rounds, Sr.	5
Roy Boggs, Sr.	6
Maxine Boggs	7
Roy and Maxine Boggs	8
Thomas Schneider	9
Jack Port	10
Harry L. Smith, Jr.	12
John A. Wood, Jr.	14
Myron H. Miller, Boxing	17
James M. Enmeier	18
Ralph M. Rickerson	20
Orlan J. Thornton	22
James E. Goff	24
Three Brave Veterans	25
Eugene Harmack	
Emil Perko	
Vinson and Flo Freeman	
Clyde F. Shindledecker	26
Myron H. Miller, Holocaust	29
Norvel A. McDonald	30
Ernest E. Cowherd	31
Clarence M. Taylor	32
Henry C. Oehmen	34
Robert D. McNulty	36
Charles E. Pennebaker	37
John F. St. Clair	38
Robert J. Byron	40
Eugene J. Denis	41
Joseph E. Ehmet	43
Morris W. "Lefty" Martin	44
William R. Ransdall	47
Millard H. Hauck	48
The Hauck Brothers	49
William I. Long	51
Georges Frederickx	52
Daniel W. Halladay	54
Edward "Ned" Burr	56
Wilburn C. Rowden	58
Alva West	62
Ethmer West	64
Frank C. Mills	66
Myron H. Miller, Patton	70
Normand R. Malo	72
William G. Jones	76
Thomas L. McHugh	77

Everett C. Deger	80
Marion B. Cooper	81
Myron H. Miller, Short Stories	82
Brigitte Bresser	84
James P. Garrett	88
Russell L. Armontrout	89
Normandy Map	90
Operation Dragoon Map	92
Franklin P. Curtiss	94
Myron H. Miller, Raymond Barnes	99
Joseph B. Jenkins	101
John C. Crews	102
Eugene Harmack	107
Tribute Team - Western Europe	108
Harry J. Kirby	110
Delmer R. Beam	112
Everett E. "Bud" Wilkinson	116
Floyd W. "Bill" Shely, Jr "	119
David Curry	120
Thomas D. Curry	121
David V. Foley	126
William S. "Bill" Spriggs	128
John E. Carroll	135
Myron H. Miller, P47s	137
Virgil W. Slade	138
Carroll O. Turner	146
Stanley P. Bielen	148
Joannes Jo. "Seppe" Op De Beeck	154
Frank A. Klepper	157
Marvin J. Schaeffer	158
Andre G. Beaumont	160
Aloysius "Al" Klugiewicz	163
Robert F. Kauffman	164
Myron H. Miller, My Grandpa	169
Letters from My Uncles	170
James F. Faber	172
Richard J. "Dick" Coyle	174
Alphonse Monfort	176
Jennings E. Barnett	180
William A. "Bill" Geppert, Jr.	182
Company K/331st - Honor Page	185
Roy "Bud" Mensing	186
Eugene J. Godin	188
Raymond H. Peloquin	191
Myron H. Miller, My Daddy	196
James F."Mac" McNabb	198
Army Buddies - Mac and Bud	202
Harold L. "Bud" Merrill	204
Dolores J. Gates Miller	206
Erich Anschutz	208

Virgil D. Mulford	210
Wilder C. Mathena	212
George E. Dosch	216
Robert A. Mitchell	220
George P. Terhanko	224
Lawrence L. Chittenden	228
Myron H. Miller, Short Stories	232
Claude K. Roberts	234
Robert C. Fergusson	237
Charles T. Davis, Sr.	238
Kenneth Moore	243
Hubert D. Kline	244
Richard Fazzio	246
Frank J. Horvath	248
William Allen	252
Ralph E. Withers	256
Dalton L. Clark	258
James W. Stokes	259
George F. Studor	260
John G. "Mac" McNamara	264
Anne R. McClure McNamara	266
Myron H. Miller, Short Stories	274
T. S. Thomason	275
Jess F. "Jay" Dudley	276
Jess and Winifred Dudley	279
Winifred "Wee WAC" Dudley	280
Bottisham Airfield Museum	282
Charles E. Rudler	284
Charles E. Harold	285
Luther A. Riddle	285
Everett "Smitty" Smith	286
Myron H. Miller, Candy Bar	289
Henry I. Tannenbaum	290
Gervis H. Kesten	292
James J. Whetton	296
Special Tribute to Men after WWII	300
Harold D. Peterson	
Robert L. Sooter	
Walter Dickens	
Irvin "Bud" Jenkins	
Paul Wohnhas	
Frank E. Ballard	
Boyd H. Miller	
Myron C. Gates	
Rector K. Gates	
Conrad L. Gates	
In the Footsteps - The Journey	303
Epilogue	318
An Artist's View	319
Index and Photo Credits	322

* Index, alphabetical by soldier, page 322.

Above: At family home in Dixon, Missouri, prior to leaving for the war c. 1942; Myron H. Miller with Uncle Lee and little brother Boyd Miller.

Right: Peaceful days on the farm after the war, c. 1946; Myron with baby sister Paula Miller Lindenlaub and Boyd Miller.

Introduction
Coming Home
as told by Boyd Miller to Jane Ballard Roth

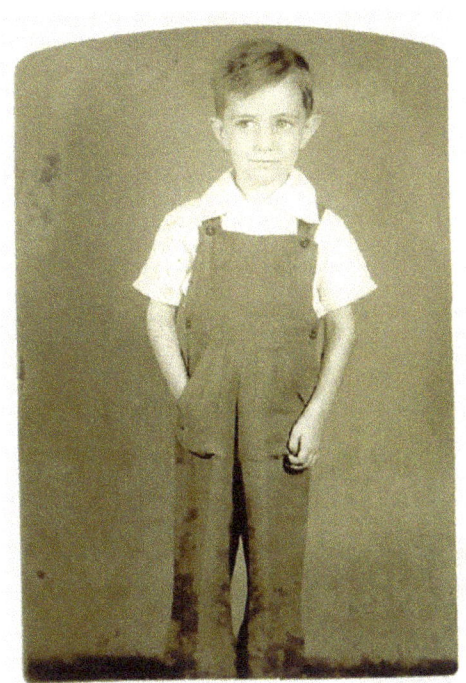

"ON NOVEMBER 14 OF 1945 when my brother returned from the War, I was five years old, and he was 27. Three days earlier, he had arrived back in the U.S. after serving a year and a half in the European Theatre Campaign, and somehow (we didn't have a telephone) he got word to us that he would be home in a few days. My mom channeled her nervous excitement into preparing all of his favorite foods—fried chicken, biscuits, mashed potatoes and gravy, apple pie for dessert. On the day he was to arrive, mine was the impatient anticipation of a little kid, asking when, when, when all day long.

"When bedtime rolled around and he still wasn't home, I was sent upstairs, where instead of going to sleep, I stared out of the window of the front bedroom into the darkness, waiting. I must have dozed off because I woke up to a commotion on the landing at the top of the stairs. I stumbled out of the bedroom stunned to see a big, tall, strong, magnificent soldier in uniform —my brother was home. The first thing he did was bend down to pick me up and hug me tight. He smelled like travel: he had been on a train from New Jersey to St. Louis and then somehow made it the last 100 miles from Jefferson Barracks to our farm in Dixon, Missouri.

"We went down to the dining room to eat and talk. My brother drank the biggest glass of milk you've ever seen and ate biscuit after biscuit, smothered in butter and jelly. 'That didn't come out even; I'd better have another one,' he joked as he buttered another biscuit. The grown-ups talked late into the night and let me stay up as long as I could. I was desperate to get some attention out of him and to pacify me, he cleaned out his wallet—brown leather, smooth with handling—and gave it to me. I couldn't leave his side, and my hand stayed on his knee until they finally made me go to bed."

The Book

The Miller Siblings' story written by Jane Ballard Roth

WE GREW UP HEARING the story of our father's homecoming filtered through the eyes of our Uncle Boyd's childlike awe. Our father's medals hung above the fireplace, and in that sense, his experience of the war was always with us. But he never mentioned it unless we thought to ask questions, which we didn't very often, being caught up in our daily affairs. Because of our ages (and our genders), the questions we asked were different, and so we each glimpsed a different facet of his experience and held notions of him as a soldier differently in our imaginations.

Moreover, our father presented a sort of contradiction: we knew him as a soft-spoken farmer, but we also knew that he had been a soldier. He had fought and suffered and likely killed. People said he was a hero, but what did that mean? Volunteering to fight? Enduring terrible conditions? Killing the enemy? When our middle brother Del was just a kid—maybe seven or so, just old enough to envision our dad as a battle-hardened hero, he asked a seemingly easy question of him, "Did you ever shoot anybody?" He looked at his little boy for just a second and then said, "I don't know, I always closed my eyes."

Even at that young age, Del recognized that the answer seemed suspicious, and it opened his eyes to the fact that being a hero was, perhaps, a more complicated affair than he had been given to understand. Years later, at our father's funeral, it was talking to people who had gone to high school with him that began to sharpen our focus. They described our father, that soft-spoken farmer, as someone who had been a tough guy and a fighter—until he returned from the war. Which one was he really? And what did it take for him to change? How could we begin to answer these questions?

Sparked by watching a documentary on World War II, Myra (the baby of the family, who had never thought to ask her own questions of our dad) started working to discover the facts of his service in Europe. Through Facebook, she soon made friends with historians in France and Germany who brought forth even greater discoveries about our father's history.

Like so many other veterans of that war, our dad had spoken very little of his experiences, mostly sharing short humorous bits and almost nothing about combat. The more we unearthed about the details of his experience, the more we were drawn into the challenge of detective work. Through our efforts and those of our new friends, we discovered the rich history of the 83rd Infantry Division, the Thunderbolt, and in particular the 331st Infantry Regiment.

It was Myra who determined that we must go to Europe to retrace our father's footsteps. Just a few months later, four of us landed in France to follow his route. Our experiences and the people we met along the way inspired this book project, which we conceived of as an opportunity to allow other families to share stories of what their own fathers and grandfathers did in WWII. From the outset, we knew that we would need the stories of many other soldiers, and we set out on a campaign to include others in helping us make this project a success. We soon discovered that it was a very common, almost universal fact that WWII veterans spoke so little of their time at war. That realization compelled us to gather these stories together before the memories are lost to time. Thus, *Soldiers' Stories* was born.

Our journey took us to Omaha Beach, Sainteny, St. Malo, the Ardennes, Luxembourg, the Hurtgen Forest, Remagen, and other places. We saw the beaches, the hedgerows, the city streets, and the towering forests that had been the scenes of terrible suffering and fighting over seventy years ago. We experienced first hand the grateful memories of French, Belgians, and Germans who were there then and the appreciation of a new generation for what those soldiers did to free Europe of tyranny.

While our father may have inspired this book, the collection of stories and images draws on the experience of many Americans who sacrificed so much for the sake of our country and its citizens. Reading their stories has helped us understand that heroes are people who allow themselves to be changed to affect the greater good. We intend for this book to honor the sacrifices those brave men and women and their families made for the sake of our nation, and we hope that it can do a small part in helping future generations appreciate our shared heritage.

The Miller Siblings:
Myra Miller
Ken Miller
Del Miller
Marshall Miller
Lynette Miller Ballard

Acknowledgments

OUR MOST SINCERE THANKS go to the many backers who contributed resources and stories to get the project started, and of course to our great friends in Europe: Jean Paul Pitou; Glyn, Elaine, Sam, and Ben Nightingale; Antoine Noslier; Gilles Billion; Willem and Vera Doms; Eddy Monfort; Eric, Nelly, and Jelle Thys; Robert Hellweg; and David Pratt. They led us on our journey of discovery, welcoming us into their homes and sharing their passion for history with us.

Without the help of Robert McNabb, we would not have found all of the stories honoring our father's buddies from the 83rd, K/331. We truly are grateful to Bob, his enthusiasm, and efforts to include the men of Company K. His extra help reviewing pages and providing solid input was instrumental in creating a quality book honoring our WWII veterans.

We would like to thank our book reviewers and additional editors: Ron Smith, Carol Turner, Michele Broxton, Tina Sterling, and Sonya Renee for their truthful opinions. Your keen eyes and unwavering support are truly appreciated.

To our friend and biggest fan in Woonsocket, Rhode Island, many thanks to Gene Peloquin for cheering us on from afar, providing stories, and being our designated first book reviewer!

NEVER FOUND

James R. Hickey, PFC, 16 INF 1 DIV, Dixon, Missouri

Name Engraved on Wall at Colleville-Sur-Mer, France

GEORGE R. YOUNG, PVT

83RD INFANTRY DIVISION, K/331ST, EUROPEAN THEATER

Submitted by Aaron Young, Grandson

GEORGE R. YOUNG, MY grandfather, never spoke about his service in the Army during WWII, not even to my father. I tried to ask him about it once. I waited until I thought he was in a good mood before I brought up the subject, but once I asked, he became very quiet. He seemed to look through me and said quietly, "Buddy, I just don't want to go back there." That was the extent of my conversation with him. I never brought it up again. It wasn't until his death in February 2010, that his story could be explored. After six years of research, we have learned much about his service. However, there is still so much more to discover.

George was living in Rosedale, Indiana when he entered the service on February 17, 1943. He registered as being an asbestos worker. It's not clear exactly where he went from there; however, through photographs found following his death, we have concluded that at one point he was with the 114th Infantry Regiment, 44th Infantry Division at Fort Lewis, Washington. Also, at some point, George had received paratrooper training from the Army Parachute School.

On June 16, 1944, George departed for England, arriving twelve days later. Less than a month later, on July 21, George joined Company K, 331st Infantry Regiment of the 83rd "Thunderbolt" Division in Sainteny, France as a replacement. The 83rd had suffered large casualties during their push through the hedgerows from Carentan to Sainteny. George was one of 63 men to join Company K that day.

George, and the rest of Company K were deployed near the village of Auxais, France, just west of the La Varde peninsula of the Taute River.

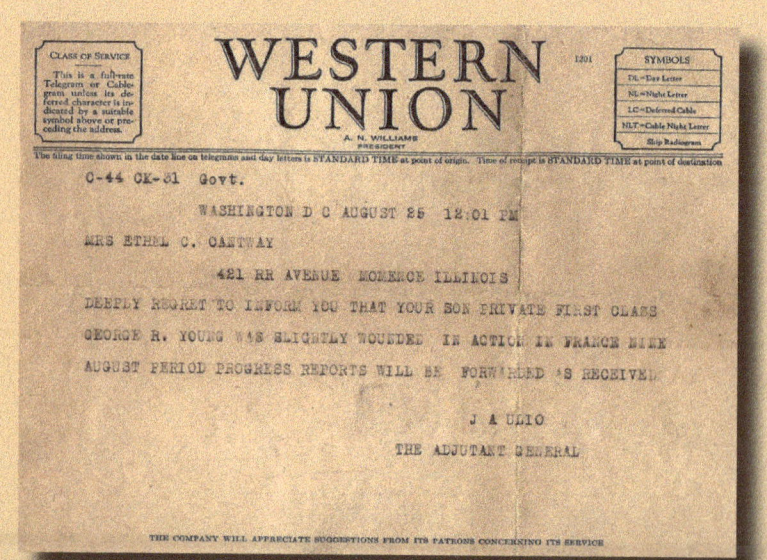

On July 25, just a few miles to the east, Operation Cobra began with "intense aerial bombardment." The next day, the 331st attacked and was slowed by numerous "S" mines, machine guns, pill boxes, and enemy tanks.

On July 27, after the Germans had retreated, the 331st advanced south through Les Alouettes, Feugères, and Le Cardonniere, and ended in the area of Le Comprond where they set up defensive positions.

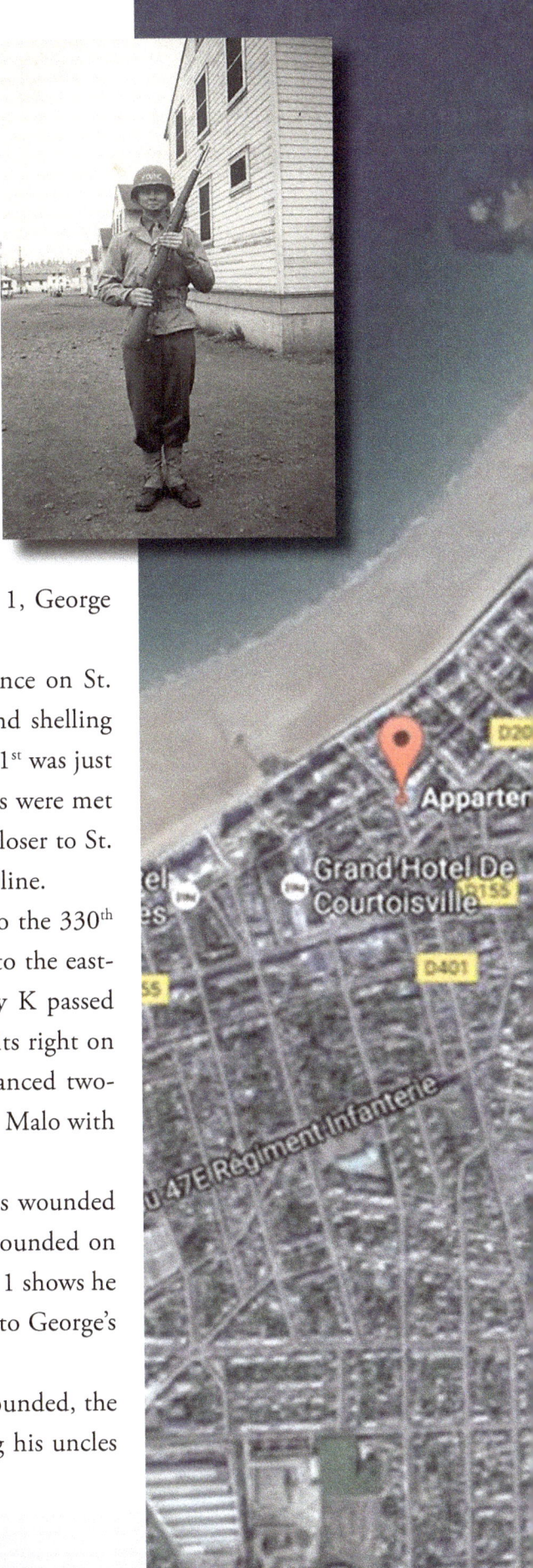

In early August, the 331st moved from Le Comprond, France, to Pontorson and occupied a line from Mont-Dol north to the coast in preparation to advance on St. Malo, France. On August 1, George received a promotion to Private First Class.

On August 5, the 83rd Division began its advance on St. Malo. Initially, they encountered light resistance and shelling from gun positions at Cancale. By midnight, the 331st was just south of Saint-Méloir-des-Ondes. The next two days were met with increasingly heavy fire as the division pushed closer to St. Malo and cleared the area to the east along the coastline.

On August 8, Company K/331st was attached to the 330th Regiment as they advanced through Paramé and into the eastern outskirts of St. Malo. On August 9, Company K passed through Company I and advanced southwest with its right on the waterfront. By nightfall, Company K had advanced two-thirds of the way across the causeway connecting St. Malo with the Citadel.

At some point during August 8 – 9, George was wounded by sniper fire. His discharge papers show he was wounded on August 8. However, the morning report on August 11 shows he was evacuated as of August 9. Also, a telegram sent to George's mother also states he was wounded August 9.

Since George never spoke about how he was wounded, the story of events is taken from my father overhearing his uncles talking about it.

The story is that George and his buddy came to a bridge abutment. When he looked around the abutment, he was shot. He stumbled into the road where he was hit again and presumably killed. George immediately ran out to get his buddy and was shot by a sniper from the second floor of a nearby building. George was shot through his left arm and into his abdomen. He was left for dead by at least two medics. When another medic was checking him, he discovered George was still alive and evacuated him to the 53rd Field Hospital.

From there, he went through a series of hospitals. As of October 10, 1944, he was at the 156th General Hospital in England. He returned to the United States on October 28, 1944. After recovering, he was finally discharged on June 15, 1945, at Camp Ellis, Illinois.

After the war, he married Ella DuCharme and lived in the Chicago area until his death in 2010. He and Ella had two children and five grandchildren.

ARLIE ROUNDS, SR.

USS Pres. Jackson, U.S. Navy, Pacific Theater

Submitted By Rick Rounds, Son

ARLIE ROUNDS, SR., UNDERAGE and seventeen, joined the U.S. Navy in August 1944. His first duty was at Camp Shoemaker, San Diego, California. His initial assignment was to guard prisoners of war for eighteen days. He served on the *USS President Jackson* class armed transport ship in the Pacific. Arlie was shipped out from Treasure Island and participated in the invasion of Iwo Jima. In November of 1944, his ship was en route to Bougainville Island with reinforcements when it was hit by three kamikazes and one 550-pound bomb, which did not explode. The marines on board rolled the bomb off of the ship and into the ocean.

Born in Grantsville, Maryland, Arlie had seven brothers, all of whom served in WWII. Ten members of the Rounds' immediate family have served in the military. Rick, retired from military service, credits his father for instilling the love of country and pride in service to his entire family. Arlie shared with his family that his favorite destination was the Philippines.

In 2002, Rick ordered miniatures of his dad's medals and presented them to Arlie as a gift which brought tears to his eyes. Soon after receiving the medals, he passed away.

ROY BOGGS, SR.

Gunnery Instructor, Army Air Corps, USA

Submitted by Jason Miller, Grandson

MYRON MILLER, WHOSE FEW stories were the idea behind this book, is my "Grandpa." I didn't get the chance to know him well. I was five when he passed away, but I've always been proud of who he was and what he did. History is important in my family, and he had a role in it that I call upon when I teach History to my high-school students. I like to capitalize it to emphasize the importance and the broad scope History encompasses. Lower-case history might be "stuff that happened in the past," but History is our interpretation of it, and those things that have deep meaning to us culturally.

Roy Boggs is my "Granddad." He also played a role in History, although a different one than Grandpa. Granddad also served during World War II, but he ended up staying stateside, which is why his stories are fascinating as well. The way he tells it, he sort of walked into his role and was chosen out of luck, but I think there was a fair amount of leadership that his superiors saw in him that got him assigned to his role as a teacher in the Army Air Corps.

He grew up on a farm in mid-Missouri, just like my other grandfather, and ended up being the right age to join up when the war came. After completing basic training and moving around the country a few times, he ended up on bases in New York City, Biloxi, and San Antonio, where he trained other men how to fire the machine guns that bristled from the noses, sides, and bellies of the big bombers. As a kid who grew up in north St. Louis County, near the McDonnell-Douglas plant where jets flew low over my backyard on a weekly basis, military aircraft have always excited me, and to know that Granddad flew on those antique B-17s when they weren't antique, but were a vital component of the war effort, gave me an immense amount of pride.

To have two grandparents who served during World War II, probably the most romanticized of conflicts in our History, is something that makes me proud. They had very different jobs, but both were important and highlight the fact that everyone has a different, but vital, role to play, whether that be in a great war or our daily lives.

MAXINE BOGGS

ROSIE THE RIVETER, STATESIDE, USA

SUBMITTED BY JASON MILLER, GRANDSON

MY GRANDMOTHER, MAXINE BOGGS, was also a contributor to the war effort. In the high-school classes that I teach, I use her as an example of Rosie the Riveter. There is, of course, the Norman Rockwell image of Rosie that almost every high-school history student has seen, but my students hear the story of Grandmother.

She was already married to Granddad when he went into the service, and since he wasn't sent overseas, she was able to move with him when he was assigned to different bases around the country. I suppose the pay from the Army Air Corps wasn't that great, because when they were stationed in New York, Grandmother got a job as an inspector in a factory that made artillery shells. I imagine her in cover-alls and a bandana just like Rosie.

The best part about this story for me is in how she related it. Before she passed, I tried to ask as many questions as I could to try to preserve the experiences but also, selfishly, so I could have stories to tell my students. In the course of one of our visits, I learned of this job. Fascinated, I basically had to interview her because she seemed somewhat coy about telling it. It's not that she was embarrassed or somehow scarred by her war experience; I came to realize that she just didn't see what she did as being that extraordinary.

So when I asked her the details of this job, she just told me that as an inspector, she and one other woman were in a small room in the corner of a massive factory space, into which a conveyor belt would bring these two-foot tall artillery shells standing on end. With her little hammer she was to tap on the pointy end of the shell and either pass it or fail it. By this point my jaw was on the floor, and I was imagining not Rockwell's Rosie but the Bugs Bunny cartoon in which the poor sap taps on the shell, and it leaves him with a blackened, blown-out face. But, of course, this was real life, not a cartoon drawing.

Did any of the shells fail the inspection!?

"No, they all passed."

Weren't you afraid of what was supposed to happen if one failed?

"Well, no, I just did my job."

ROY AND MAXINE

TOGETHER IN TEXAS, WHAT A GAS! USA

SUBMITTED BY JASON MILLER, GRANDSON

GRANDDAD FLEW IN BOMBERS and Grandmother was Rosie the Riveter. I guess you could say they had it easy because they weren't overseas, but I don't see it that way. Neither of them saw combat; their stories point to the extreme level of involvement on the American homefront and the moral nature of World War II. It touched everyone's lives, and everyone was involved in a pretty direct way, whether it was school kids collecting scrap metal out of alleys or housewives rationing food, or farmers upping production to feed the troops. These contributions were necessary and point to the relative unity of purpose Americans had during the war. Almost everyone made sacrifices and did so willingly, all for a cause they recognized as important and bigger than themselves.

A funnier story related to the sacrifices people made, but also showing some of the fun-loving nature of my grandparents, involves gasoline stamps and parties. Of course, gas was rationed during the war; Granddad's bombers needed to fly, after all. But Grandmother and Granddad had a car when they were stationed in Biloxi and later in Texas. Granddad says this made them among the most popular folks on the base because they could drive into town when they had leave time. It also gave them the freedom to party when leave time came around.

The reason they were so popular there is because they were the only ones on the base that had a car, and everyone wanted to be their friends so they could catch a ride to anywhere that wasn't on base. I imagine life on an Army base would be pretty boring, and I know these were all young-uns in their early twenties.

Why were they the only ones with a car? Well, in addition to the country's coming out of the depression as a result of the war, rationing of gas was a real drawback to having a car. It just wasn't worth maintaining one when you couldn't use it that much due to the fuel limitations. But Granddad had a way around that. He had virtually unlimited access to gasoline in the form of his father back on the farm next to the Missouri River outside of Boonville. You see, farmers didn't have limits on gasoline. They needed to keep those tractors running so the troops, and eventually Western Europe, could be fed. So Great-Granddad always had extra gasoline stamps to mail to his son on the Army base so they could party when they had time off.

THOMAS SCHNEIDER

Fort Richardson, U.S. Army Air Force, Alaska, USA

Submitted by Christina Andrew, Granddaughter

THOMAS SCHNEIDER WAS BORN in 1920 and served as a radioman in the U.S. Army Air Force during World War II. He grew up in Chicago and was stationed at Fort Richardson near Fairbanks, Alaska and was the first person on the base to receive the news of the attack on Pearl Harbor. The news was particularly hard for him, his best friend and other childhood friends were among those killed in the attack.

After the war, he married Pauline and settled in the St. Louis area and started a family. An interesting fact is that Pauline worked as a nurse at Jefferson Barracks hospital during the war. The couple had three children: Mary Catharine, Clifford, and William.

Using skills he learned in the Army; he established an electronics repair shop. Sadly, he suffered from the guilt of surviving when his friends were killed in the war. He continued to suffer until his death in the 1970s.

JACK PORT

4TH INFANTRY DIV, 12TH REG, E CO, EUROPEAN THEATER

Submitted by Eric Zelt, Friend

SITTING HUDDLED WITH THIRTY-FIVE other soldiers in an LST (Landing Ship, Tank) approaching the Normandy coast, Jack was cold and wet, a little seasick, and a lot of scared. Prayers and cries for mothers and families arose from the men around him, as Jack and his mates, members of Echo Company, 2nd Battalion, 12th Regiment, 4th Infantry Division (ID), dashed ashore at Utah Beach on the cool morning of June 6, 1944. Being defined by a single event in life isn't something most of us think about, or would even want, since it's usually history, or at the very least, posterity that defines our memorial moments in time; how interesting to observe how many veterans of D-Day are marked by just such a single distinction. Couldn't these veterans benefit from being appreciated through the broader prism of the lives they built and the other legacies they left, rather than just their military accomplishments?

For nearly three hundred days after that fateful landing in France, Jack and his mates battled fear, bombs, German machine guns, Wehrmacht soldiers, hunger, cold, and anger. The 4th Infantry Division was in contact with the enemy for over 190 days of their mission. They fought in every major battle that the U.S. Army waged as they marched from Normandy through Germany: D-Day, the Bocage, Operation COBRA (the Breakout), Huertgen Forest, and the Bulge. Jack was wounded, patched up, and sent back to his unit. Among many achievements, the 4th ID liberated the

vital port of Cherbourg and marched with pride down the Champs-Elysées as liberators of Paris. Jack and his mates saw their last combat duty on May 2, 1945, against SS troops near the Tegernsee in southern Germany, a scant 6km from the Austrian border.

On July 12, 1945, the men of the 4th ID finally set foot again in America, landing in the New York harbor. Even to this day, as Jack shares his experiences with fellow veterans and others, I am struck by his use of the word duty. It comes up often and

defines not only his perspective regarding military service but also that of so many of his colleagues. There is no chest thumping or bravado of any kind. On the contrary, among Jack and his mates, there is deep humility, a collective mourning of brothers lost to combat and time, and celebrating with joy their enduring achievements in serving the cause of liberty. Jack shuns the label "Greatest Generation," pointing instead to all the technological achievements of the last twenty years as having had a greater impact on the world than any fighting he may have done. Then again, would the free Europe and America we enjoy today exist at all, if not for Jack and his mates?

Once back home, Jack built his life with the same perseverance that allowed him to survive as a soldier. He ran a successful clothing business, raised a family, and served on the

San Diego County School Board for over twenty years. He invested in local businesses, co-founded a bank, and remains an active Rotarian. Jack volunteers with local literacy programs and speaks often in his community on his World War II experiences. Every June, Jack flies back to Normandy in honor of his mates who never made it back home, who never got to have families, or play tennis, or grow old with loved ones. His first stop in Normandy is the long flat stretch of sand known as Utah Beach, where past and present merge, where history and potential collided over seventy-two years ago. For Jack, there isn't talk of "I can't," or "I won't," but there is always "I will ... "

HARRY L. SMITH, JR., SGT MAJ

USS War Hawk, 1279th Combat Engineers, Pacific Theater

Submitted by Ron Smith, Son

THERE WERE, OF COURSE, the lighter moments—an unexpected wrestling match with a water moccasin while on maneuvers in Louisiana; making fudge with Army buddies in a foxhole during a "Nighttime Charlie" raid on an island in the South Pacific; a hammock hung in a foxhole to provide more comfort during Japanese air raids at the Clark Field air base in the Philippines.

But nothing during Harry Smith's 1,691-day World War II adventures could trump the memory of a January 10, 1945 boat ride in the Lingayen Gulf during the invasion of Luzon—a major step in the American liberation of the Philippines.

Harry Lyman Smith, Jr., whose marathon World War II experience started on February 6, 1941, and ended on a Sunday, September 23, 1945, was a naïve 22-year-old farmboy from Independence, Missouri, when he was drafted by a National Guard unit—the 110th Combat Engineers—and assigned to Camp Robinson in Little Rock, Arkansas, as a lowly private. Just short of four years later in January of 1945, he was a battalion Sergeant Major with the 1279th Combat Engineers when he was awakened by a 4 a.m. explosion that rocked the transport ship *USS War Hawk* and created panic.

"They made us all get out and go on top of the ship—everybody," Harry said six decades later. "And then they eventually got ropes down over the side. So, we climbed down into another small boat for a landing. They crowded a bunch of us in there so tight you couldn't really squeeze anybody else in."

The explosion was caused by a "Shinyo" suicide motorboat, laden with several tons of explosives. It rammed the portside of the *War Hawk*, blowing a 25-foot hole that killed a reported 61 men. Safely evacuated from what was feared to be a sinking ship, Harry said the fear factor only got worse.

"And then (they) took us out and started circling, out in plain sight, in open seas. They waited for other boats to congregate there and then go all in at one time, but in the meantime, Japanese planes started coming in. There were three of them. They were dropping bombs, trying to hit the ships. And we were out there in plain sight."

Harry, whose plan to announce his engagement to Kansas City girl, Ruth Boland, was disrupted on December 7, 1941, by the bombing of Pearl Harbor and his subsequent extended war service, recalled thinking he might never see his sweetheart again.

"We thought they hit our boat," he said, "because it started smoking. But evidently the boats were putting smoke out to camouflage. But eventually, after they circled awhile, they took us on in."

Harry estimated there were forty to fifty ships in the Gulf, ranging from destroyers and battleships, to airplane carriers, transports and other vessels.

"It was just like the Fourth of July," he recalled. "That's just what it looked like. All the different ships in the harbor. It was a big gun battle."

The *War Hawk* suffered damage to its engine room and was dead in the water. The crew struggled to keep the ship afloat and eventually restored partial power. After a long, slow journey to Lehti Gulf, more extensive repairs were made, and the *War Hawk* eventually returned to service. Not so for two other landing crafts that were sunk by Kamikaze boats on the same day.

> *"It was just like the Fourth of July."*

JOHN A. WOOD, JR.

623RD MEDICAL CLEARING COMPANY, EUROPEAN THEATER

Submitted by Christine Smith, Daughter

With their transport ship anchored in a channel enveloped by heavy nighttime fog, members of the Army's 623rd Medical Clearing Company could only imagine the disturbing sights they would confront the next morning.

John A. Wood Jr., a native of St. Louis, Missouri, arrived at Omaha Beach on the morning of July 18, 1944—a month and a half after the D-Day invasion of Normandy. He was dropped off in chest-deep water, unable to swim because of the file box he carried above his head to shore.

He negotiated an obstacle course of discarded military gear, sunken ships, and German barriers. He carried a full pack during the seven-mile hike through areas scarred by naval and air bombardment to the marshaling area, where his unit received orders to operate a dispensary in Barneville-Carteret, France.

Over the next two months, John would tend to sick and wounded soldiers in hospitals and holding stations on a meandering journey through Normandy, Rennes, Le Mans, and the far western edge of the Brest Peninsula before making stops in Luxembourg and Belgium. While camping in pup tents just north of Bastogne, John recalled listening to broadcasts of the 1944 World Series between his hometown Cardinals and Browns.

John, who worked as an accounting clerk for the Wabash Railroad in civilian life, spent 168 hours training as a medical technician, followed by a month more of classwork and on-floor training at Billings General Hospital in Indiana. But nothing could prepare him for the onslaught of misery he would encounter near the end of 1944 when his unit was attached to the

110th evacuation hospital near Esch-sur-Alzette (south of Luxembourg City) during the Battle of the Bulge.

In a December 23, 1944, letter to future wife, Leola Kayler, John expressed frustration: "If you have trouble reading this, blame it on the damn Germans as we are having an air raid and a blackout, so I am writing by the light of a coal lantern I bought."

But he did not mention the trail of amputations, shrapnel surgeries, and other bloody horrors he must have witnessed. He steadfastly refused to discuss that period of his Army service, even after the war.

The government's Medical Department Office of Medical History (VII Corps) put that refusal in perspective. The 400-bed evacuation hospital where John worked received most of the American casualties from the southern flank of the Bulge. The hospital at one point was treating 300 new patients per day with a surgical backlog of 300. Tents were pitched in a paved courtyard to treat the sick and lightly wounded.

The hospital handled more than 5,000 patients in one month and reported a mortality rate of 1.5 percent among the more than 2,200 admitted for surgery.

MYRON H. MILLER, S SGT

83rd Infantry Division, K/331st, European Theater

Submitted by Del Miller, Son

SOME CALLED THE YOUNG man Billy, for there in the backwoods of the Ozarks that was the old-timey nickname for the devil himself. My father earned his reputation with a massive right uppercut worthy of some local fame and a fearlessness regarding fisticuffs that saw any number of opponents out cold on the floor.

But the small town tough often comes to grief out in the big wide world and you might imagine that was his fate when the government "requested," as he put it, that he join the Army.

Off to basic training he went and his world became one of foxholes and target practice and physical training. And physical training was a very favorite thing of his company commander who, in his civilian life, had been a semi-professional boxer of some renown. It was his idea to teach his men about the fine art of fighting.

He would stand in the ring and call for a volunteer. Said volunteer would tie on his gloves, step into the ring and hit the canvas a moment later, since raw recruits were no match for a real boxer. This went on for days. But my father watched carefully and saw, what he told me was a weakness in the Captain's technique … an opening, as it were.

So one day, he volunteered. He climbed into the ring and the fight began with the two fighters circling each other. The Captain closed and threw a left jab, but my father ducked and stepped back. The captain followed with a right, but Dad ducked that one too, and another left came after that.

In that fleeting instant between that right and that left, Dad saw his chance and threw a right-handed punch that started near his right kneecap and ended two feet on the lee side of the Captain's jaw. The Captain responded by losing consciousness and falling heavily to the ground.

From that day onward physical training did not include boxing.

JAMES M. ENMEIER, COL

83RD INFANTRY DIVISION, HQ, DENTAL SURGEON, EUROPEAN THEATER

Submitted by Gretchen Stiers, Granddaughter

COLONEL JAMES MERLE ENMEIER was a career dental surgeon in the United States Army. He enlisted at Camp Atterbury, Indiana on January 15, 1941, and was commissioned as a 1st Lieutenant. He was stationed with the 13th Infantry Regiment at Fort Jackson, South Carolina for two years and joined the 83rd Infantry Division as part of the European Theater mobilization effort in December 1942. Several months before the 83rd sailed for England in April 1944, 1st Lieutenant Enmeier was promoted to Major. As a dental surgeon at the rank of Major, he served with the 83rd Headquarters medical unit, performing both routine dental work and surgery as needed on the war front. He and his fellow Thunderbolts landed at Omaha Beach ten days after D-Day, stormed the hedgerows in Normandy, fought through Brittany and Luxembourg, and survived the cold and snow in both the Hurtgen Forest and the Battle of the Bulge.

After the Germans had surrendered in May 1945, Colonel Enmeier spent his last months in Europe at the 83rd Infantry Division Rest Center in BAD Harzburg, Germany and with the 99th Infantry Division headquarters medical unit in Kirtzengen, Germany. He was shipped home in September 1945 and spent the remaining three months of his WWII service at Camp Atterbury until he was released from active duty on December 24, 1945.

After two years of private dental practice in Vincennes, Indiana, Colonel Enmeier reenlisted in the regular army at the rank of Major. He continued to serve his country until his retirement July 25, 1969. During his service, he was stationed at Fort Knox, Kentucky (1947–1950); Nuremberg and Kaiserslautern, Germany (1951–1954); San Antonio, Texas (1954–1955); the Presidio of San Francisco, California

(1955–1959); Washington, DC (1959–1962); Seoul, South Korea (1962-1963); Fort Eustis, Virginia (1963–1967); and Fort Gordon, Georgia (1967–1969). He was promoted to Lieutenant Colonel in July 1951 and Colonel in August 1961. Colonel Enmeier died on April 27, 1975, from lung cancer and was buried with his family in the Vincennes City Cemetery in Indiana.

Sadly, Colonel Enmeier's personal records and photos from his World War II service were lost in two separate warehouse fires, but his daughters, Brenda Jane Stiers and Barbara Ann Bunting, remember a few stories that he shared over the years. In addition to pulling teeth and performing dental surgery, he served as what is now known as a M.A.S.H. doctor. One time in France, when no medical doctor was available, he performed an emergency appendectomy to save a soldier's life. He spoke about being indebted to a French farm family that hid him in a hayloft during a battle. He also spoke about the horrors of being part of the medical team that first walked into Langenstein, a subcamp of the Buchenwald concentration camp, after it was liberated by his fellow soldiers of the 83rd Infantry Division.

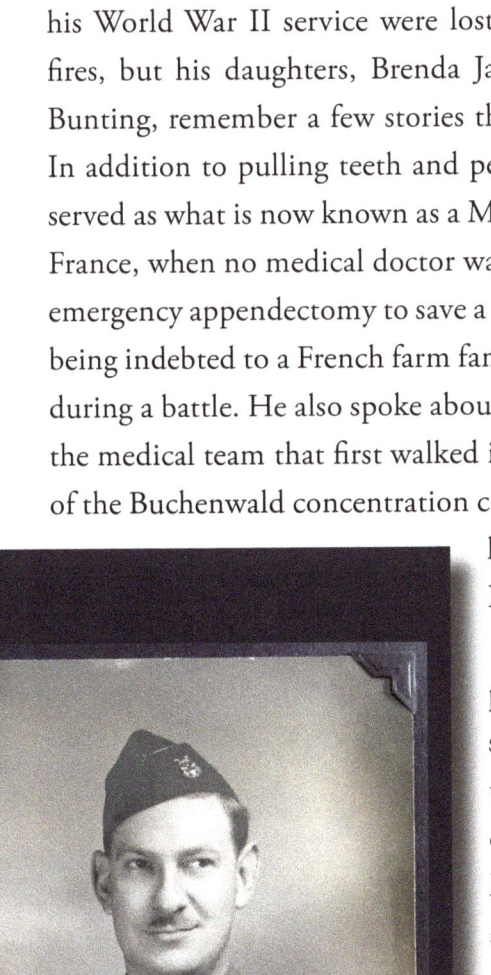

Colonel Enmeier was a patriot and a hero. He was a stern, stubborn man with a terrific sense of humor who deeply loved his family and his country. He had scars and undoubtedly nightmares, but he forged on after returning from WWII. By learning about his life and the lives of all the men and women who served during WWII, these stories become a richer part of our heritage and legacy.

Major Enmeier Decorated For Duty Overseas

MAJOR JAMES ENMEIER

Major James M. Enmeier, 83rd infantry division, has been awarded a certificate of merit in the recognition of conspicuously meritorious and outstanding performance of military duty, and a citation for outstanding performance of duty as division dental surgeon from July 1, 1944 to Dec. 31, 1944, in France, Luxembourg, Germany and Belgium.

Major Enmeier's division also has received a Presidential citation for outstanding performance of military duty under freezing conditions in the Ardennes offensive. Men of the division now may wear four bronze battle stars on their European theater of operations ribbon, for action in Normandy, Duren, Germany, the Ardennes and Neuss.

Major Enmeier, son of Paul Enmeier, former county clerk, formerly was a practicing dentist in Vincennes. Another local boy, Maurice Vachett, also is in the 83rd division.

The 83rd captured 20,000 German prisoners at Beaugency, France, earlier in the war.

Major Enmeier sailed for Wales in April of last year. He crossed the channel with the division in July. They were at Carentan, St. Malo, Brest, Dinard, Dinan, Rennes Orleans, Beaugency, Metz, Duren, then back to Aachen and the Ardennes, and then spearheaded and won the Ninth army race to the Rhine river at Neuss, on March 9.

His parents and wife and two daughters, Brenda and Barbara, reside in Vincennes.

RALPH M. RICKERSON

USS Neosho (AO-48), U.S. Navy, Pacific Theater

Submitted by Denise Rickerson Colley, Daughter

RALPH MONROE RICKERSON, MY father, served on the *USS Neosho (AO-48)* from the ComServ Ron 10 (one of two ComServ Ron squadrons created by Admiral Nimitz to provide mobile service) and supplied fuel, food and other sundries to the fleet combat unit as it moved across the Pacific. They also delivered mail and transported the wounded (for medical care) and the dead to aircraft carriers (for their final destination—home). In addition, they built docks in designated areas in the Pacific, such as on the Island of Ulithi, to be used for repairs to ships in the fleet. The Neosho traveled with destroyers, battleships, and aircraft carriers and was the first Oiler to fuel two of these ships at the same time, a difficult feat when the weather was bad and the seas rough.

Thirteen battle stars were awarded to this ship during WWII, among which were the American Campaign Medal, the Asiatic-Pacific Campaign Medal, the WWII Victory Medal, the Naval Occupation Service Medal, the Philippines Presidential Unit Citation, and the Philippines Liberation Medal.

Some of the campaigns by the *USS Neosho* include the capture and occupation of Saipan, June to August 1944; 2nd Bonins Raid, June 1944; the capture and occupation of Guam, July to August 1944; the Tinian capture and occupation, June to August 1944; the Western Carolina Island operation, September to October 1944; the assault of Philippine Island, September 1944; the Leyte operation, October to November 1944; the Luzon operation (China coast) Formosa attack, January 1945; the Iwo Jima operation, February to March 1945; the Hollandia operation, April 1945; the Okinawa Gunto operation, June 1945; and the 3rd fleet operation against Japan, July to August 1945.

My father was twenty-nine years old when he enlisted in the U.S. Navy. At the time, he was married with three small sons. His younger brother enlisted in the U.S. Army at the same time. My father was gone for eighteen months. Mother and three older brothers went to California from Missouri to meet him when his ship docked in November 1945. My parents went on to have four more sons and one daughter (me).

He didn't talk much about his time in the Navy, but there were a few stories my brothers and I remember him telling when he was older. He talked about the numerous times he crossed the equator and the "King Neptune" Ceremony perpetrated on all new sailors crossing the equator for the first time. He talked of listening to Tokyo Rose on the radio. He would imitate how she talked, and it would make us laugh. The story we all remember best was when he was in Tokyo Bay at the time of the signing of the instrument of surrender by the Japanese.

The Neosho was just north of Japan, August 1945, after the second atomic bomb was dropped on Nagasaki, Japan. Ships were allowed into Tokyo Bay by invitation only. My father remembered coming into the bay and the innumerable sharks, so nobody wanted to get into the water. He told of their ship being near enough to the *USS Missouri* to watch the Japanese officials board. He and his mates took turns looking through field glasses to see what was happening.

My father told about the "little Japanese" who wore glasses and was dressed in a black suit with a tall black hat. This "little Japanese" stood ramrod-straight, not looking left or right, then he went up to the table and bent over to sign his name. We now know this was the Foreign Minister of Japan, Mamoru Shigemitsu. When he had finished signing, Fleet Admiral Chester W. Nimitz, USN, General MacArthur, and other U.S. officers signed the paper. My father talked of the airplanes whose engines roared as they flew over the ships and all the shouting, whistling and yelling by the sailors onboard. Ralph Monroe Rickerson lived to be ninety-one years old and, although he didn't talk much about his time in the war until he was older, he did like reminiscing about some of his fellow shipmates, especially that day in Tokyo Bay.

ORLAN J. THORNTON, SR MSGT

GUNNERY INSTRUCTOR, ARMY AIR CORPS, EUROPEAN THEATER

SUBMITTED BY JAMES T. THORNTON, SON

MY FATHER, ORLAN JAMES (Jimmy) Thornton was born December 29, 1923, on a farm near the small town of Tarkio, Missouri. His father, my grandfather, died when Dad was sixteen. Dad had to drop out of high school to help his brother run the farm. When his mother remarried several years later, Dad was able to fulfill his desire to see the world. He had little money and jobs were scarce during the Great Depression, so he joined the Civilian Conservation Corps (CCC) in 1940. Never one to shy away from food, he became a cook—a hobby he enjoyed for the rest of his life. He also loved to play baseball and even had a tryout with the St. Louis Cardinals. But, of course, World War II came to America and Dad became a soldier in 1943.

The Army saw fit to send him to the Aerial Gunnery School after basic training, and Dad made the best of it. He was very good at the job, and after a stint as a gunner in coastal patrol planes (during which he helped sink a U-boat), Dad became an instructor in B-24 Bombers. He later started a school to operate and maintain the fire control system on B-29 bombers, but Japan surrendered before Dad could deploy.

Since the Army Air Corps no longer needed his services and he now had technical training, Dad became an electrician and was sent to Europe as part of the occupation force. He enjoyed seeing new parts of the world but was dismayed at the war's destruction and inhumanity. He became teary-eyed decades later when telling me of his visits to Auschwitz and Buchenwald.

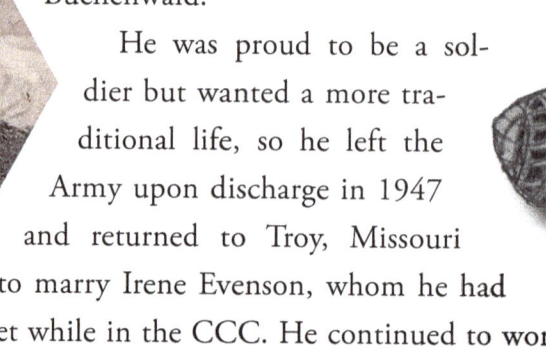

He was proud to be a soldier but wanted a more traditional life, so he left the Army upon discharge in 1947 and returned to Troy, Missouri to marry Irene Evenson, whom he had met while in the CCC. He continued to work as an electrician in the construction industry until the Korean War broke out in 1950. He was recalled to the U.S. Air Force and assigned to the newly constituted Strategic Air Command in a Civil Engineering Squadron. Since he had nearly eight years in the service after the Korean War was over, Dad decided to make the Air Force a career. He earned an Associates Degree through correspondence courses and served in numerous assignments both at home and abroad, including South Vietnam, where he earned a Bronze Star for his actions during the Tet Offensive in 1968. He completed a long career as a Senior Master Sergeant upon his retirement in 1971.

Dad never considered himself anything other than a regular guy. He was a loving and patient father and reveled in his roles as Uncle Jimmy and later as Paw-Paw. Although he was proud of his service in three wars spanning nearly three decades, Dad took even greater satisfaction in raising his family to be **honest** and **hard-working** citizens of the greatest country on earth— America.

> *As to my leadership qualifications, I just want to say that whatever success I enjoyed as a leader can be attributed to just two or three simple things. First, it was due to all the great people who worked with me and for me. It just seemed that the good Lord always sent me the people I needed at the time I needed them.*

Colonel Robert H. York

Commanding officer of the
83rd Infantry Division, 331st Regiment
from Normandy to the end of WWII

JAMES E. GOFF, CPL

106TH INFANTRY DIVISION, RECONNAISSANCE, EUROPEAN THEATER

Submitted by Carol Turner, Friend

JAMES E. GOFF WAS a Corporal in the 106th Infantry Division. He enlisted on March 24, 1943, at the age of nineteen. A year later, he would be crossing the English Channel and wading through the surf to enter the European Theater of Operations at La Havre, France.

The 106th trudged across France and Belgium, arriving to relieve the 2nd Infantry Division in the Ardennes near the town of St. Vith on December 9, 1944. Less than ten days after arriving on the continent, thousands of German artillery pieces and rocket launchers announced the beginning of a deadly and costly battle which would become known as the Battle of the Bulge.

Vicious fighting trapped two combat teams on the Schnee Eiffel. The valiant men inflicted a tremendous toll on the German forces. Out of ammunition, water, food, and medical supplies, the regiment was forced to surrender on December 19th. More than 6,000 men became prisoners of war, including James Goff.

At a family Christmas party, James's parents and his sweetheart, Delores, received the devastating news that he was missing in action. By that time, James Goff had been marched to the overcrowded prisoner of war camp, Stalag 3A, near Lukenwalde, Prussia. For over 178 days Corporal Goff would suffer from lack of food and water, and would experience physical and mental atrocities. Stalag 3A was liberated by the Russian Red Army on April 22, 1945.

James seldom spoke of his war experiences after returning home to St. Clair County, Illinois. Instead, he concentrated on living. He was a loving and devoted husband and raised a beautiful daughter, Ruthann. He was the Keeper of the Clubhouse on Parker Lake where

he fished to his heart's content and barbecued to the culinary delight of everyone. He was a gifted wood worker, designing lawn ornaments for every season: bunnies for Easter, hearts for Valentine's Day ... even a big white reindeer at Christmas. After retiring, James became the doggy daycare for his grand dog, Samantha.

James Goff was a good man who served his country and his family well.

THREE BRAVE VETERANS

St. Louis Gateway Chapter Veterans - Battle of the Bulge

Interviewed and Written by Sela Roth, WWII Descendant

AT 96, EUGENE HARMACK is the oldest member of the St. Louis Gateway Chapter of the Battle of the Bulge. He was also in the 83rd Infantry Division, HQ, 329th. His job was communications at the headquarters. He vividly remembers Operation Cobra, when bombs were being dropped on Germans to get them out of the way for the Americans. Eugene told me that during his service he and his fellow soldiers had two enemies: the Germans and the cold. He had seventy percent disability because of the five feet of snow surrounding him, freezing his limbs. When speaking about memories in France, Eugene told me about seeing some women's heads being shaved because they had collaborated with the enemy. It was a way that the French could identify and punish these women. Eugene spent a total of one and a half years overseas fighting.

EMIL PERKO WAS A 93-year-old WWII Veteran who died in June of 2016. He served in the 106th Infantry Division, 422nd Regiment, Company H. After he was sent to Europe to fight, his unit was nicknamed "the sitting ducks," as the reinforcements of ammo and other necessary supplies never came to them. Eventually, they were forced to surrender to the Germans because of a decree stating that the whole infantry would be slaughtered if no surrender came. Then, over 6,000 Americans were shoved onto a dark train and sent to POW relocation camps. Once the train transported them to this snowy forest, they were forced into cold buildings with only mats to sleep on. As for food, all that they were given was thin soup, boiled carrot tops, cabbage, and other unrecognizable vegetables and occasional bits of horsemeat. After a considerable time living like this, the malnourished and scrawny POWs were discovered by Allied forces who took them out of captivity. Soon Emil and others from his infantry were taken to a ship bound for New York. Emil then took a train back home to St. Louis, Missouri.

VINSON AND FLO FREEMAN are a couple who met in 1946 at a sorority party at Washington University. Vin was in the reconnaissance section of the 83rd Infantry Division, HQ 329 BN INR. His job in the INR was to make sure that soldiers in his infantry knew where to be and that they knew where the enemy was. Though he was able to sleep indoors, Vin has very vivid memories of zero-degree weather and members of his infantry losing seventy percent mobility at times from frostbite. Vin told me that men who had to sleep outside would put down their blankets and coats in the frozen foxhole and sleep with their sleeping bags resting on top of them. He also recalled watching a soldier in his unit die while guarding their headquarters. "It was the scariest part because it could have been any of us," was what he told me when I came to visit a meeting of the St. Louis Gateway Chapter Veterans of the Battle of the Bulge.

CLYDE F. SHINDLEDECKER

USS Barnstable (APA-93), U.S. Navy, Pacific Theater

Submitted by Eric Zelt, Grandson

IN WESTERN PENNSYLVANIA, CLYDE Shindledecker (my granddad) lived a spartan life of hard work, simple pleasures and struggle. His father was a tenant farmer, and he worked on the B&O Railroad crew. Early photos show a handsome man of slight build with a smile and a crew cut. The Japanese attack on Pearl Harbor in December of 1941 wrought huge change in the lives of all young men in America. Clyde, being a little older and having two young children, was not among early draftees to fight the new war. A few years passed and the war dragged on. Our nation needed more men to fight; so in January 1944, at the age of 28, he was drafted to serve his country. Granddad went into the Navy, taking his basic training at Great Lakes Naval Base.

Upon completion of radar schooling in San Diego, Granddad flew to Hawaii where he joined the crew of the *USS Barnstable* and set sail for the South Pacific Theater. When we were growing up, Granddad never talked about his war experience, and we didn't know enough to bring up the subject. His naval service simply never came up. What we discovered came to us in small bits over many years. My mother, Nancy, relayed his involvement to us incrementally, but we were left with many more questions than answers. Like so many of his generation who didn't talk about their service, he just completed it. Granddad saw his participation as a duty to be executed as best he could for the greater good of his country.

Honoring Clyde's contribution and telling his story has taken on renewed importance as I work with veterans of the European Theater to preserve and relate their stories for future generations. After going through some of his diaries, letters, and dusting off further personal recollections from family, we are proud to know a little more about Granddad's service.

Clyde Shindledecker spent two years in the Navy, coming home finally in November 1945. His ship and crew played vital roles in two of the most significant battles in the Asian Pacific Theater, the Battles of Leyte, One and Two. The first battle of Leyte was General Douglas MacArthur's triumphant return to the Philippines. Granddad had a different flavor of the war than ground combatants: his ship worked as a troop transport, shuttling men into LST's (Landing Ship, Tank) who then drove them to the beaches being stormed. The LST's returned loaded with dead and wounded soldiers. His ship would then shuttle casualties to hospital ships and then bring fresh troops back. After a kamikaze pilot blew up a ship very close to his in the formation, he took an active part in rescuing victims from the Pacific waters. After Japan surrendered, Granddad and his mates shuttled troops into Japan for the Allied Occupation. He was proudest of his Philippines Liberation Medal with two battle stars and the role he played in freeing the Philippine people from Japanese occupation.

His war tenure touched him in ways we can never understand. Despite coming from a long tradition of deer hunters, Granddad would never again fire a gun or hurt any creature. A picture of the *USS Barnstable* always hung over his sofa, and we seldom saw him without his "WWII Veteran" hat. He was the kindest, most thoughtful man I have ever known. Clyde Shindledecker was a deeply private man who lived the rest of his long life just as he executed his Naval commitment: caring for others with compassion while revering life in all its forms.

MYRON H. MILLER, S SGT

83rd Infantry Division, K/331st, European Theater

Submitted by Marshall Miller, Son

ALL MY DAD WANTED to be was a farmer. His dad was a farmer, and his dad before him was a farmer.

Before the United States declared war in 1941, he was a twenty-three-year-old young man helping my grandpa run a 160-acre farm in central Missouri. In addition, he worked full time in construction at Fort Leonard Wood, about twenty-five miles away. The last thing he and nearly everybody he knew wanted to do was to get involved in a war thousands of miles away to help people he didn't know. The Great Depression was still very fresh in everyone's minds, and the primary goal people were concerned about was just surviving. Pearl Harbor changed everything.

By the time my dad was drafted, the US was fully involved in the preparation and execution of war on a global scale. For most of his contemporaries, their world consisted of a very small part of this global catastrophe. Going off to fight in Europe or the Pacific was not on many wish lists, but like millions of young men when called to duty he marched off to war.

As I get older, I see how memories can become hazy. The details get scrambled and what you remember doesn't always match the facts. But one memory is indelibly etched in my mind.

I was twelve or thirteen years old, and I clearly remember Dad and I were sitting in the living room watching TV. I was on the couch and he was sitting in his overstuffed chair. I don't recall anyone else in the room, but in my memory, it was just Dad and me. We were watching a documentary on the Holocaust ... my first exposure to that awful chapter in human history. Needless to say, I was stunned.

Throughout the program, not a word was said. Dad sat and watched without comment. I didn't know what to think. I do remember glancing over now and then, wondering what he was thinking, knowing he was there, and knowing he had to have seen and done things I knew nothing about.

As the program ended, Dad cleared his throat and very quietly explained to me why it was necessary that he had to fight. I know I can't get his exact words, but this is how I remember them.

"You know, I walked and fought all the way across Europe and didn't understand. I thought, why are we over here? This isn't our war. Why do we have to fight these guys? Then, I walked into a concentration camp, and I knew why. Hitler was one man who needed to be killed."

NORVEL A. MCDONALD

84th Infantry Division, E/335th, European Theater

Submitted by Elizabeth Fadel, Daughter

My father, Norvel August (NA) McDonald, was truly a part of the Greatest Generation! He served in the US Army with the 84th Infantry Division. He never spoke about his time in the service, and it's no wonder why.

He passed away in 2010, and it was then I decided to do extensive research on his military history including actually walking in some of his footsteps. I went to Omaha Beach, where he landed in November of 1944, and areas he fought through on the Siegfried Line. My trifecta will be traveling to Belgium one day where he fought in the Battle of the Bulge!

He fought all the way from France in 1944, to the Elbe River in May of 1945, where German soldiers swam across to surrender to American soldiers instead of Russian soldiers. He took part in some of the hardest fought battles in Europe and fought with the 84th Infantry for over 180 days.

He was awarded a Purple Heart, a Bronze Star with three oak clusters—one for each battle he fought—and a Combat Infantry Badge, to name a few. His photograph is in a book written by Lt. Theodore Draper, Dad is eating a K-ration in the snow somewhere in Belgium.

He was always good at taking things apart and putting them back together again. It turns out that he was part of a mining platoon where he actually took mines apart and set them off! Later he was in small mortars, sending them screaming across to the enemy.

His division liberated two POW camps and he served until he was discharged in 1946. After all he had been through, he didn't have enough points to go home—a system the Army used to discharge soldiers. Three battles and he still couldn't go home!

I am blessed beyond words to have the ability to do this research on my dad for our family to have for generations! Our little piece of history ...

—A Proud Daughter!

ERNEST E. COWHERD, PFC

31st Infantry Division, 167th Regiment, Pacific Theater

Submitted by Barbara Cowherd, Daughter-in-Law

PRIVATE 1ST CLASS ERNEST Cowherd was born July 6, 1923. He was a graduate of Purdy High School in Purdy, Missouri and was attending the University of Arkansas until he was drafted into the Army on October 14, 1944. He went to Fort Roberson, Arkansas for training and was shipped to Mindanao, Philippines, April 13, 1945, and arrived May 5, 1945.

Ernest was sent to the front lines of battle and immediately faced harsh conditions and difficult terrain. In less than two months, he was wounded on June 24, 1945, with shrapnel in his leg and hip and a broken leg. He was the only one of a group of men to make it out alive after encountering fierce resistance. Carried out of the jungle, he made it to a stretcher where medics then transported him to a field hospital. He stayed in the field hospital in the Philippines until September and then was flown to Vaughn Army Hospital in Chicago. Flat on his back for six months while recovering from his severe injuries, Ernest was discharged on February of 1946.

He was awarded the Purple Heart, The Bronze Star, Asiatic-Pacific Theater Ribbon and the Victory Medal. It took him 63 years to receive his Bronze Star. He had forgotten that he was never awarded the medal until his grandson brought up the issue. Finally, in 2008 he received the missing decoration for his wartime act of bravery that happened back in 1945.

After his discharge from the Army, he came back to the family farm and established a dairy farm and attended the Agriculture Vocational School for Veterans in Monett, Missouri. Ernest married Mary Jeanette Eden on May 2, 1948, and they had seven children.

In addition to running a large dairy operation, he was a Registered Holstein Breeder and with the family, participated in many Holstein shows and sales. Ernest served for many years as a 4-H leader, the Barry County Extension Board, the Federal Land Bank Credit Board, and the Cassville Board of Education, serving six years as President of the Board. A well-respected community leader, Ernest was a member of the Cassville Methodist Church and served on the Board of Trustees and Administrative Board.

CLARENCE M. TAYLOR, CPL

European and Pacific Theater

Submitted by Glenda Taylor Hunter, Daughter and Terry Taylor, Son

EVERY MILE REVEALED SOMETHING new. He was just a country boy from the hills of Tennessee whose grandest view of the world had been the city of Nashville. He found himself on a train traveling through places he had only read about in books and magazines. With his own eyes, he was saw the city of New York, the Empire State Building, Yankee Stadium, and the Statue of Liberty. It would have seemed like a great vacation, except he was just one of a thousand other young soldiers riding a train to the harbor to board a ship for North Africa.

He thought about his young wife. It hadn't been that long ago that he had met a beautiful girl, Rhea, at the soda fountain in Centerville, Tennessee. They had only known each other a few months before eloping to Kentucky to get married. As the only son of his widowed mother, he had not been drafted. However, his new marriage changed his draft status and Uncle Sam called him up to the war. He would soon find himself on an unimaginable journey that would cause many young men to lose their lives.

How could the Atlantic Ocean be so big? The waters seemed to go on forever.

As a boy, his water escapades had been limited to the muddy rivers and lakes of Middle Tennessee, where the shore had never been more than a stone's throw away. Now he was in the middle of the ocean without any sight of land. Their convoy of ships finally arrived in Casablanca. The city was as exotic as he could ever imagine. Arabs, Canadians, Brits, and French expatriates, as well as German and Italian prisoners of war, would cross his path. Every sight, sound, and the smell were so strange.

As the war would go on, he would find himself back over the Atlantic, across the United States, and then on to the Pacific Ocean heading to the jungles of Okinawa.

Cartoons were drawn by Clarence Taylor and sent to his wife Rhea in 1944.

He would be strafed by a Japanese fighter plane and survive a great ocean typhoon. An incredible change of life for a young man whose greatest adventures before the war had been hunting squirrels in the backwoods of Tennessee. Eventually, he would finally make his way back home to his wife for a new start. Like so many others of his generation, his life would be forever changed by events over which he had little control but would cause him to have a whole new view of the world.

HENRY C. OEHMEN, PFC

83rd Infantry Division, E/331st, European Theater

Submitted by Connor McNulty, Grandson

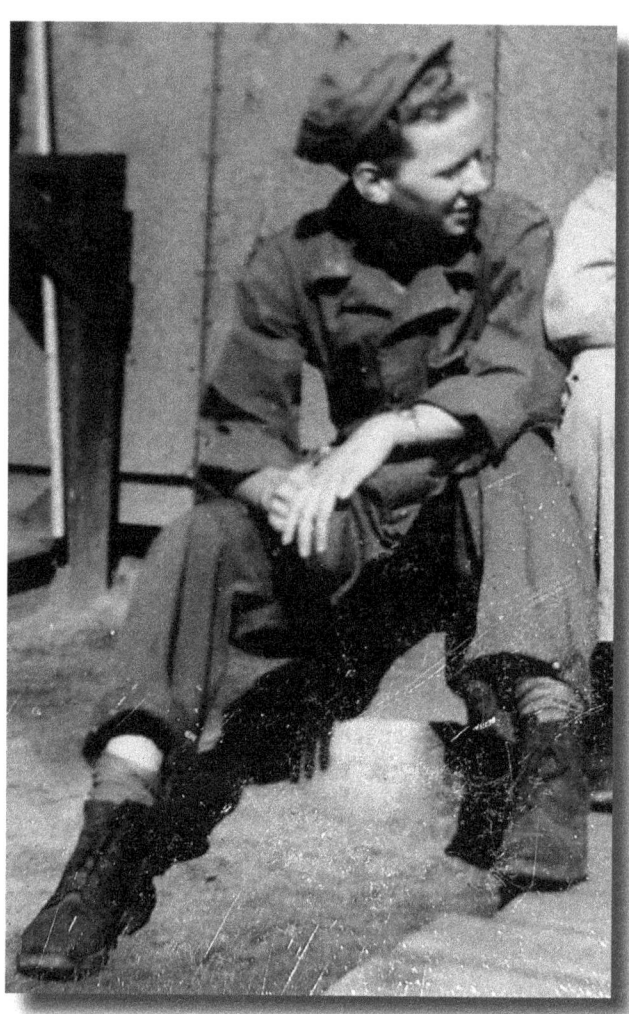

THE STORY OF MY journey to learn about my grandfather begins in 1991. I was born in late September. Both of my grandfathers are veterans of World War II. By mid-October of that year, two weeks after I was born, our family laid to rest Pfc. Henry C. Oehmen, a veteran of the Battle of the Bulge and my maternal grandfather. He was sixty-five years old when I was born, and while he was very sick, he was notified about my birth, the birth of his second grandchild and was very pleased with the news that I was born. Those two weeks that we shared together on earth have become a time of year that I cherish very much.

I had a wonderful New England upbringing. When I was born, so was an unquenchable curiosity about the man, the father of my mother, and the soldier that was my Grandpa Hank. Young boys are almost immediately enthralled with adventure, violence, and brotherhood. Heroes captivate us. The he-men of the world are people all young boys aspire to become. At the time, I had not realized, but I have come to discover, that I am related to a few. Whether it was a new action figure or the classic Hollywood war films, each broadened my imagination and served to stoke my curiosity.

I certainly asked at a very early age if any of the men in my family were soldiers who had fought in a war. I can recall my brother's imagination as well. When we were young, he would proudly and confidently proclaim, our grandfather had "killed Adolf Hitler," either an amazing stretch or the truth, I had to get to the bottom of things. The yeses I received from our family became very deep down, a red-hot spark that I have fueled and taken care of for my entire life. It was incumbent that I learn everything I could about the life my grandfather led but not just as a grandfather, but as a young soldier who fought through the darkest time in modern history.

An amazing influence on my life and my journey to connect with him was the spouse he left behind. My Grandmother Rose, his life partner for over forty years, was truly my best friend.

They met at a dance after the war and were married sometime after. He left his hometown to live with her and her family in the town I was born, raised, and still currently live. That was very telling to me how much he cared for her. In my research, I've uncovered a letter addressed to Pfc. Henry Oehmen stating that he once proclaimed to the sender, "If he ever were to make it home alive, his greatest aspiration was to get married and to start a family." I was in awe that this was the woman to fulfill his goal and also fully grateful that I was part of his ambitions.

I was so proud to be reminded at every visit how much I resembled her late husband. Of the three grandchildren he left behind, I was the only one to have light blonde hair and light blue eyes. Those were his features that she admired. I was also the only grandchild who had never met her husband. As I grew older, I spoke on the telephone with my grandmother almost every evening. Our daily conversations almost always reverted to the topic of my grandfather. Despite my age, I think I understood that she was alone now and that the joy her husband gave her would never be replaced. I had hoped that with the new joy of a grandson, I would help her mourn the loss of her husband.

Every winter storm or annually during the summer, we would travel across town to shovel snow or maintain the lawn at my grandmother's. Thank goodness, Father and my older brother could only accomplish those tasks. As soon as work would start, I always found myself sneaking into the house to share a visit with Grandmother instead. To step into her house was to step back in time. She lived alone and everything was the same. She had calendars still hanging on the walls in the basement from the twenties. Before the work outside was finished, I made sure to carefully seize my opportunity to ask her if we could explore the attic. I knew that's where his precious belongings were kept.

There was so much evidence that I needed to investigate.

What was the Battle of the Bulge?
Why was his heart purple?
Had I grown enough to fit into his uniform?
Did I look as sharp in it as he had?
Who are these men in the photographs alongside him?

His Heart was Purple . . .

I was unfortunately reminded often, how much his military service was a mystery to her. Like most veterans who came home from the battlefields, he simply wanted to start his new life and to forget the pain and suffering that he had the fortune to make it out alive. I felt almost nosey at times about delving into a topic which was so difficult for anyone to have dealt with. The spark inside me, the physical connection I have with this man, still have always transmuted those thoughts. My drive to know about his part in the war is both my connection and my infatuation. I only wish to comfort the pain that this young man had to endure.

ROBERT D. MCNULTY

Yeoman 3rd Class, U.S. Naval Reserve, Pacific Theater

Submitted By Connor McNulty, Grandson

I CREDIT PART OF my interest in the grandfather I never knew; because of the amazing life I had growing up with my paternal grandfather, who is still living. Robert McNulty, my father's father, is a Navy veteran of the Pacific Theater and today is eighty-nine years old. He has shown me the love of 1,000 grandfathers and I may never be able to express how much he has meant to me. Because of the breathtaking role he has played in my life, I know how incredible it would have been if I were able to experience a similar relationship with Grandpa Hank.

My journey has been a long one and I aim to carry it with me into my future. I have answered many of my questions thus far, but still my mission will continue. I've met so many people who are on similar journeys. I was invited to the White House as Hank's descendant. It has taken me the farthest away from home I've ever been and I only intend to venture farther. Like so many young men before me, I intend to arrive in Europe and with me I will carry this great responsibility that I've been born with. I will whole-heartedly be sure to see it through.

CHARLES E. PENNEBAKER, 1ST SGT

Greenland Base Command, U.S. Army Air Force, European Theater

Submitted by Myra Pennebaker Rollins, Daughter

First Poppy donation made

From left: Kathryn Rushing, Auxiliary President, and Charles Pennebaker Submitted

Making the first Poppy fund donation was Charles Pennebaker. Pennebaker served in World War II after enlisting in the Air Force. Most of his time was spent in Greenland where he said it was cold, lots of snow, windy and just cold. After serving three years, he was honorable discharged with the rank of 1 Sgt. He came back to St. Louis and worked in construction most of his life.

He was called to preach in 1970 and later retired as a pastor in the Dixon area after 20 years. He is a veteran who served his country proudly. Pennebaker is over 90 years old and still serving whereever he can.

The American Legion Auxiliary Unit 298 will be out in the community on May 21 and 22 asking for donations to the Poppy fund. These funds are use to help veterans

JOHN F. ST. CLAIR, PVT

U.S. Army, Pacific Theater

Submitted by Cari St. Clair Wickliffe, Daughter

WHEN I WAS A young girl, my father would say, "Little girls don't need to hear about war," bypassing my questions. Typically, this occurred while we were watching a war movie on the television. Much of my understanding of Dad's service comes from pictures and a sense of community with his VFW buddies living in and around Lesterville, Missouri.

The headshot of Dad in his uniform is powerful, as it invokes a sense of contentment and readiness to serve. There is a pureness I did not expect, considering what lay ahead. Although perhaps at that stage, it was actually based on not knowing what was ahead. Other pictures of Dad are from combat situations showing the cost of battles and the toll on survivors.

What I remember most, is the gift of camaraderie and family born by his VFW buddies. Granted, growing up in small town, most people relied on one another; however, these men shared a unique, unspoken bond. It went beyond drinking beer, smoking cigarettes, and arguing politics. They made it a sense of pride and accomplishment for us to memorize Dad's dog tag number, 37132796, and to know the privilege of bringing them home. These men and their families were just part of our family sharing holiday gatherings and river time. They naturally provided an extended sense of security, support, and strength.

I am so thankful for my father, a veteran, and all of the others who selflessly let me see what they so gallantly did for our entire country.

37132796

No. 10—ROBERT J. BYRON, Greater Chicago, Ill., Lodge No. 3.

ROBERT J. BYRON, SGT

302 Transport Wing, Army Air Corps, European Theater

Submitted by Patrick Leullier, Grandson

MY GRANDFATHER, SERGEANT ROBERT J. Byron, served in the European Theater. He enlisted on March 1943 in Chicago, Illinois as an Army Air Force 405 Clerk Typist for the Headquarters and Headquarters Squadron 302 Transport Wing. His unit was based at Grove Berkshire (Royal Air Force, Station Grove, Great Britain). In 1944, after the Invasion of Europe, he was in Paris, France and later in Belgium in 1945.

The story goes ... after the war, Robert was going from Belgium to France with some of his buddies when he met my maternal grandmother. They were married in Paris, France, in 1945. I think it is interesting that my grandfather came from the United States to help save our country during WWII and then stayed after meeting his bride.

His service from 1943-1946 started in the Army Air Corps/Basic Training at Chanute Field, Illinois. Robert served in the 302 Transport Wing. His last service was as Branch Adjudant General Corps; Adjudant General (Enlisted).

His Honorable Discharge indicates that his years of battle were in the European-Africa-Middle Eastern Theater, Rhineland Campaign from September 16, 1944 to March 21, 1945, and in Central Europe from March 22 to May 11, 1945.

He received the European-African-Middle Eastern Theater Medal, Good Conduct Medal, American Theater Medal, WWII Victory Medal, and Bronze Campaign Stars (For Central Europe, Rhineland, and Nothern France).

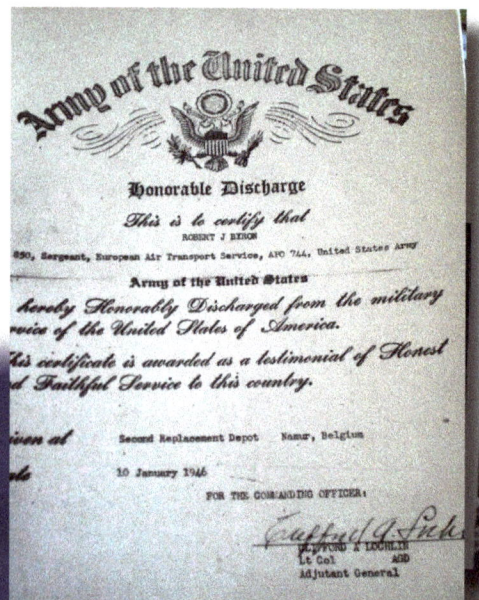

EUGENE J. DENIS, PFC

83rd Infantry Division, B/330th, European Theater

Submitted by Patrick Leullier, Adopted Grave

EUGENE DENIS' GRAVE WAS given to me when I subscribed to Memory Flowers, a project of The Patton Foundation founded by Helen Patton, the granddaughter of General George S. Patton, Jr.

On the Memory Flowers Normandy Facebook page, it explains that through the French Association, Les Fleurs de la Memoire, over 3,700 French families and schools have adopted over 10,000 American graves in Normandy and Brittany of the American serviceman killed in France during World War II. The Association members agree in writing to place flowers on the American's grave at least once a year, if possible on the American Memorial Day, to remember the sacrifice of these brave men. However, for the most part, the American families of the servicemen, and Americans in general are totally unaware that the French are doing this.

I am the proud grandson of a WWII veteran, Robert J. Byron, and in turn, honored to take care of Eugene's grave for his family. For more information or to make a donation go to www.thepattonfoundation.org or @MemoryFlowersNormandy on Facebook.

JOSEPH E. EHMET, S SGT

83rd Infantry Division, K/331st, European Theater

Written by Del Miller on behalf of The Miller Family

MY FATHER TOLD MY mother how he was wounded and she, in turn, related to me another story of war, this one sadder than most.

He sat on the edge of a trench which had belonged to the Germans just the day before. Tomorrow Company K would join the last push to the Ruhr River and, at last, bring to a close the Battle of Hurtgen Forest.

He told her that he was sitting there cleaning his rifle just a few feet from another soldier who was also preparing for battle. The mortar shell landed between them, wounding my father and killing that other soldier.

We read the morning reports for Company K and there was only one man who was reported killed on that day … S/Sgt. Joseph Ehmet.

My father must've known Joe very well, as he was likely my dad's squad leader, sitting next to him in the same trench and all. Searching further we found that my dad joined Company K on the same day Joe did. Both of them were replacements and they probably rode in from Carentan on the same truck.

But that was in Normandy, half a year earlier and half a continent away. Joe and my dad fought all through Normandy and across Brittany, they fought together through the Hurtgen Forest, the Battle of Gey and up onto this lonely hill.

Think of the stories they shared and the bond which must have grown between them; two mid-western boys thrown into a terrible war. They had to be more than friends, much more than friends. Then my dad lived, and Joe died.

So we tried to find out more about Joe so that we might call his family. He was born in Covington, Kentucky, an only son who never married, his parents long dead. Whom do we tell?

We found some people named Ehmet who still lived in his hometown, but they'd never heard of Joe. I'm so sorry that Joe's mother never knew what happened.

But at least we know.

MORRIS W. 'LEFTY' MARTIN

49TH ENGINEER COMBAT BN, U.S. ARMY, EUROPEAN THEATER

SUBMITTED BY KERRI MILLIGAN FRENCH, NIECE

LEFTY WAS THE FOURTH of seven children born September 3, 1922, to Levi and Minnie Martin in Dixon, Missouri. Times were hard for the Martin Family even before the Great Depression. The family moved several times during Lefty's childhood, and they settled in an area around Maries County, Missouri called Wheeler. When Lefty was a child, he became proficient at throwing rocks at wild rabbits in the field near his home. The rabbits he hit ended up on the family dinner table.

His formal education ended at the eighth grade. At that time, his brother Bill was working for the Depression-era Civilian Conservation Corp. At the age of fifteen, Lefty, who lied about his age to get into the program, joined his brother working for the CCC. His work in construction projects for the CCC foreshadowed his later service during WWII with the combat engineers. At about that time, he also began playing baseball for town teams in central Missouri.

In 1940, Wally Schang, a former major league catcher, saw Lefty pitch in Rolla, Missouri for a Dixon town team. Lefty pitched two shut-outs and struck out 43 batters in a single afternoon.

Impressed by what he saw, Scout Schang referred Martin to the front office of the Chicago White Sox. In 1941, the White Sox invited Lefty to try out. Lefty was 18 when he began his professional baseball career that lasted 17 years with an interruption during the years of 1943-1945.

As he was beginning his ball career, a war was raging across Europe and the Pacific Ocean. In response to this situation, the United States instituted its first peace-time military draft. The 1940 Selective Service Act required men between the ages of 21 and 35 to register for military service. Lefty was exempt from the draft during his first season of professional ball in 1941. After Pearl Harbor, the age brackets for the draft were changed to require men between 18 and 45 to register. Morris was inducted into the U.S. Army on January 2, 1943.

Morris Martin was assigned to the First Army's 49th Combat Engineers in World War II. He participated in Operation Torch, Operation Overlord, Ste.-Mere-Eglise, The Normandy Invasion at Omaha Beach, Operation Cobra, Bastogne, the Bridge at Remagen, and the Battle of the Bulge.

He didn't pick up a baseball from the time he left the U.S. for service in WWII until he came home in 1945 to recover from his war injuries. His first injury was shrapnel to his neck, left hand and arm while on guard duty near St. Lo, France. He stayed on the front lines despite his injuries. Late in the year of 1944, he was involved in the Battle of the Bulge in the Ardennes Mountains of Belgium. He suffered frostbite in the bitterly cold temperatures, but he remained with his unit until he was seriously injured in combat in 1945.

On March 23, 1945, at a crossroad near Bonn, Germany, he was shot in the leg. The wound nearly cost him his leg. Lefty was evacuated to a hospital in Saint-Quentin, France. He was extremely fortunate to be under the watchful care of a nurse who looked at his chart and discovered he was a professional baseball player. The nurse recommended he resist the recommended amputation of his leg. She told him there was a "new" drug that would fight the infection of gangrene. He took her advice and was treated with over 150 injections of penicillin. The recovery was long and painful, but he was fortunate that the "new" medication was successful.

Lefty spent two months in the hospital before being sent to Fort Dix, New Jersey. From there, he went to Camp Carson, Colorado where he was given furlough at the end of September 1945. While on Furlough, he met his wife, Leona, whom he married in 1945.

Lefty was discharged from the Army in 1945 with two legs intact thanks to a nurse in France and the power of penicillin, a pitching hand that had been hit by shrapnel, and battle scars beyond those that were visible on his body.

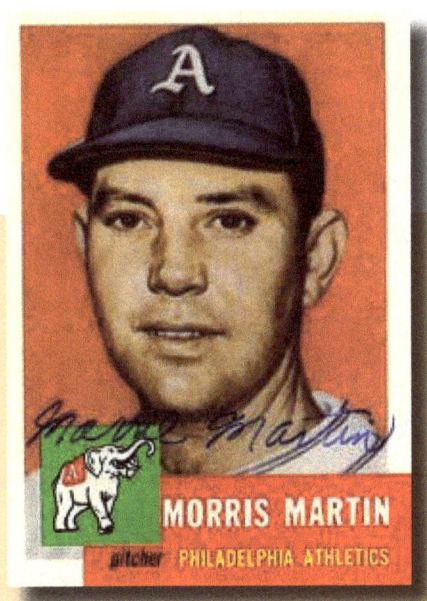

"I faced Mickey Mantle, Joe DiMaggio and Frank Robinson. But the best hitter I ever faced was Ted Williams," Martin told The Missourian. "He had great eyes. You could never fool him."

After his discharge, he was decorated with an EAME (Europe, Africa, Middle East) Ribbon with five Bronze Stars and a Purple Heart with Oak Leaf Cluster (wounded twice in battle).

Lefty returned to baseball in 1946. He survived a world war to rub elbows with teammates like Jackie Robinson, Duke Snider, Nellie Fox and Stan Musial.

Although Lefty enjoyed talking about his baseball career, he didn't like to talk about his role in WWII. He took part in a conference held in New Orleans in 2008 about baseball and WWII that stirred up painful memories about his wartime experience. Shortly before his death on May 24, 2010, he made a statement that showed he understood how important his wartime service was, "We had a job to do, and we did it. I don't have regrets about the time I missed in baseball. I'm proud of what we did. I'd do it again."

No matter what part of his life he liked to remember, he lived a life worth remembering.

He was a true war hero.

A left-handed pitcher, Martin played for eight different professional teams during his career, including 21 games for the St. Louis Cardinals during the 1957-58 seasons.

WILLIAM R. RANSDALL, 1ST LT

Fighter Pilot, U.S. Army Air Force, European Theater

Submitted by Bill L. Ransdall, Son

WILLIAM RUSSELL RANSDALL WAS born on December 4, 1919, in Augusta, Kansas. He died on July 6, 2009, in Waynesville, Missouri.

For most of his childhood, he lived in Waynesville, Missouri. Then he went to Augusta, Kansas to finish high school. He enlisted in the Army Air Corps on December 23, 1940. He went to pilot school in Yuma, Arizona, where he fired the highest gunnery score ever recorded at that time. In World War II, William attained the rank of First Lieutenant. He flew seventy-six combat missions as a fighter pilot in P40s and P47s and was once shot down behind enemy lines and was listed Missing in Action (MIA). After three days, he was found by a French Patrol and returned to his unit. He was awarded the Distinguished Flying Cross.

On August 12, 1945, he was honorably discharged from the service. After the war, he settled in Waynesville where he married Marjorie L. Roach and had a son named Billy Lee Ransdall.

NOTE FROM BILL L. RANSDALL:

Dad was an avid supporter of Fort Leonard Wood and the military families. He was a corporate member of AUSA (Association of the United States Army). He often traveled to Washington, D.C. to attend the national conventions and rode the bus with the military personnel.

He was asked to testify at the public official hearing for the building and permitting of Cannon Range at Fort Wood. A Brigadier General (Air Force), conducted the meeting. Dad was in total support of the project and spoke of the importance of training, having served as a fighter pilot himself.

After the meeting, the General told my dad that he had attended flight school but was washed out because of his eyesight. Dad responded that he always wondered what happened to those guys that washed out, now he knew, they made Generals out of them! They both had a good laugh and we now have Cannon Range!

MILLARD H. HAUCK, T4 SGT

Engineers, U.S. Army, European Theater

Submitted by Harlond Hauck, Son

EFFORTS WERE MADE WHENEVER possible to not have brothers land at the same time. Therefore, Fred Max Hauck was in the first wave on D-Day as a duck driver. The duck got hit by a shell in the back and was disabled, which then floated in the English Channel for a day before being rescued. However, the rescuers would not take them to the beach where they wanted to go after floating a day (dry land); instead, the rescuers took them back to England. They were then sent back to France soon after.

My dad, Millard Hauck, went in a couple of days after D-Day and was assigned to drive a fuel tanker since his dad had worked on a pipeline (not sure how the army thought that qualified him to be a fuel driver, but that is what they told him nonetheless). The Germans quickly figured out that it was more efficient to blow up the fuel tankers rather than trying to take out all the tanks. So, after about a week, he had lost over half the people he had started with. One day, the Captain came through asking if anyone had any heavy equipment experience. Dad raised his hand, even though he had never seen such a large piece of equipment. He quickly figured out how to start the monstrosity and drove it the rest of the war. His group got lost (I think during the German push-back later that year). They crossed a river with several pieces of heavy equipment and could then see an encampment that was not supposed to be there. The Germans had retaken that side of the river. His group immediately scraped off the coating on the headlights and retreated as fast as they could.

Throughout his time with the big machinery, his group had built airfields for Patton's drive, but his army was moving so fast, most of the time the airfields were not even used. My dad was the last one back home because his unit was attached to Patton's occupation force.

Hauck Boys Home from WWII
Fred Max   Bessie   Frank X.
Millard   Edwin   Egland

THE HAUCK BROTHERS

Brothers from Dixon, Missouri, Pacific and European Theaters

Submitted by Harlond Hauck, Son and Nephew

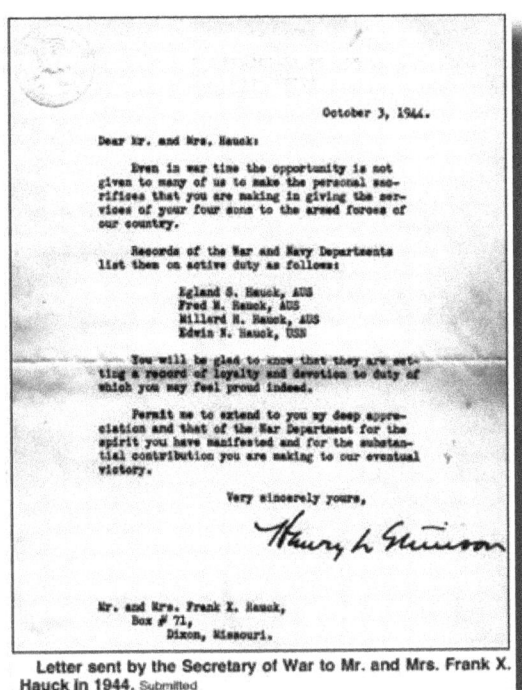

Letter sent by the Secretary of War to Mr. and Mrs. Frank X. Hauck in 1944. Submitted.

I CAN REMEMBER FRED Max taking me on his shoulders down to the depot each day to meet the train to see if Dad was on it, finally making his way home. Everyone says at three-years-old, you can't remember these things, but I think I can because everything was so dramatic during that time. I really didn't have a concept of a dad, but I sure enjoyed the ride on Fred Max's shoulders. I can also remember going with Mom and Grandma Hauck to Jefferson Barracks for Dad to muster out. They say I can't remember that, but I told them how we sat on the beautifully manicured grass in a big swale ditch waiting on him. So, they think maybe I could somehow remember. I also vividly remember getting kicked out of Mom's bed, to which I took a dim view; and I remember crying all night several nights because of this terrible wrong.

I remember an old story Dad and Fred Max used to laugh about. Dad found an old, abandoned, shot-up car which he fixed up. To transport the car, he would open the big earth scraper and drive the car inside and take it with him.

Dixon family presented 5-Star Banner in honor of sons' service in WWII

The four Hauck brothers who served during World War II, from left: Millard, Egland, Edwin and Fred Max. Photo submitted.

still living; a gold star would represent a son lost during service.) At that time, their four sons: Egland Sutton Hauck, Fred Max Hauck, Millard Hale Hauck (all members of the U.S. Army) and Edwin Nile Hauck (Egland's twin and a member of the U.S. Navy) were listed as being on active duty by the records of the War and Navy Departments. Their sister, Frances, married a military man, Jack P. Geise, who became a colonel in the army. The couple was later stationed in Germany and Italy after World War II was over. The original banner included four stars, but a fifth was later added to denote Mr. Geise's involvement, as well.

Recipients of the banner usually hung it on a string and displayed it in the windows of their homes, so others could easily recognize their sons' contributions to the war effort. Eventually, Bessie Hauck had her banner framed to preserve it. In her later years, Bessie moved in with her son, Edwin and his wife, Inez. Eventually, after her death, her grandson—Tony Hauck (Edwin's son) found the framed banner in some items he was going through which belonged to his parents. Tony, who lives in the Tulsa, Oklahoma area, made a trip to Dixon to deliver the family heirloom to the only remaining son of Bessie and Frank Egland and his wife, Carmen.

Egland Hauck, holding the memorial banner his mother and father received during their sons' military involvement during World War II. Photo by Susan E. Hohman.

Fred Max stayed in the reserves, so he got called up in the Korean war, even though he was the oldest of the siblings and much older than all the new recruits. Edwin served in the Pacific where his ship got hit (he wouldn't ever talk about it) and his twin, Egland, served in Europe. The youngest in our family was Francis, the only sister.

Francis' husband, Jack Geise, was an officer who eventually became a colonel. Francis met him when he was stationed at Fort Leonard Wood. He had graduated from Military School and served on Eisenhower's staff most of the war. The family word is that he is the person who Eisenhower dispatched to deliver Patton's stand-down order in Italy after the slapping incident. He did that reluctantly. They were married after Dad had shipped out, but somehow Fred Max met him after the invasion, brought him down to meet Dad and they all three were able to stay in touch through Jack's position and would meet periodically through the rest of the war. Jack and Francis were stationed for many years at various embassies after the war ended.

Millard Hauck with his three oldest grandchildren playing in the sand at Omaha Beach. Three previous trips to the beaches of France, he tried to find his landing point but left disappointed. On this, the fourth trip, we were all packed into a small car driving up and down the beaches all day. Suddenly my Dad, in a quiet, subdued voice said to pull over. I don't remember him saying another word. This was it–he had finally found the landing point. It was exactly as he had described it, down to the locations of the gun emplacements (most were still there), ridges and valleys. Guess something like that would stick in your mind. He was really happy to have found it and you can see in the picture, very reflective.

WILLIAM I. LONG, PFC

83rd Infantry Division, E/331st, European Theater

Submitted by Carol Long Buckley, Daughter

PRIVATE FIRST CLASS WILLIAM Irvin Long was born in Shamokin, Pennsylvania on February 14, 1915. He married Amy A. Vought on November 21, 1941, and was inducted into the US Army on November 13, 1943. He traveled to England, then went to the continent where he served in combat in France, Luxembourg, Belgium, and Germany, with Company E, 331st Infantry, 83rd Infantry Division.

He was killed in action in the Huertgen Forest near Gey, Germany on December 10, 1944. He had been awarded the Combat Infantryman's Badge, Good Conduct Medal, and the Purple Heart. His daughter, Carol Jeanne, was born one month after his death. His wife Amy received the notice of her husband's death three days after she gave birth to his daughter.

Carol and George Buckley had the privilege to travel to Holland to visit her father's grave at the American War Cemetery in Margraten, Netherlands, where over 8,000 American soldiers are buried. They met Tanja and Rico Bronneberg, who had adopted his grave and faithfully cared for it for many years. They attended the Memorial Day Ceremony together and found it heartwarming to realize how wonderfully the people of Holland have honored and cared for their fallen American liberators.

Foundation for Adopting Graves American Cemetery Margraten, http://www.adoptiegraven-margraten.nl/en/

GEORGES FREDERICKX

Teen During the Occupation of Belgium

Submitted by Jelle Thys, Grandson

MY GRANDFATHER, GEORGES FREDERICKX, was born April 8, 1923, as the second child in a family of seven children. He was the oldest son of Emiel Frederickx and Celina Helsen; his sister was two years older.

The family had always lived in Putte, Belgium, and was living there when the war broke out on May 10, 1940. Celina Helsen had fled the country with her siblings and parents during World War I as well, and it was decided the family would join the long line of fugitives trying to stay out of the grasp of the German Army. At 17 years of age, Georges was not old enough to join the Belgian Army, so he fled together with his family. The Germans caught up with them, however, and on May 28th, Belgium capitulated. A few weeks later, the family decided to move back to their hometown of Putte.

As the war progressed, the Germans were drafting larger and larger numbers from their workforce. Because of this, they started to look for new able-bodied young men in their occupied territories to fill in these vacant spots. First, they set up a system where men from the occupied countries could volunteer, but this proved of little success. This forced the German government to start enforcing these young men to go to work in Germany. One of those young men that the Germans wanted to employ in their war industry, was my grandfather, Georges

Frederickx. Because of the workforce regulations, Georges was required to go sign up and leave on a later day. Like most of the young men, he signed up but when the time came around to go to the train station, he had changed his mind. He had now become what we in Dutch call a "werkweigeraar," literally, someone who refuses to go to work.

Being a "werkweigeraar," Georges and several of his friends automatically became fugitives, which meant they had to go into hiding. Because of the rural nature of Putte, they managed to always stay in the area. The local population supported the young men and farmers allowed them to work their fields in exchange for some food or a place to sleep. Sometimes, they would even dare to go sleep at home, however, there was always a risk involved in doing so. The German police would actively search for the men that refused to go to work and would organize razzia's in the middle of the night. My grandfather's older sister recalls how the Germans went to work:

> *"The Germans would pull up in their truck in the middle of the night and turn our house upside down. They would even storm into my, or my sisters' rooms, pulling away the sheets as we were still in our beds. They wanted to make sure we were not hiding our brother in any way. When Georges stayed at home, he would not sleep in the house, however; he would sleep outside in the bomb shelter. This would give him a chance to run if the Germans raided our house."*

All in all, most of the "werkweigeraars" of Putte managed to stay out of trouble rather easily. A friend of my grandfather testified to this as well:

> *"We could go into the bar at night with little problems and we would even go into town when a fair or something similar was going on. We just tried to stay out of trouble and lay low. Many times, I also slept at home and even worked on our own farm and whenever the Germans were planning a razzia, the local policeman would warn my parents. In the summer, when we were sleeping outdoors we could hear the German trucks from miles away so that made it easy to stay out of their grasp."*

My grandfather, Georges Frederickx, stayed in hiding until Putte was liberated early September 1944. After that, he would go to work for the U.S. military unloading supplies from trains onto trucks to be brought to the frontline. He married my grandmother in the 1950s and together they had three children, two girls and a boy, Gerda, André, and Nelly (my mother). My grandmother passed away in 2001. My grandfather suffered a hemorrhage in May 2009 and spent four weeks in the hospital before passing away. It saddens me deeply that I never got to speak to him in person about his experiences during World War II.

DANIEL W. HALLADAY, COL

Captain, 83rd Infantry Division, K/331st, European Theater

Submitted by Whitney Halladay Whitelaw, Daughter

I AM VERY PROUD to be the daughter of Daniel Whitney Halladay (Dan, to his military friends and Whit, to others). I am sorry that my brother, Steve Halladay, is no longer living to make contributions to this narrative as he attended several reunions with Dad and would have memories relating to the 83rd Infantry Division.

While I knew that Dad had served in both World War II and the Korean War, it was not something discussed in our home. I do remember that shrapnel in his back surfaced and was removed throughout his life—apparently, I thought that was normal. Many of my friends' parents had been in the war; we really did not understand the level of sacrifice they made to allow us to live and grow up in a free country.

My dad's life and value system were greatly influenced by his military experience. My brother and I, our children and grandchildren have been directly and indirectly impacted by his pride in being an American, his honor in serving his country and his strong belief in always doing the right thing. His was a life well lived and we, his descendants, are grateful to have been part of that journey.

Background
- Date of Birth: October 13, 1920, in Santa Ana, California
- Date of Death: July 12, 1980

Military
- Active in the United States Army during both World War II and the Korean War
- Awarded the Silver Star, Bronze Star with two Oak Leaf Clusters, Commendation Medal, Purple Heart with Oak Leaf Clusters and Combat Infantryman's Badge
- United States Army Reserve, Fayetteville, AR from 1955-1966
- Retired from the Army with the rank of Colonel
- Appointed to the Board of Visitors to the United States Military Academy from 1970-1973

Education
- Bachelor of Arts Degree from Pomona College in Claremont, California in 1942
- Master of Arts Degree in Social Sciences and Education from Claremont
- Graduate School in 1947
- Doctor of Education Degree in Student Personnel Administration and Administration of Higher Education from Columbia University in 1955

Career
- Dean of Students, University of Arkansas from 1955-1966
- President of East Texas State University from 1966-1972
- President Texas A&I University from 1972-1976
- Acting Chancellor of Texas A&I University System from 1976-1977
- Chancellor of the University System of South Texas from 1977-1980

CAPTAIN HALLADAY

SO YOU'RE AN ENLISTED man, sent to a war where your captain sends you and your men into mortal danger every day. The captain decides who will charge the machine gun nest and who will be exposed to deadly fire. How could you not feel bitterness toward him? How could you not hate him?

Thirty years after the war, my father spoke to Daniel Halladay on the phone. I don't know the reason why he called, but they spoke at length. After the call, I asked about Capt. Halladay and my father told me, "Daniel Halladay was the best soldier I ever knew. He was terrific."

Del Miller, son of Myron H. Miller, S/Sgt

EDWARD 'NED' BURR, COL

1st Lt., 83rd Infantry Division, 324th FAbn, European Theater

Submitted by Ned Burr, Self

ON THE MORNING OF July 4, 1944, in Normandy France, E Company of the 331st Infantry Regiment, 83rd Infantry Division began an attack on the German defenses. I was assigned to this company as a forward observer from the 324th Field Artillery Battalion. No sooner had we begun our advance when we received a heavy amount of fire of all forms from the enemy. The company commander asked me to request a re-fire of our artillery barrage. In my effort to make radio contact, my radio operator and I were hit by fragments from a small shell. The fragment that hit me, entered my body in the back of my left armpit and exited under my left shoulder blade–the explosion blew me off of the side of the road eight feet down into the road. That fall bruised some ribs, so when I came to, it hurt a bit to breathe. I climbed back up the side of the road to check on my radioman, but as I started to help him, realized that I was in trouble myself. I stumbled back along the side of the road and fortunately came to a dirt ramp which led me down out of the line of fire and into the arms of some of the men who had been with me earlier. I collapsed and, as I learned later, the guys carried me back to the battalion aid station.

My story at this point, relates entirely to the medical support organization the Army had put in place to save men like me who were wounded in action. There was a doctor assigned to that aid station and he took action to stop the bleeding and to give me a large injection of morphine. I was then placed in a field ambulance, which took me back to an evacuation hospital, which had a full operating capability. I only regained consciousness twice before I ended up in a hospital bed—once as I was put into the ambulance, and once while I was on a stretcher on my way to have x-rays taken. I did not stay awake for very long either time due, I'm sure, to the morphine. As I look back on it, I find it a bit amazing that there was a doctor on the front lines and a tented, but major hospital facility only a few miles back of those same combat lines. The fragment that

went through me did not hit any organs or bones, but my loss of blood was large. Somewhere along the path of my medical care, I received a transfusion of 2,000 cc's of whole blood. That blood came from Americans (like my beloved wife), who made regular donations to the blood bank. There again, a hospital thousands of miles from home had large supplies of different types of whole blood on hand.

My medical journey was not complete. I had a relapse while recovering in the Evac Hospital, in that the sutures on the wound on the back of me opened, and if not for the action of an alert nurse, I might have bled to death in that bed. Finally, I was carried to Utah Beach, loaded onto a landing craft, and then on to a beautifully equipped hospital ship. Once back in England, I spent the night in a holding facility and the next morning I was on a hospital train headed for the General Hospital in Cheltenham. I don't remember much about the details of the trip. As I mentioned previously, morphine was applied liberally. I believe–of course, it suppressed the pain, but I also think that it was an aid to the staff in keeping patient complaints to a minimum. The care I received was superb. I was on the road to recovery when I arrived at Cheltenham on or about July 15th and I was discharged and ordered to rejoin my unit on September 1st.

The photo below is the area where I was wounded in 1944. Back then, it looked nothing like this; it was a terrible, scarred battleground. I love how this scenic picture shows the countryside today, free of war—beautiful!

Watch the video of Colonel Edward "Ned" Burr on The Washington Free Beacon being interviewed: Five World War II Veterans Tell Their Stories. http://freebeacon.com/culture/5-world-war-ii-veterans-tell-their-stories/

WILBURN C. ROWDEN, T SGT

452ND BOMB GROUP, U.S. ARMY AIR CORPS, EUROPEAN THEATER

SUBMITTED BY CAROL ROWDEN MILLER, SISTER

WILBURN ROWDEN GREW UP in Vienna, Missouri and served in the U.S. Army Air Corps as a B-17 Radio Operator assigned to the 452nd Bomb Group. His plane was shot down over Germany in March 1944; he was captured and remained a prisoner of war until April, 1945. In 1999, he wrote about his experiences of fifty-five years earlier. Today, he lives in Jefferson City, Missouri.

Brothers from Vienna, Missouri, Wilburn C. Rowden (L), Herbert V. Rowden (R)

March 6, 1944: Target, Berlin ("Big B"). We didn't make it to Berlin. In the vicinity of Hanover, Germany, ME-109 fighters hit us and damaged our aircraft. The first time they hit our #2 engine and set us on fire. We dropped out of formation to feather the engine and were hit again, the #3 engine was knocked out, the radio room and nose were shot up, and we were still on fire. I recall pandemonium in the aircraft. We were losing altitude, and our pilot gave us the order to bail out. Fire had destroyed two parachutes, and with only one spare, we were one chute short. Our pilot, MacDonald, came on the intercom and told the navigator to come to the cockpit and take his spare chute and for all crew members to jump, "Bail Out!" The navigator protested, but MacDonald told him that he was in command and if anyone could make a crash landing with the aircraft in the condition it was, he could. So we all bailed out and left the pilot alone to fly or crash the plane.

We were at approximately 30,000 feet. Our tail gunner had to be pushed out as he was injured and passed out due to lack of oxygen. So some of our crew pulled the handle to his parachute and pushed him out. The ball turret jammed and had to be cranked manually to a position so the gunner could get out.

I remember pulling my ripcord and felt the jolt when may parachute opened. As I was floating down towards earth, I assessed my plight, realizing I still had my ripcord handle in one hand and my G.I. shoes in the other.

A German fighter buzzed me on the way down and I could see the pilot looking at me. I thought he was going to get me in his slipstream and spill my chute, but he didn't. I thought if I had my .45 pistol, I might have shot him. I felt helpless. He was probably relaying my position to ground by radio.

I landed in a small clearing at the edge of a field. My parachute caught in top of a small tree which bent over due to my weight and let me down easily. The timber was dense and dark around the clearing, a good place for me to hide. I thought, as I had been instructed, if possible I would wait until dark to move. First, I attempted to get my parachute out of the tree to hide it. It was then that I discovered that I had been hit in my arms and legs. I noticed blood coming through my clothing and it hurt to move my arms and legs. Then I noticed some German Air (Luftwaffe) soldiers moving in on me. They were spread out carrying their rifles in the ready position. We had been instructed to be taken by soldiers rather than civilians, if unable to escape or evade. So, realizing I could not run, I sat down on one of the tree stumps and awaited them.

I was bandaged after dark and much later I was placed in the bed of a truck, along with some other captured airmen and moved to a hospital in Hanover. I was placed in a room with six or eight bunks with some other injured airmen. We had a very young captured Russian soldier assigned to take care of us. Because I couldn't move my arms or legs, he fed me the single skimpy meal we got daily.

On about March 10th, I was moved by train to a hospital in Frankfurt. I remember riding on the train with only a blanket to wrap up in and getting pretty cold. I saw some of my crewmembers and learned that our co-pilot, Lieutenant Godsey from Richmond, Virginia and Lieutenant John Harris, our bombardier from Salmon, Idaho, had not been heard from. We learned later that civilians had killed them. I remember the joyous reunion with Lieutenant Moskowitz, our navigator and our pilot, Lieutenant MacDonald who had crash-landed the plane and survived. Upon arriving at Frankfurt, I was separated from the rest of our crew and taken to the hospital. This was the last time I saw any of our crew while in Germany.

On March 23, 1944, Wilburn was moved to Stalag Luft #6 in East Prussia near the Baltic Coast. Living conditions were primitive and the weather cold. Food was poor and meager but was supplemented by Red Cross parcels. By Summer, the Russian army advance was nearing the camp and on July 15, 1944, Wilburn and the other POWs started their move to Stalag Luft #9 at Gross Tischau, in North Central Germany.

When we entered the compound, we were held in the enclosure at the front entrance where we were searched and processed and assigned to barracks. We were held in the vorlager for two days where we were strip-searched. We were ordered to undress completely, and all items of our clothing were laid flat on a table and each seam, lapel, and pocket were felt and bent by guards. They looked in our mouth, nose, ears and all parts of our bodies where anything could be concealed. One of the POWs was carrying a small compass in his mouth. When ordered to open his mouth, he swallowed the compass. We retrieved it a few days later.

There were approximately twenty-four men to each room. We soon became friends and a lot of us were nicknamed. Such names as Curly, South Side, Proff, Silent Ed, Lonesome, Poco, Horizontal Harry, and mine was Crooner. I was held in this camp from July 18, 1944, to February 6, 1945. We were aware of the progress of the war. We had traded cigarettes from our food parcels for a radio that was hidden from our guards. Each day, one of our guys would come to each room and read a BBC news bulletin. We had a plan that if a guard came into a room while the news bulletin was being read, the paper would be thrown into the stove and burned. The Red Cross food parcels were a great help to our well-being and morale. Besides food and cigarettes, they also furnished items of clothing, books, and recreational equipment. Also, we occasionally received mail and some packages from home which were a joy. However, by the time we received the packages, the cookies were stale and most of the time in crumbs. In one of my parcels were some snapshots of friends and family, which I still have and some clothing items that I was glad to get and dress up and wear out.

On February 6, 1945, Wilburn and the other POWs were marched out of Stalag Luft #9 on a move that would cover some 500 miles in 87 days and end in Bitterfield, Germany.

My buddy and I began to make preparations. We each took a shirt and sewed the tail shut and brought the sleeves down and sewed them to the tail to make a knapsack. This way, we could carry items in the pack and drape our rolled blankets over the top. We hit the road, the sorriest looking group of stragglers you ever saw. We were wearing all the extra clothing we could obtain and carrying our other provisions and personal items. Some simply carried a small roll or package, others, like myself, had a makeshift pack.

Soon the extra food we were carrying was used up, and we began to rely on scrounging along the way. We were usually housed at night in a village or courtyard that was surrounded by a fence or wall, thus making it easier for the guards to control us. The courtyards usually had barns where we could sleep in the hayloft or stalls in the hay, probably where we picked up some of our body lice. During these stops, we managed to trade with some local people for food, using cigarettes or candy from our food parcels. At one stop, we had a G.I. watch that belonged to one of our guys which I traded for sausage and bread.

Somewhere, I remember a German guard at a road junction gesturing and shouting as we passed, that Roosevelt was dead. "Ja, Roosevelt kaput, dead," and gesturing across his throat. This caused us a lot of concern and worry and was a topic of discussion amongst us for a while, wondering if this might affect our status.

We were marched through the line and turned over to the American 104th Division (Timberwolf). Some Canadian soldiers approached one of our guards and reached out and took his gun. That was when I knew for sure this was the real thing. The first American soldier we saw was greeted, hugged, kissed and hand shaken until his arm and shoulder hurt. What a happy day! Our German guards were held in an open field surrounded by our soldiers. I did not have any sympathy for them. As we moved across the bridge over the river into Bitterfield, a lot of POWs threw their blankets and other items into the river. I decided to keep mine, not knowing if I might need them again.

For an adventure that began with my induction into the Army on January 7, 1943 and ending on November 3, 1945, I, a backwards country boy, saw a lot of the country and had obtained a great deal of experience. Looking back, I can say that I am proud to have served my country.

Wilburn C. Rowden

ALVA WEST, T3 SGT

456th Dukw Co, Amphibian Truck Co., U.S. Army, Pacific Theater

Submitted by Mark West, Son

AMERICAN, MISSOURIAN, FARMER, FAMILY man, World War II veteran. Alva West, my dad, was born in 1919 and passed away May 16, 1992.

Born in a log cabin, located near where the West family originally settled near Meta, Missouri, he was a descendant of one of the first settlers in Missouri. Dad lived most of his life near Chilhowee where he and his older brother worked long, hard days with their father during the Great Depression. He was picking corn, by hand, in Iowa the day Pearl Harbor was bombed.

In the Spring of 1942, he got a letter in the mail from the U.S. Government saying that his friends and neighbors had selected him to serve in the military.

He reported to the draft board in Clinton, Missouri on April 23, 1942. His induction into the U.S. Army was on April 24, 1942 at Jefferson Barracks, Missouri. He was sent to Fort Dix, New Jersey for basic training and on April 29, 1942, he was assigned to Aberdeen Proving Ground, Aberdeen, Maryland, Company A, 2nd Ordnance Training Battalion, where he received heavy maintenance training.

On November 11, 1942, he traveled to Rice, California en route to the Mojave Desert for assignment to the 86th Ordnance Company, which was part of the support for General George Patton's armored maneuvers, desert training.

While he was there, he was asked to seal a tank. Patton asked Dad and another solider to drive it under the Colorado River. The other solider refused, and Patton got in to complete the ride under the river.

Bob Hope, who was on base to entertain, asked to go on a tank ride. Dad asked him what kind of ride he wanted. He said "give it everything you got."

Dad offered him a helmet and he refused. Dad took the tank over the obstacle course and Hope banged his head a time or two.

In 1943, the Armored Division was transferred to Camp Kilmer, New Jersey. A casual camp preparing to ship overseas. When given a physical checkup, Dad was diagnosed with the residuals of scarlet fever and quarantined. He did not ship out to Africa with his armored unit.

Once released from quarantine, he was sent to Moulrieville, South Carolina, near Fort Moultrie, for Amphibian Truck Training. He was given hand-to-hand combat training by a marine sergeant. The Amphibian Truck Company operated special land/water vehicles known as DUKWs ("Ducks").

The entire company was shipped by train to San Francisco and the 456th Amphibian Truck Company Embarked October 12, 1943 to the Pacific on the USAT David C. Shanks. The ship crossed the equator on October 20, 1943.

The Unit arrived on Guadalcanal (an ordnance resupply) on November 5, 1943. They travelled to the Gilberts and Mariana Islands before arriving in Peleliu.

The Battle of Peleliu occurred from September 15, 1944 to November, 27 1944.

The first day Dad arrived on Peleliu, he lost his field pack. He dug a fox hole with his mess kit spoon, with Japanese machine gun fire hitting the sand in front of him. During his time on Peleliu, he saw a marine disintegrate when he stepped on a land mine. He welded metal doors shut to keep the Japanese from shooting at them. When zagging his Duck across an air field, a Japanese machine gun cut loose and shot the steering wheel out of his hands and sprayed 114 bullet holes into the hull of the Duck. At the end of Peleliu, he had not changed clothes, showered, or shaved in 69 days. When he took his shoes off, the bottoms of his feet came with them.

In December 1944, he returned to Guadalcanal. On Christmas 1944, his company was quarantined by a doctor for being unfit for battle with battle fatigue and were given hospital rations. Upon release from the hospital, they were issued 50 new DUKWs. They did maneuvers and hauled supplies during their time on the island. When the unit set sail again, they picked up men and joined the armada/fleet headed to Okinawa.

On April 1, 1945, Easter Sunday, they landed on Okinawa. It was the largest amphibious assault in the Pacific and the bloodiest battle in the Pacific.

Brothers from Chihowee, Missouri,
Ethmer West (L), Alva West (R)

Dad endured, but had trench foot from wet feet because the antibiotic he was issued did not work. He shaved with lye G.I. soap and placed it in his socks and cured the trench foot himself. He lived through a typhoon and Kamikaze planes. When the surrender was announced on August 1945, soldiers began shooting into the air in celebration. Dad was worried about dying from the celebration fire and had to take shelter.

Dad returned to the States and separated from the Army in December 1945 at Jefferson Barracks, Missouri. He finally made it home two days before Christmas 1945.

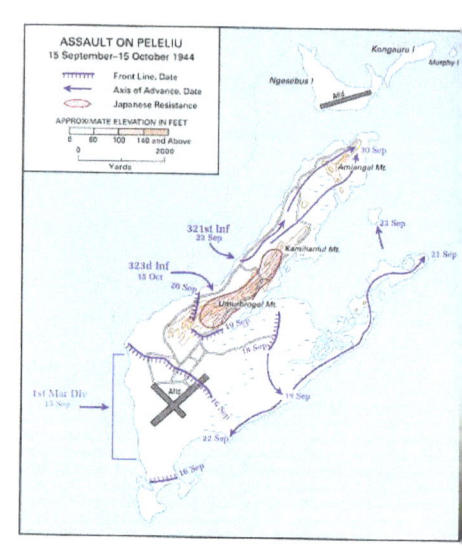

ETHMER WEST, CPL

35TH INFANTRY DIVISION, H/137, EUROPEAN THEATER

SUBMITTED BY MARK WEST, NEPHEW

ETHMER WEST WAS MY father's brother. I never met him as he was killed in action on July 19, 1944, while fighting in the hedgerows of Normandy.

My uncle began infantry training during April 1942 and was assigned to the 4th Platoon, Company C, 54th Infantry Training Battalion, at Camp Wolters in Mineral Wells, Texas. This was the largest infantry replacement training base during WWII and the same facility where Audie Murphy trained.

- In early 1943, he assembled with the 35th Infantry Division at Camp San Luis Obispo.
- April 1943, he moved with the division to Camp Rucker, Alabama.
- November, December 1943 and January 1944, Ethmer was at the Tennessee Maneuver Area.
- Afterwards, he was moved to Camp Butner, North Carolina for final training which finished with Mountain Maneuvers in West Virginia.
- After West Virginia, the regiment was reviewed in a Combat Team Exercise by Secretary of War Patterson and Senator Harry Truman.
- May 4, 1944, they were moved to Camp Kilmer New Jersey.
- May 11, 1944, sailed past the Statue of Liberty, on SS Thomas H. Barry on the way to Europe.
- May 24, 1944, ship docked at Avonmouth, England; sent by train through Exeter to Bodmin Road and Newquay.
- July 4, 1944, moved the unit to Plymouth and Falmouth.
- July 6–7, 1944, loaded and shipped out from both Plymouth and Falmouth.
- July 7–8–9, 1944, landed at Omaha Beach.

At this point, Ethmer was assigned to the 35th Infantry Division, 137th Infantry Regiment, Company H as a light mortar crewman. According to the combat history timeline found on the website, 35thInfantryDivision-memory.com, the137th was assigned to beach defense.

COMPANY RESTRICTED
MORNING REPORT ENDING 2400 25 July 194 4
STATION Hemel T4665 Lambert Zone 1
ORGANIZATION Co H 137 Inf Regt Inf

SERIAL NUMBER	NAME		GRADE	CODE
01313277	McLean, Charles S	Inf	2 Lt	A
	Asgd & Jd fr 92 Repl Bn Date of Rank			
	6 Mar 1943 Comp AUS Race W Prin Dy			
	Inf Unit Comdr 1542			
36116900	Polzin, Harold A	653	Cpl	
35125296	Bryant, Theodore L	653	Cpl	
	Above 2 EM Promoted to SGT			
36561761	Brunsel, Andrew	607	Pfc	A
	Fr LWA Dropped fr Asgmt to RTD			
37145130	West, Ethmer	607	Cpl	M
	Fr Dy to KIA as of 19 July 1944			
35441679	McCleese, Warren	504	Pfc	M
	Fr Dy to LWA Dropped fr Asgmt as of			
	17 July 1944			

RECORD OF EVENTS
MAP USED ST LO SHEET 6F/2

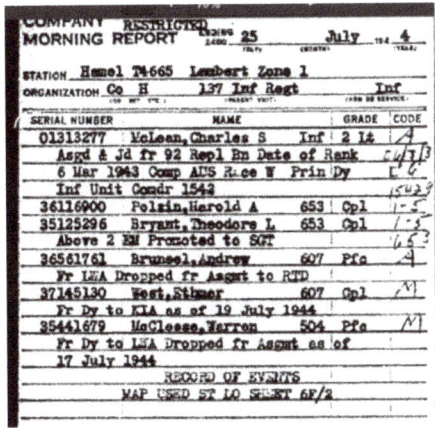

- July 8–9, 1944, prepared for battle.
- Afternoon July 9, 1944, unit movement began forward to relieve the 119th Infantry Regiment of the 30th Infantry Division in the vicinity of Le Meauffe north of St. Lo.
- July 10–18, 1944, hedgerow battle and daily battles ending with heaviest fighting on the last two days and the division taking St. Lo after a retreat by German forces on the 18th.
- July 19, 1944, patrolling rear areas, clearing out scattered enemy, clearing minefields and reorganizing forces for defense.
- July 19, 1944, recorded as Ethmer Killed In Action (KIA).

19 JULY 1944 - With St. Lo taken, and the Corps mission completed in eight days of fighting, 19 July was a period of patrolling rear areas and cleaning out scattered Germans, clearing minefields, and reorganization of forces for defense of areas occupied. The Germans, from their positions across the river, continued to shell our troops with mortar and artillery fire, and shortly before 2300 Wednesday night, single-engine enemy bombers flew over the regimental area dropping flares and butterfly bombs. On this day our losses were 9 killed, 11 wounded and 1 missing. Clearing the area boosted the number of prisoners captured to 54 for the 19th. On this day also the Corps Commander issued a commendation for the fine showing of the 35th Division in their part of the operation.

QMC Form 14

- 1948, Deceased returned from LaCambe-Insigny, France.
- February 11, 1948, interned Lot 11, Grave 1026 of the Jefferson City National Cemetery, 1042 E. McCarty, Jefferson City, Missouri

Ethmer grave
Ethmer was borned aug 25 1917
was killed in acion in France
on July 19. 1944 age 26 years
10 months 24 days
was brought to U.S.
in February and buried
in National Cemetary
Feb 11 1948 at Jefferson
City Mo.

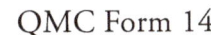

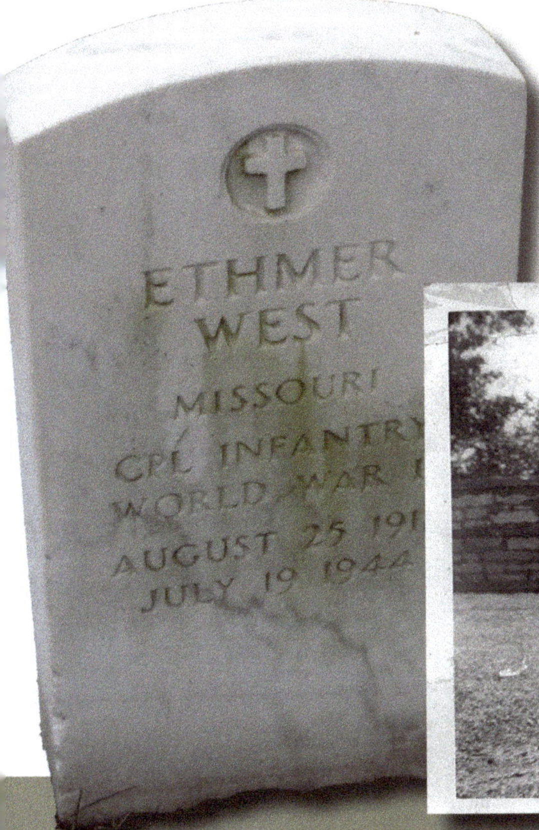

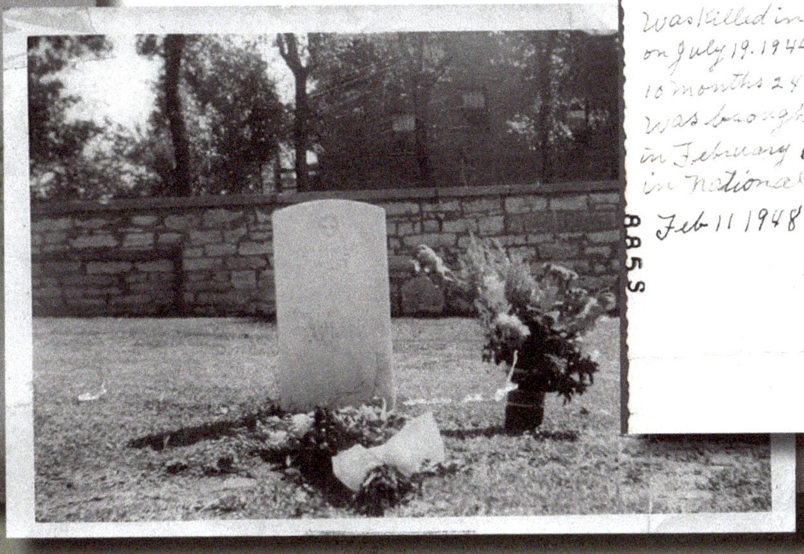

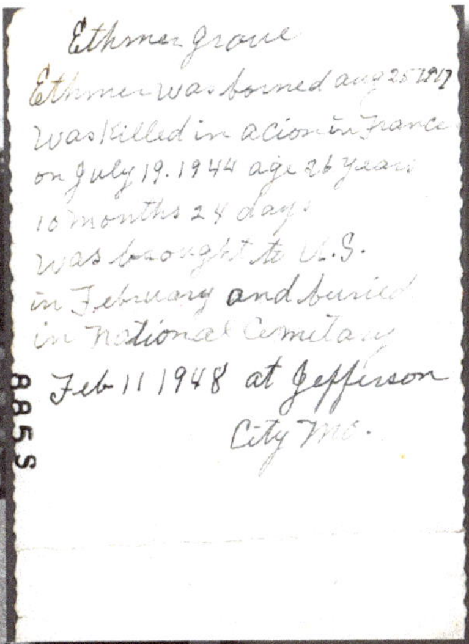

FRANK C. MILLS, PFC

83rd Infantry Division, K/329, European Theater

Submitted by Judy Mills Self, Niece

OMAHA BEACH OR COLLEVILLE de Mer, France stretches for five miles. The beach splays itself like the palm of your hand; with the access inlets resembling your fingers and the guarding cliffs standing firm and strong like a callused palm. The ocean spray whispers the many hidden mysteries held on these embattled shores.

Those whispers caught my attention in 2007. During an American Battlefield D-Day tour, the guide asked whether any participants were descendants of World War II veterans. I recalled my Father mentioning an Uncle Frank who was killed in World War II during the Battle of the Bulge. The guide inquired as to the Division. Embarrassed, I had no idea, as my family rarely mentioned my Uncle Frank. However, I never really asked about him either. What did his sacrifice on the Battlefields of Europe mean? Where was his "sense of place" in all of this? Where did he belong?

As the tour continued, walking the hedgerows of Normandy, and as I sat in the bloodstained pews of Angoville-au-Plain, my mind began to whisper more questions. Was Uncle Frank here? Was he one of the few who survived "Purple Heart Lane" in Carentan? Did he wade through the flooded marshes of Sainteny and Auxais? Who was this man who managed to survive until December 17, 1944? My intuition told me there was more to the man and to his story than just his name, Frank Mills.

Upon my return to the States, I decided to discover what, if any, information I could find on Uncle Frank. Pulling out a box of family memorabilia, I discovered an Army response letter to my father answering his request for more information regarding Frank's death. Fortunately, his military ID number was referenced as well as a notation that he was killed-in-action in and around Guzernich, Germany. I could find no other family items mentioning Uncle Frank; no photographs . . . nothing. Not knowing what direction to take my investigation, I placed a call to a colleague, John Bauserman, who wrote the World War II book, *The Malmedy Massacre*. As a military expert, he used his sources and my uncle's military ID number to determine his membership in the U.S. Army 83rd Infantry Division. However, no other information was available.

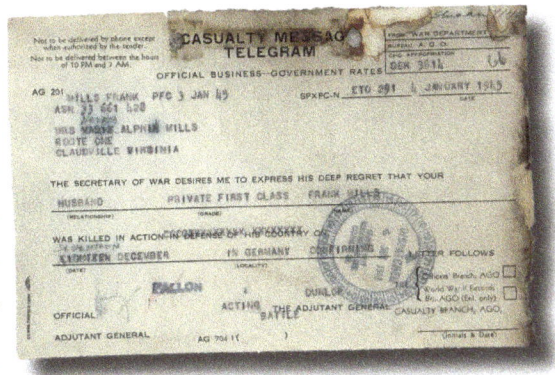

In 2008, World War II records were still classified and sealed. Only the veteran, the next of kin, or an appointed designee by the next of kin could access military records.

Dead-end? Perhaps. Uncle Frank had a daughter whom he'd never met. As a "war orphan," she was born during his deployment. I contacted her asking if she would give me permission to trace her dad's footsteps during his World War II service. Her reply was a simple, "No." Honoring her request, I abandoned my active quest, but the whispers of Omaha Beach kept pulling me back to Uncle Frank's mystery.

In 2014, the World War II military records were declassified; I revived my search for Uncle Frank. Then, another roadblock appeared. When I requested documents from the St. Louis, Missouri military archives, I was informed my Uncle Frank's records were among those damaged in the 1973 fire. Disappointed but hopeful, I returned to Normandy, France, in 2015

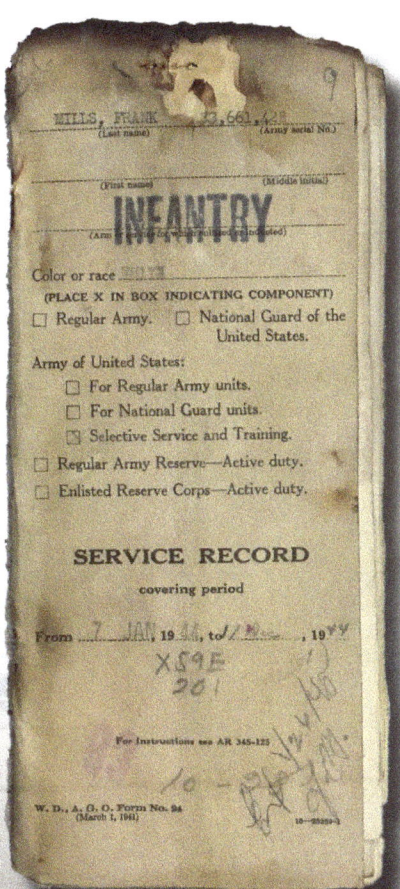

and 2016 for assistance. I made contact with a local World War II expert, military historian, and guide, Sean Claxton. His extensive experience working for the British World War II archives in London provided access to additional records. Sean discovered my Uncle's death certificate and found he was a member of the 329th "Buckshot Regiment." But his Battalion and Company were still a mystery. Sean requested the Individual Deceased Personnel File (IDPF), hoping to solve the puzzle. Early searches of after-action reports, morning reports, and other primary sources did not contain my Uncle Frank's name. Some indicators pointed toward his membership in the 2nd Battalion Headquarters Company, but there was no firm evidence. Sean, my husband, Sam, and I hiked the paths and pastures of Normandy following the 2nd Battalion. As I sat in an old, overgrown machine gun nest, I wondered how had he survived the horrendous fighting of the hedgerows?

In June 2016, I discovered the U.S. Army 83rd Infantry Association. I combed their website with the announcement of their 70th Reunion for the end of July in Arlington, Virginia.

Consulting Sean, he urged me to attend the reunion and contact the group for research assistance. The Senior Vice President, Lawrence Scheerer, responded to my email inquiry after forwarding Uncle Frank's information to members (descendants and veterans) including the Association's European Chapter members. Immediately, their vast network went to work. From Missouri to Belgium everyone weighed-in to help find Frank Mills. Finally, one week prior to the Association reunion, the IDPF arrived, revealing Uncle Frank was in the 329th, 3rd Battalion, K Company. Within thirty minutes of distributing this updated information to the 83rd network, Willem Doms of Belgium located the last action of Uncle Frank. He could locate the spot within 1,000 yards to where he was killed outside of Birgel, Germany. Willem offered to guide me on a hike of the last footsteps of Uncle Frank from the Hurtgen Forest to outside Birgel toward Rolsdorf.

What was Uncle Frank's "place" in this group of incredible men labeled by military historians as "the finest group of infantrymen who ever fought" (General George S. Patton) to the "Ragtag Circus" (Life Magazine)? I now know he received at least two combat medals, as well as a rifleman medal, and could be eligible for more awarded posthumously. I know he was considered an "old man" among his band of brothers as he had just turned 30 years old. I know Uncle Frank was offered several promotions, but he turned them down. I know he survived some of the most vicious, continuous fighting of the European Theater.

He landed on Utah beach with the 53rd Replacement Battalion joining the 83rd, 329th, 3rd Battalion, K Company as a "Replacement" on August 15, 1944 fighting in the house-to-house combat of the fortress, Cite d'Alet, of St. Malo in Brittany. He patrolled Angiers in the Loire Valley. He marveled as the 329th accepted the largest surrender of German forces at any one time, 20,000. He retrained the replacements in Luxembourg. He dug in the snow and shivered through the -20 temperatures of the Hurtgen Forest, shell bursts raining shrapnel down upon him. He must have felt optimistic as he crossed from Belgium into Germany thinking the end of the war might be near. I know this was a man I would have been proud to call Uncle.

But most important, I know there is much more to discover. As I invited his daughter, Dianna Mills White, to attend an impending ceremony to honor her father, she found the open box of his memorabilia. Among these treasures was a Purple Heart. The Purple Heart lay untouched for seventy-two years but now is opening doors to more information about this courageous man. The Purple Heart symbolically beats, reuniting a family. My sister, Jane Marie Mills, has now joined the search for Uncle Frank, discovering the pivotal document containing his enlistment date. The strength of one man remains even after all of these years.

In September 2016, under the auspices of French military historian, Jean Paul Pitou and the mayors of Sainteny and Auxais, France, a memorial ceremony was held to honor Frank C. Mills as a member of the U.S. 83rd Infantry for his part in liberating Sainteny and Auxais from Nazi occupation in 1944. Also, Glyn and Elaine Nightingale, citizens of Auxais, welcomed us to view a memorial in their garden to the 83rd. They opened their home to total strangers to toast his memory.

My Uncle Frank has found his sense of place. He belongs in my heart and in the hearts of the people of France, Luxembourg, Belgium, and Germany.

Response to the Mayors of Sainteny and Auxais, France:

"Je suis très touchée par cet honneur. Au nom de toute notre famille, je souhaite vous remercier pour votre gentillesse et votre générosité. Aujourd'hui, grâce à vos actions, vous touchez le sens le plus profond de l'humanité. Soixante-douze années se sont écoulées, mais, en toute honnêteté, nous pouvons dire, 'Plus ça change, plus c'est la même chose'."

English translation:

"I am very touched by this honor. On behalf of our family, I wish to thank you for your kindness and generosity. Today, through your actions, you touch the deepest sense of humanity. Seventy-two years have passed, but in all honesty, we can say, 'The more things change, the more they stay the same'."

MYRON H. MILLER, S SGT

83RD INFANTRY DIVISION, K/331ST, EUROPEAN THEATER

Submitted by Lynette Miller Ballard, Daughter

MY DAD ALWAYS HAD a self-deprecating sense of humor and never bragged about anything unless he did so by making a humorous remark. About the time the movie *Patton* came out, with George C. Scott playing General George S. Patton, Daddy said he saw the General once. He said that General Patton reviewed the troops, and Daddy's platoon was one of those reviewed. He said everyone was very nervous to do a good job, and they performed their best for the General. Daddy said that after the drill, General Patton said, "Best damn bunch of Boy Scouts I ever saw."

Just this year, I learned about how important a responsibility it was for my dad's platoon to be chosen. The story was written up in The TTF. "A representative regiment of the 83rd Division marched in review before the 3rd Army Commander, General George S. Patton, when he visited the Division area on Monday, July 30th as part of his regular scheduled tour of inspection among combat troops under his command." General Patton arrived in a C-47 Troop Carrier at precisely 10 o'clock at Pocking Air Base. He was greeted by a Guard of Honor, composed of members of the 83rd. Maj. General Robert Macon, 83rd Divisional Commander, and his staff greeted the General, complete with a seventeen gun salute and the 83rd Division Military Band.

From there they proceeded to the reviewing stand where General Patton met the regimental staff and reviewed the troops. On the way to the stand, he stopped to talk to at least one soldier in each company, asking questions about their military decorations. Patton addressed the assemblage saying, "Never have I seen a more perfectly aligned group—bar none." He went on to say, "I believe you will end this war sooner than you think." He said, "I am talking to you, not as your Army Commander, but as an old man to a group of young men!" He talked about military preparedness, his main theme, which he believed would prevent another war.

Before going on to Passau, General Patton stopped to view a demonstration that was specially planned for him along the Pocking-Passau Highway. The General stood on a high promontory overlooking the site where the problem was to be run off. He was given the "situation." The demonstration began with mortars and light machine guns opening up the assault on the objective. The 3rd platoon of Company K attacked through a clump of woods.

This assault proceeded by a rifle grenade bombardment of the enemy, supported by machine guns. When each assault and each successive objective was taken, the support fire was lifted to allow troops to advance. The offensive was temporarily stopped in its attack upon a heavily fortified position. "S/Sgt Myron Miller, squad leader, led the initial assault of the 3rd platoon." The story in The TTF concludes: "In reference to the assault problem that he had just witnessed, General Patton seemed outspoken in his amazement at the amount of firepower that such a small unit was able to put down."

I was thrilled and amazed to learn how my father was chosen to be a part of such a complex demonstration—and how General Patton admired the work of all involved. The story my father told was typical of him—simple, without drawing attention to his part in an important military event. I believe that the "Boy Scout" comment may have actually been said and that the Army journalist paraphrased it for the final printed account.

NORMAND R. MALO, T SGT

83rd Infantry Division, K/331, European Theater

Submitted by Judy Bolzani on behalf of The Malo Family

Permission was granted by Pat Ferron and Eugene Peloquin to reprint Normand Malo's war history which was part of the Veterans History Project by Norwich Connecticut 5th Graders in 2002. The story of Normand Malo was written by Brittney Gagne, Argennis Olivo, and Lashea Wade and is from the publication, *Learning Through Living Histories: Veterans Stories as Written Through the Eyes of Norwich Children*, copyright 2002 by Norwich Public Schools, Greater Norwich Community Leadership Team. This outstanding book project was funded by the Norwich Children's First Initiative. It features twenty-four stories of WWII veterans. We are proud to include their work in *Soldiers' Stories*. Please note that this story is intrepreted and written by fifth grade students and may have resulted in minor imperfections in content.

JUST IMAGINE BEING IN a war like World War II. Well, our class had had the chance to meet and interview a veteran from WWII. Here is some information that we have gathered from our veteran. We are going to tell you about Normand Malo's life, his childhood, and his wartime and post-war experience.

When Normand Malo was a child, he loved math, reading, and spelling. I think Normand likes math because he likes to figure out a lot of problems.

Did you know that he went to a school called Saint Ann School? He spent his childhood in Woonsocket, Rhode Island. He spoke French for 12 years. Till this day, he still speaks French to his family. Did I mention that he loved sports like baseball, and ice-skating? One thing he liked to play was Hide and Seek and Tag with his best friend, Bob Chabot. When Normand had free time, he had a paper route at age 12. Some of his favorite foods were meat loaf and French toast. The food that he does not like is cheese. He had a big family, with five sisters and one brother.

Radio reports announced that Japanese aircraft attacked Pearl Harbor on December 7, 1941. As a result of this attack, Normand Malo entered the army in 1942. He trained first, and then he went to Camp Atterbury, Indiana, and Camp Breckinridge and received his dog tag #31244203. During the war, daily life for soldiers was very hectic because they didn't know when the next attack was going to appear. One of his duties in wartime was as a scout. He had to go on

patrols to look for German soldiers. His responsibility in the Army was also as a French interpreter, which is a person who translates French for the English or vice-versa. Normand was promoted to Sergeant in charge of forty men. When he was in the Army, he served in France, Luxembourg, Belgium and Germany.

The most interesting thing he experienced during the war was serving as a Communication Sergeant. He laid telephone lines to many outposts on front lines. Some of the people he remembers the most were his officers, Lyman Coker and Captain Daniel Halladay. Some of the things that he remembered about them were their calmness and bravery. "One day in a battle in Luxembourg, I saw my First Lieutenant, Lyman Coker, get killed right next to me by a German sniper," stated Normand. It was the biggest loss for him.

While Normand was in Normandy on June 26, 1944, he watched his friends being injured and dying during attacks by the Germans. Then in July of 1944, he was hurt close to his eye while in the hedgerows in Normandy, France. The second time he was wounded in the right leg at Roer River in Germany. He said, "Till this day it still hurts." Also, he thinks they left a piece of the shrapnel—that is like a piece of metal—near his eye. He had to sleep in a pit, which caused his back to hurt during the day while he was on duty. While in the pit, Normand could hear the sound of gunfire and warring tanks over his head.

It's been reported that how brutal the war was. When Normand came back, he said that everything was still the same. Normand continued working at Taft Pierce Manufacturing Company

My dear friend Normand Malo was a salt of the earth soldier and leader of troops. Unheralded heroes, Norm and all of the Thunderbolts.

Eugene Peloquin, lifelong friend of Normand Malo (pictured).

in the stockroom in Woonsocket, R.I. in 1945. He even became the foreman of the stockroom and continued to work there until 1983, when he retired after 42 years.

One day, Normand got a call and they told him that he earned two Bronze Stars and a Purple Heart. Now we will tell you why he earned the awards for the electrifying drama he went through. He earned the Purple Heart because of being wounded in Normandy and Germany. He earned his first Bronze Star for the service from December 25, 1944, to May 1945 in Belgium and Germany. He showed exemplary service as a Communication Specialist in the 331st Infantry Regiment of the 83rd Infantry Division. He received his second Bronze Star because of the heroic action in connection with the military operation against an enemy of the United States (the Germans) on December 23, 1944, in Germany. Normand, who was a squad leader, would not stop on his mission to place the relief elements on the right flank of his company, even though shell fragments wounded him. During the mission, there was a lot of fighting going on with the Germans. All this courage showed his devotion to his duties as a sergeant and that's why he received his Bronze Star. In conclusion, special memories for Normand were all the things that he did in the war like being in charge of forty men and having to see his 1st Lieutenant Lyman Coker die right next to him. Also, when Normand was in the war, he had got drafted and his rank was Tech/Sergeant. Normand missed talking to and seeing his family while he was in the war. That must have felt very devastating to not see his family or friends, and he always wrote home every week and to former buddies of his company every year. He also attended an army reunion so he could see his old time friends. Writing this has been a great experience for us.

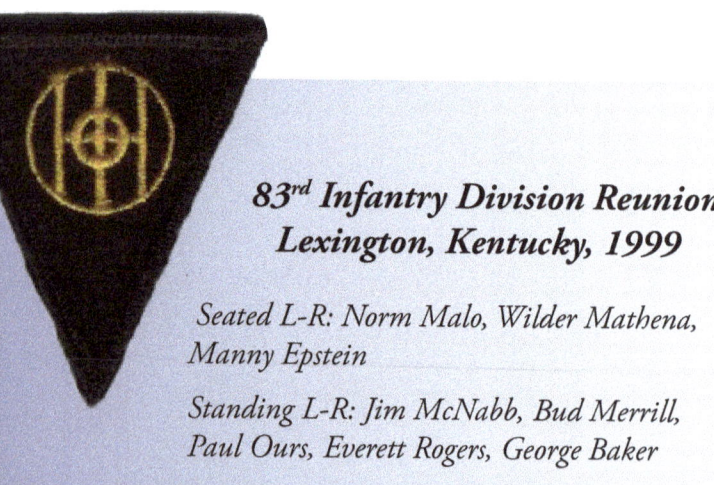

83rd Infantry Division Reunion
Lexington, Kentucky, 1999

Seated L-R: Norm Malo, Wilder Mathena, Manny Epstein

Standing L-R: Jim McNabb, Bud Merrill, Paul Ours, Everett Rogers, George Baker

DATA SHEET: NORMAND R. MALO

Branch of Service:: Army
Date entered: 11/11/42
Place entered service: Providence
Date discharged: 11/15/45
Highest Rank Held: Tech/Sergeant
Unit Assigned to: 83rd Infantry Division--Camp Atterbury, Indiana

What wars, theaters, campaigns, or locations were you in?
World War II, European Theater (4) Campaigns: Normandy–Brittany, Rhineland–Central Europe, France, Luxembourg, Belgium, Germany.

What were your general duties, skill or rating?
French interpretor, Scout, Platoon Sergeant.

Did you have combat service? When were you first under fire?
6-26-44 in Normandy hedgerows.

What were your feelings in combat?
Very scared at the sight of so many buddies dying and being wounded.

Did you receive any injuries, wounds or illness? Were you captured?
Wounded in face 7-14-44 in Hedgerows of Normandy, France.
Wounded a second time in right leg near Roer River, Germany on 12-15-44.

What was daily life like?
Very hectic, not knowing when next attack would be coming.

Did your equipment work? How was it compared to the enemy's?
Combat boots could have been better.

What was your unit like? How were your officers?
Unit was very will organized as a company and very well trained.
The officers were very efficient and brave.

Did you receive any decorations, medals or recommendations?
Received two Purple Hearts and two Bronze Stars.

What was the most interesting thing you experienced during your service?
Serving as communications sergeant, laying telephone lines to many outposts on front lines.

What persons do you remember from the service and why?
My officers–Lyman Coker and Captain Daniel Halladay.
For their calmness and bravery under enemy fire and leadership.

What experience left the greatest impression on you?
The biggest loss was seeing my officer 1st Lieutenant Lyman Coker get killed right next to me by a German sniper in Luxembourg.

Did you perform any unusual service or duties?
Served as French interpreter translating for officers.

WILLIAM G. JONES, SGT

90TH INFANTRY DIVISION, U.S. ARMY, EUROPEAN THEATER

Submitted by Dr. Rhonda Jones, Daughter

MY DAD, WILLIAM GILBERT Jones, was drafted his junior year in high school in Kentucky. He was a replacement soldier in the 90th Infantry Division and served as a Sergeant in Patton's Army. Dad participated in the invasion of France in June of 1944, was wounded, and has a Purple Heart.

After the war, he worked for many years and retired from Allied Chemical Corporation in Metropolis, Illinois. He always had a passion for basketball, especially Kentucky basketball, and introduced me to the game. Like him, I also played in high school, and he and I share the love of our Kentucky Wildcats. We follow them and have attended tournament playoffs together. He also has a passion for the St. Louis Cardinals as do I, and we follow them together, as well.

His music career started when he retired. He took up the piano and from there, taught himself how to play the fiddle, guitar, banjo, and other instruments. He now plays two to three times per week at jam sessions with his buddies. His wife of two years, Jean, is there with him every step of the way with her homemade goodies.

He mows his yard, drinks coffee every morning with his friends, and still does more than most people who are twenty years younger. I am so blessed to have such a special dad. He helped me through my college years, and without him and my mother I might not be where I am today. I think I hit the jackpot when it comes to parents.

Dad will be 92 years old on December 14, 2016.

THOMAS L. MCHUGH, CPL

2539th Army Air Force, 1705 Ord Corps, European Theater

Submitted by Carol Turner, Niece

EVERY SUNDAY MORNING, Rosalie McHugh walked to Holy Angels Church, usually with a niece or two trailing behind or hopscotching at her side. She prayed daily for the safety of her husband, Tom, fighting in the Mediterranean, always keeping her Novena candle lit at a side altar. After the service, the small group would stop at Beyersdorfer's Bakery which provided the much-needed therapy that only excellent pastry could give.

Rosalie and Thomas McHugh never had children of their own. Their memories were passed down from nieces, and eventually to great nieces, of their rather large extended family. This is how I, their great niece, came to be honored with the ownership of a rusty, footlocker containing some of my Uncle Tom's "Army stuff." An emotional journey began with the opening of the reluctant trunk lid.

The trunk was a treasure trove of memorabilia from the War. There were dozens and dozens of photos, some creased and folded. Uncle Tom's personal memorabilia, such as campaign ribbons, chevrons, medals, two silver cigarette cases, local newspapers and newsletters touting stories of baseball and firemen's picnics were included; handbooks, prayer books, Tom's musty service garrison caps, ties, even his army-green socks! The true treasures, however, were hundreds of letters, lovingly bound by strings and ribbons.

Aunt Rosalie and Uncle Tom were thought of as an older couple who laughed often, loved the family unconditionally, and loved each other. The insights of the cherished letters transformed them into young, newlyweds struggling with the profound effects of the War. Like so many other young couples torn apart by great distance, the letters described their loneliness and nagging fears and uncertainties. They spoke of the severe shortage of housing, maneuvering a truck in the harsh, rocky terrain of Italy, the long hours of my aunt's job, and the lack of cigarettes. But most of all, the letters told of their undying love for each other and their need to be reunited ... in their home ... and to be a family again.

Saturday, evening
August 11, 1945

My Sweetheart,

Pretty soon V-J Day will be here, dearest, maybe tomorrow morning. Gosh, Tom, just think what that means. It means that it won't be long until we can say good-bye to Army-life, and "hello forever" to your wife and home, honey. Does that sound good to you? It sounds Heavenly to me... Honest...

Sunday, evening
August 12, 1945

Tom, My Darling,

Honey, I'm missing you now... terribly much...

Mom, Dad, Elsie, and I had dinner and I couldn't help talking about you. We are here in the living room and at 9:33 PM, there was a News Flash: "Japan accepts the surrender terms of the Allies." Then three minutes later, a bulletin from United States Flashed:

"Our Washington Bureau advises that they did not send the flash which came on our leased wires."

Gosh, that is a heck of a mistake to make. Crowds on Broadway went wild! Around here, auto horns started blaring throughout our neighborhood but stopped at the retraction. It is now eerily quiet...

St. Louis, IL
Tuesday, evening
August 14, 1945

Hello Darling:

Here I am again, and this time I'm writing from the office. All day long we've had a radio on and turned it up whenever announcements were on. It has been heartbreaking in its teasing. I have always said I wouldn't believe it until Truman announced it, but the country at large is already celebrating, as you know. Then around noon, bulletin cam:

"Very Urgent: The Japanese Legation said that the coded cables it received this morning from Tokyo do not contain the answer awaited by the whole world."

It is now 5 PM and we are told that Truman now has the Reply, and it is just waiting until the Big Three can get together on the telephone to arrange a time to announce it simultaneously to their respective countries. Well darling, he can't announce it too soon to suit us all. I just wish we could be together on V-J Day, but darling, we'll have the rest of our lives together as soon as you get out of that uniform. It is a beautiful uniform, Tom, and you look wonderful in it, really, but oh man, how you can strut in your civies!

It is 5:15 PM now and we are expecting the word any minute over the air and are afraid to go on our way home for fear we will miss it, but we'll be going along anyhow pretty soon. This suspense during the last hour, since we know Truman has the message, is almost too much. I long to grasp your hand and you'd keep me under control. I'd be okay just being with you...

I love you dearly, honey, with all of my heart, always, and miss you terrifically. I hope it won't be long before they see fit to discharge you and allow you to graduate into a civilian again.

All my love,
Your own Rosalie

Home
August 14, 1945
Peace Day
10:30 PM

My Dearest Tom,

Well, Peace is finally here, honey, and oh, Tom, never in my life have I missed you more than I did tonight. My heart is definitely with you.

Lewis and Adele came by for Mom, Dad, El, and I. We drove through East St. Louis, and darling, the town left its hair down! We drove down Collinsville Avenue and on to St. Louis. The mob on 8th, 9th, 10th and Grand was terrific! Traffic was guided off Washington Avenue to side streets since the mob of humanity was too dense. People were dressed crazily and paraded in the streets; cars were overloaded and they even rode on the tops. Lewis turned his burglar alarm on the car and left it on for the whole drive. Cars had old hardware and tubs tied to the back of them and tin cans, too—anything that would make a noise.

We didn't return home till 9:50 PM. I was hoping you might get a line through to me tonight but, of course, you couldn't. I tried to phone your folks but couldn't ever get the Long Distance operator as the lines were too crowded. The telephone company just broadcast a plea to not use the phones except for emergencies as they are overloaded.

Well, I've talked with you, and perhaps I can sleep now. The last few days of tension and excitement have been running too high for restful sleeping. I hope to see you in my dreams, dear. Tell me about how you celebrated, dear.

I love you so very much, Tom. Please take care of yourself for me, dear.

All my love,
Your own Rosalie

Tuesday evening
August 15, 1945

My Own Darling,

Gosh honey, the first 24 hours of peace is past and gasoline rationing has stopped, canned fruits and vegetables are no longer rationed. The Manpower Commission has released labor; no more jobs are frozen. It's all very wonderful, but nothing is complete because you are not here. It will be swell when you are here. You'll never know how I ached to talk to you Monday night or today.

How did the men celebrate, dear, and what did you do? I have never felt so far away from you ever as I did Monday night. I needed to be with you. Now we must be patient and mark the time until you are discharged and home again. Nothing is complete without you, dear, just nothing. I'm afraid this gal really loves her husband . . . don't you think?

I do love you, darling, with every breath. Please take care.

All my love,
Your loving wife, Rosalie

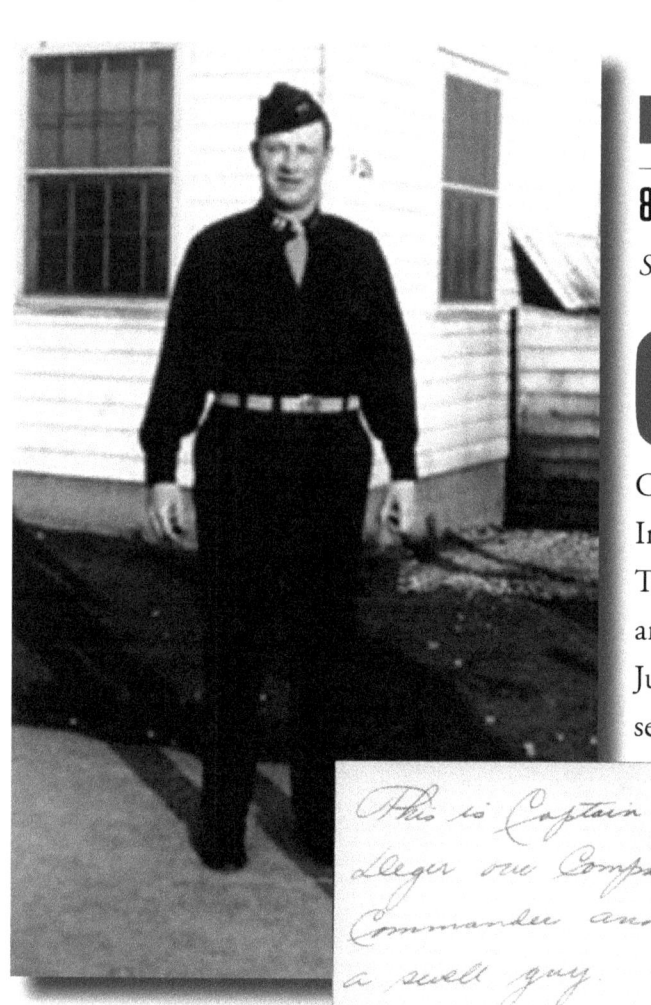

This is Captain
Deger our Company
Commander and
a swell guy

EVERETT C. DEGER, CAPT

83rd Infantry Division, K/331, European Theater

Submitted by Robert McNabb, Friend

CAPTAIN EVERETT C. DEGER—nicknamed Duke—was from Nebraska and a college graduate. He was the Commander of Company K at Camp Atterbury, Indiana and all through training in Kentucky and Tennessee. He shipped out with his unit overseas and engaged in battle. He was wounded early in July 1944 during the Normandy campaign and sent directly home to the States with a "million-dollar wound" (if the wound was serious enough, the soldiers were shipped back to the States and never returned to combat).

Captain Deger returned home to run the family business and served on the boards of the Fairbury State Bank and Fairbury Cemetery Association. He passed away in August of 1983.

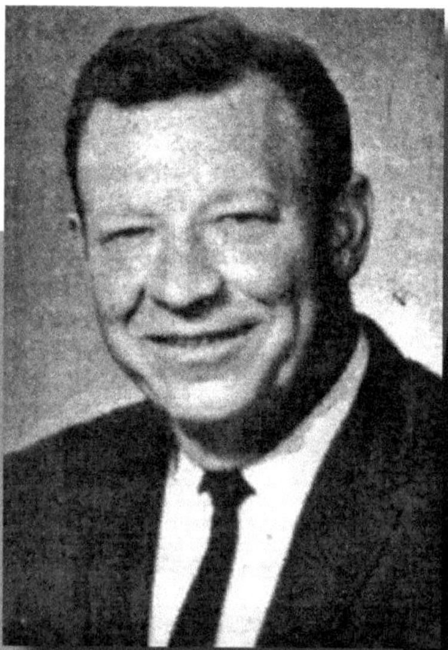

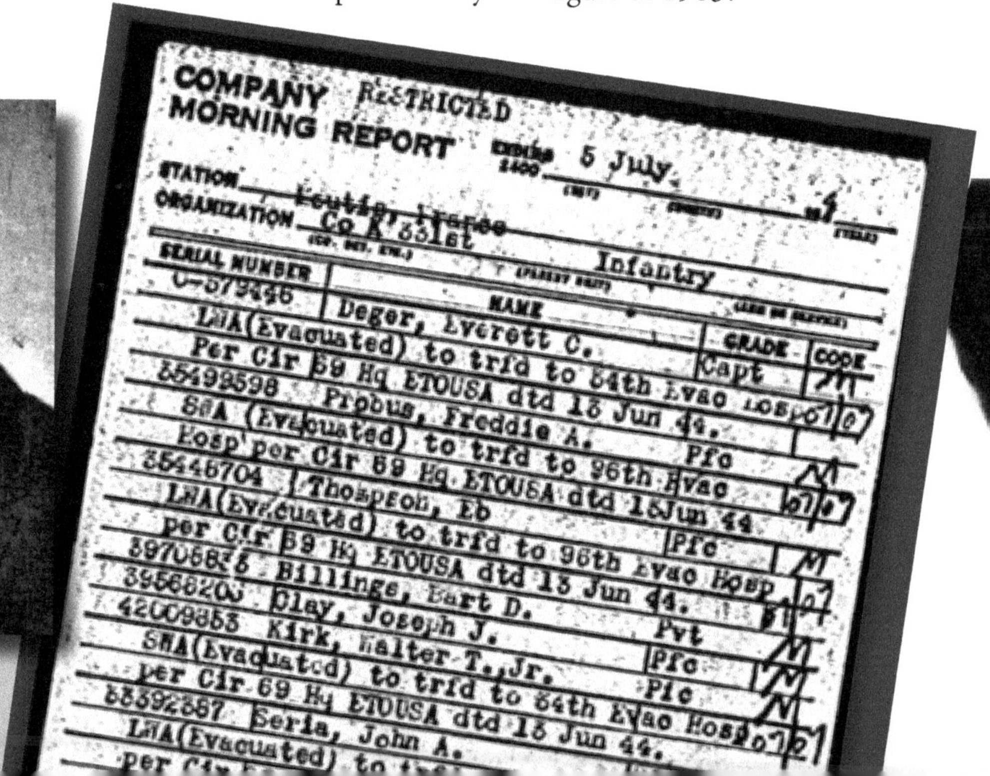

COMPANY RESTRICTED
MORNING REPORT ENDING 2400 5 July

STATION Loutin, France
ORGANIZATION Co K 331st Infantry

SERIAL NUMBER	NAME	GRADE	CODE
O-579446	Deger, Everett C.	Capt	
	LWA(Evacuated) to trfd to 24th Evac Hosp per Cir 69 Hq ETOUSA dtd 13 Jun 44.		
35492598	Probus, Freddie A.	Pfc	
	SWA (Evacuated) to trfd to 96th Evac Hosp per Cir 69 Hq ETOUSA dtd 13Jun 44		
35446704	Thompson, Eb	Pfc	
	LWA(Evacuated) to trfd to 96th Evac Hosp per Cir 69 Hq ETOUSA dtd 13 Jun 44.		
39706876	Billings, Bart D.		
39568200	Clay, Joseph J.	Pvt	
42009853	Kirk, Walter T., Jr.	Pfc	
	SWA(Evacuated) to trfd to 24th Evac Hosp per Cir 69 Hq ETOUSA dtd 13 Jun 44.	Pfc	
33392387	Seria, John A.		
	LWA(Evacuated) to trfd ... per Cir ...		

MARION B. COOPER, MAJ

Capt, 83rd Infantry Division, K/331, European Theater

Submitted by Cynthia Cooper Snipes, Daughter

MARION B. COOPER WAS born in Hillsboro, Indiana on June 13, 1915, and entered the service on February 19, 1942, in Flint, Michigan. He went through basic training at the Presidio and graduated from Officer Candidate School at Fort Benning, Georgia on October 23, 1942.

By March of 1944, he had been promoted to Company Commander of Company I, 3rd Battalion, 331st Infantry, 83rd Division. Captain Cooper led Company I overseas to Omaha Beach in Normandy, where they remained in a defensive position until July 4th when Company I attacked the Germans in the hedgerows. On July 15, 1944, near Sainteny, France, he earned the Silver Star for heroic action and his first Purple Heart.

After getting out of the hospital, he rejoined the 331st Infantry, 83rd Division, in France in September 1944 as the Company Commander of Company K. On January 11, 1945, orders came in to attack Petite Langlir downhill at night through waist deep snow. Captain Cooper told the Colonel who gave the order that he would go down the hill alone, but he would leave his men on the hill. The Colonel relented and battered the town with artillery until sunrise. Company K then moved into the town and captured 114 Germans.

He participated in battles and campaigns in Normandy, Ardennes, Northern France, and the Rhineland. Captain Cooper was wounded in the hand in Hemmerdon, Germany, during a counterattack on March 12, 1945. Captain Cooper received a Purple Heart with Oak Leaf Cluster, a Silver Star, a Bronze Star with Oak Leaf Cluster, and the Combat Infantry Badge for his services and injuries while overseas. He was discharged from the service in September 1946 as Major.

As a civilian, he worked for the Elston Bank and Trust Company for 31 years, retiring in 1980 as Senior Vice-President and Director of the bank. With his wife Mary Ellen, they have three children and eight grandchildren. He was the Director of the Montgomery County Historical Society. Major Cooper passed away in June 2000 and was interred with full military honors in Hillsboro, Indiana.

MYRON H. MILLER, S SGT

83rd Infantry Division, K/331st, European Theater

Short Stories Written by Del Miller, Son

Hedgerows

ON MY FATHER'S FARM you cleaned up the fence rows. Sumac, briars, and multi-flora rose would grow up around the fence posts and entwine themselves through the barbed wire.

Dad hated that brush beyond reason and we would find ourselves in the fields every year chopping and tearing out, burning every root and every branch even if we had to rebuild the fence afterward. I was never sure why he so hated having some brush in his fencerows. I mean, the fence could fall down and you would still have a row of brush, but a cow couldn't get through. Who needs a fence?

And then I was in Sainteny, France in the Bocage region of France. Standing in the sunken road where my father once fought with unseen Germans on just the other side of this hedgerow, firing their guns at him through the brush.

I think I know why we had to clean up those fences.

The Doorway

HE CROUCHED INSIDE THE doorway, figuring out how to run through it into the street outside. At the end of the street, a German machine gun was firing large caliber bullets at a very high rate of fire right down the street. His job was to destroy that machine gun nest, but the task was complicated by the hail of bullets coming his way.

He hoped there was an alcove or another doorway across the street that he could dash into for cover as he zig-zagged up the street toward the target. But the gunfire was so heavy, he couldn't even stick his head out of the doorway to look.

Very, very carefully he twisted his head around the door facing, just another inch and could maybe see if there was safe haven on the other side of the street. Just another half inch to go and ... Bam! Bam! Bam! A storm of bullets hit the door frame six inches above his head blowing to dust the wall he was hiding behind.

He sprinted across that street and promptly tripped and fell, bouncing his helmet off his head, as enemy fire kicked up spouts of dirt and lead as they hit the pavement all around him.

Scrambling on his hands and knees while simultaneously grabbing for his helmet which bounced erratically just out of reach, he sped across the street scooting along on hands and knees while trying to grab the elusive helmet as it skittered just ahead of him.

He made it most of the way across the street and lunged through the doorway snagging the helmet as he did so and as the bullets pounded the ground behind him.

What a job.

Don't say you can't.

IF I EVER TOLD my father "I can't," he would always say, "Don't say you can't because you will." Of course, then he would just smile and help me out. As I got older, I understood how a simple lesson my Dad received in training camp would shape my own life.

He was a brand new enlisted man freshly arrived at basic training. His platoon leader spotted each man to a location and instructed them to all dig themselves a foxhole. My dad soon realized that his position was sited directly on top of a granite slab that extended several yards in every direction.

To put a foxhole in there would require a jackhammer, not an entrenching tool. Realizing the futility of trying to dig a hole in a boulder with a 2-foot long shovel, he sat down and waited for further instructions. Soon his sergeant was standing over him shouting:

Sergeant: "Soldier, I told you to dig."

Dad: "You can't dig in solid rock."

Sergeant: "Don't say you can't soldier, because you will!"

My dad rather loved this story because he apparently thought that his sons could benefit from learning never to say, "I can't."

So I asked him, "Did you dig the foxhole?"

He looked at me funny and said, "Of course not, you can't dig in solid rock!"

Did you shoot anybody?

I WAS JUST A KID, maybe seven or so. Just learning that my dad was a hero. A battle-hardened soldier of the greatest war.

I asked him a question, a seemingly easy one, "Did you ever shoot anybody?"

He looked at his little boy for just a second and then said, "I don't know, I always closed my eyes."

Yeah, sure.

Walk down that road.

NOW HE AND THE other replacements jumped from the bed of the truck and straight into the battle for Normandy. My father was a replacement arriving less than a month after D-Day, and now he was at the front. The sound of constant gunfire spilled from the nearby woods, exploding artillery shells boomed over the next hill. All around him were the wounded and the dead, awaiting transit out on the very truck they had just arrived on. It was all so horrifying to a green soldier.

They reported for duty and then were led off in the direction of war, the sounds of battle growing louder and louder until it sounded as if they were in the middle of hell itself. Then he was placed into a squad, and only minutes later the lieutenant walked up to my dad's new sergeant and gave the first orders my Dad received in battle. The Lieutenant pointed down the path and said, "Walk down this road until you're fired upon," and with that, he turned and hurried off.

That's when my dad began to learn about war.

BRIGITTE BRESSER

Survivor, Japanese Internment Camp, Java, Indonesia

Submitted by Brigitte Bresser, Self

I WAS A LITTLE girl when the Japanese invaded Java, Indonesia. I lived in a gorgeous house in Saradan on Java. Most of us Dutch people lived in big houses. The day we heard that the Japanese soldiers had invaded Java, my parents tried to escape with us. We were at that time, a family of seven—five kids and my mother and father. My father planned our escape with two loyal servants who went with us, trying to help us escape from the Japanese invaders. The male servant was our cook and the female servant, was our nanny. The plan was to disguise ourselves as a farmer's family. So the day we escaped, we went with a farm wagon pulled by an ox. We had to leave everything behind, even our beloved dog, Nero. My father was disguised as a wounded farmer and he pretended that he couldn't speak. My mother was the farmer's wife. Together with the servants, she did the talking. When we were traveling the land, we saw a lot of dead bodies in the river Solo. It made a great impression on us kids.

After a couple of months traveling the land, we came to a small village where we stayed for a while. When we lived in the village, a young girl helped us do chores. Our cook told us it was a bad idea, but my mother felt sorry for the girl and took her in as a kind of housemaid. The day my mother found out that she stole money from us, was the day that my mother told her to leave. A few days later, we were picked up by the Japanese soldiers because the girl had betrayed us. She was holding a grudge, so she told the Japanese soldiers where we were.

My father was sent away to a concentration camp and we were sent back home. When we came home, the house was completely empty. They had robbed us blind when we were away. Fortunately, our dog Nero was still at the house. So coming home didn't feel as bad as we thought it would be without my father. But during our escape, they had taken all of our friends to the concentration camps. The only ones who were left in peace were the German families. They could stay in their houses because of the alliance that Japan had with Germany. We thought we had good fortune, but there was nothing to eat, so we had to go into the fields to search for vegetables and rice. We asked the farmers for food, and some of them were my father's old workers, and they helped us get by. But it was a struggle to get food on the table every day. Sometimes, we even had to steal to be able to eat. This was very hard for my mother.

One day, the Kempeitai (this is the Japanese Gestapo) came to my mother. She had to go to their office because they were searching for young women to work in their brothels to satisfy the needs of the Japanese army. My mother went, but she took all of us children with her to their office. When we arrived, the officer took one look at us and decided they didn't need my mum. The officer was feeling sorry for us children, so that's why he didn't send my mother away in the brothel. He asked her where we lived. My mother told him, and he said, "Because you are Dutch, you need to go to a concentration camp, there you will be provided for." We were put on a train. Our dog, Nero, couldn't come with us, but he ran behind in the rain until he couldn't run anymore. That's the last that I ever saw of our dog. I never saw our cook or nanny again. They weren't taken away because they were Indonesian citizens and the Japanese Government wasn't at war with them. A few hours later, we arrived at the woman's camp. It was already dark. We lived in a huge barn, so there wasn't any privacy. Sheets divided the barn, and each family had their own quarters, and we slept on the wooden floors. Every morning, we had to remove the fleas from our bodies. At the camp, they gave us rice and sugar. It wasn't much, but at least we could survive. Fortunately, my oldest brother could stay with us because he wasn't twelve yet.

My mother and my oldest sister worked there as a washerwoman to get some extra cash. My oldest brother had to clean the latrines, but he didn't get paid. All the boys had to take care of the latrines. Because the latrines were built over a ditch, the boys could go out into the fields and look for food. The younger kids could go to school once a week. This is where I learned to speak Japanese, but I have forgotten all of these Japanese lessons. The whole time that we stayed there, we had to come out every morning. The Japanese soldiers would hoist the flag and we had to bow our heads and greet the flag. We had to sing the Japanese anthem whilst hoisting. One day, a Dutch lady yelled, "Long live the Queen." For that, she was punished and had to stay out in the burning sun all day with no water or food. One day, a Japanese soldier came by and offered my mother a cigarette. My mother told him she didn't smoke. But he kept pushing the cigarette in my mother's hand. Finally, she realized it was a letter from my father all rolled up like a cigarette. My father had sent her this note. The note said that my father got tortured by the Japanese because my father knew where all the military bases had been. He had worked for the department that had to destroy all evidence of the existence that the KNIL had been there. But my father pretended not to know and played dumb. Because of that, they started to hit him on his knees repeatedly. My father struggled with the effects of that torture for the rest of his life. Sometimes he couldn't walk anymore because his knees became so swollen. My father never talked about this traumatic experience, but some nights he woke up screaming because of the nightmares.

The longer we stayed in the camps, the more diseases broke out. The children got dysentery, lice, and other diseases. My mother saved a lot of the children because she knew how to make medicine from plants and herbs. When we were living in Saradan, our cook taught my mother how to use plants and herbs to heal. She put this knowledge into practice at the camp to save the children from certain death.

After three years of living under poor conditions in the camp, we were freed. The Japanese had gone, from one moment to the next, and Indonesian guerrilla warriors took over the camp. So freedom was relative.

After a little while, the Australian Army and the Indian Army came with big open trucks. We were loaded in the back and stood until we arrived at a big building. There, we were led to an enormous room where they sprinkled powder over us so we would be decontaminated. They gave us clean clothing and asked my mother where she wanted to go. My mother said she wanted to go to her foster mum in Jakarta—the capital of Indonesia.

When we were in Jakarta, the Red Cross helped us to be reunited with my father, who was also liberated. My mother was told by the Red Cross and a nephew—who had been sent to work on the Burma railroad—that all of her brothers were killed whilst working on the Burma railroad, and they were buried underneath the railroad. Her nephew was the only one of her family that survived. Every morning the men were taken from the camp and had to run to the railroad where they had to work. The work was horrific. If they didn't or couldn't work—because they broke down—they were beaten with sticks. If they didn't get up, they were left behind and nobody was allowed to help them. If they died, the workers had to bury them. They had to work quickly because they wanted the railroad to be finished real soon. During the work, they didn't get food or water. Our nephew told us that there is a dead body buried underneath every sleeper on the railroad track.

We had the good fortune that our whole family survived the war and were reunited after the war, but we still live with the effects that the war has had on us. All the women in our family have the shakes (shaking hands) because of malnutrition in the camp. For my family and me, the war is over, but if I look at the world we live in nowadays I feel like we haven't learned the lesson yet.

Hopefully, my children and grandchildren will never have to live in fear of being at war. I am sharing my story with you in hopes that others will see what kind of devastation war brings and that in the end, war can be eradicated from our lives.

Many years after the war, Brigitte's parents celebrated their 50th wedding anniversary. Despite the horrors they lived through, they were still a close and happy family.

Standing L-R: Brigitte, Ewald, Ingrid, William, Beatrix, Robert.
Seated L-R: Emilia, Ferdinand, Yvonne.

JAMES P. GARRETT, S SGT

566th Signal Company, European Theater

Submitted by Jerry and Dewey Garrett, Sons

THIS PAGE IS DEDICATED to the memory of James Perry Garrett, of Richmond, Missouri, known as JP to family and friends. He was born March 27, 1908, and died at the age of 94 on July 22, 2002. The photos tell his story.

He and his wife, Mildred Pauline Blaine Garrett (1910 - 1986), raised two sons, Jerry Blaine Garrett, and Dewey Nelson Garrett.

JP's treasured uniform and other items from his military service were donated by his sons to Glyn Nightingale in 2016. Glyn lives in England and is proud to serve as caretaker and honored to display JP Garrett's uniform among his WWII military collection.

February 1945 (L-R), S/Sgt Constable, Pfc Hasty, S/Sgt Garrett, M/Sgt Polaske, S/Sgt Holmes, and T/Sgt Gates

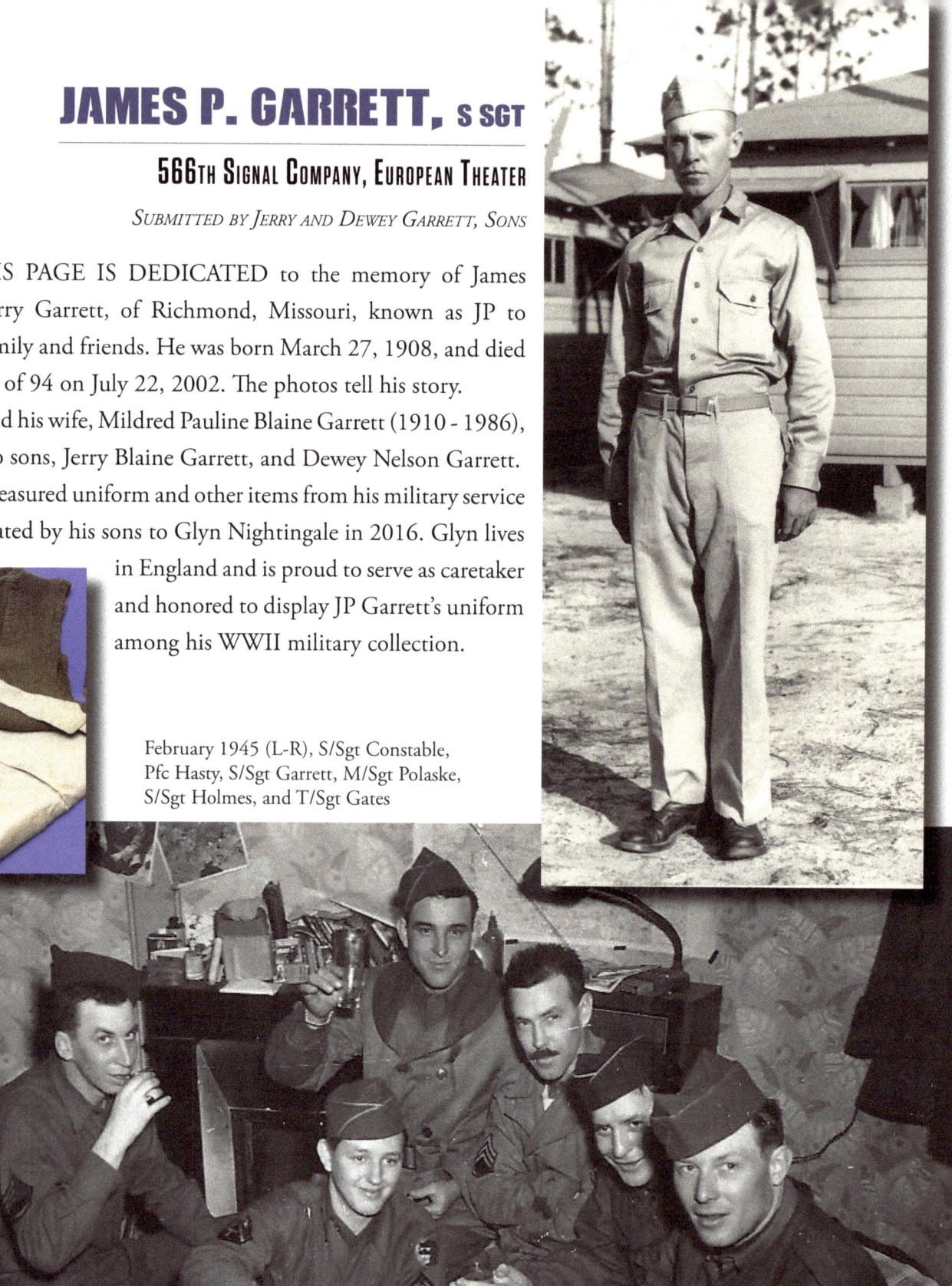

RUSSELL L. ARMONTROUT

USS Springfield (CL-66), U.S. Navy, Pacific Theater

Submitted by Robbin Martin Denham, Granddaughter

OUR FAMILY IS PROUD and honored to share our special WWII veteran from Centralia, Missouri, Russell "Leonard" Armontrout. He is pictured in his Navy uniform with his wife, Louise. Leonard served on the *USS Springfield (CL-66)* in the Pacific Theater during WWII. While living at the Missouri Veterans Home in Mexico, Missouri, he was fortunate to participate in the Central Missouri Honor Flight from Columbia. Leonard passed away the day after Thanksgiving in 2015 at the age of 93.

CHERBOURG–ROUEN MAP

First Edition, War Office Copy 1941

From the Collection of Thomas Shipley, Sr.

PANORAMIC BEACH SKETCH

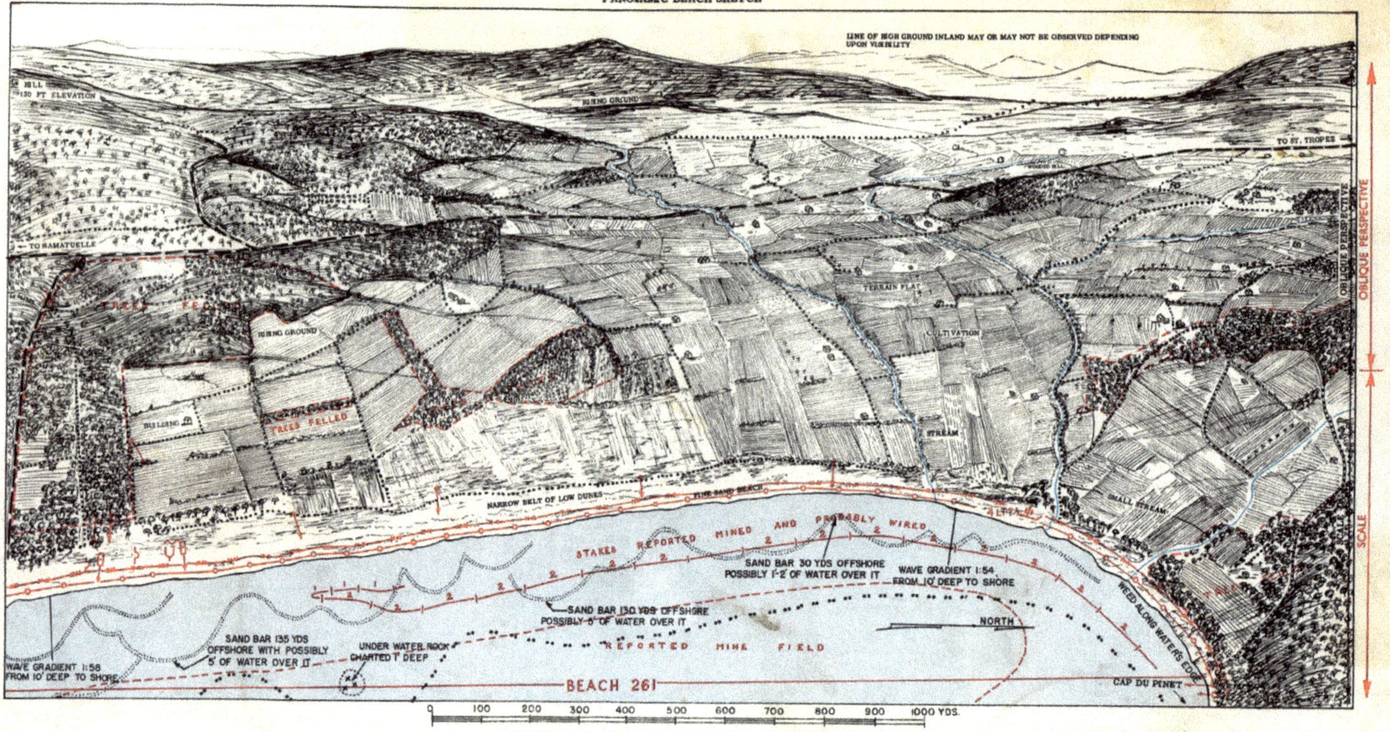

No. P—4
BEACH 261 (North)

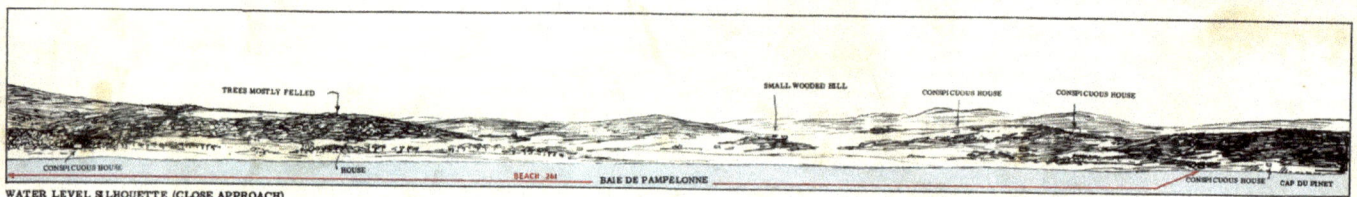

WATER LEVEL SILHOUETTE (CLOSE APPROACH)

WATER LEVEL SILHOUETTE (DISTANT)

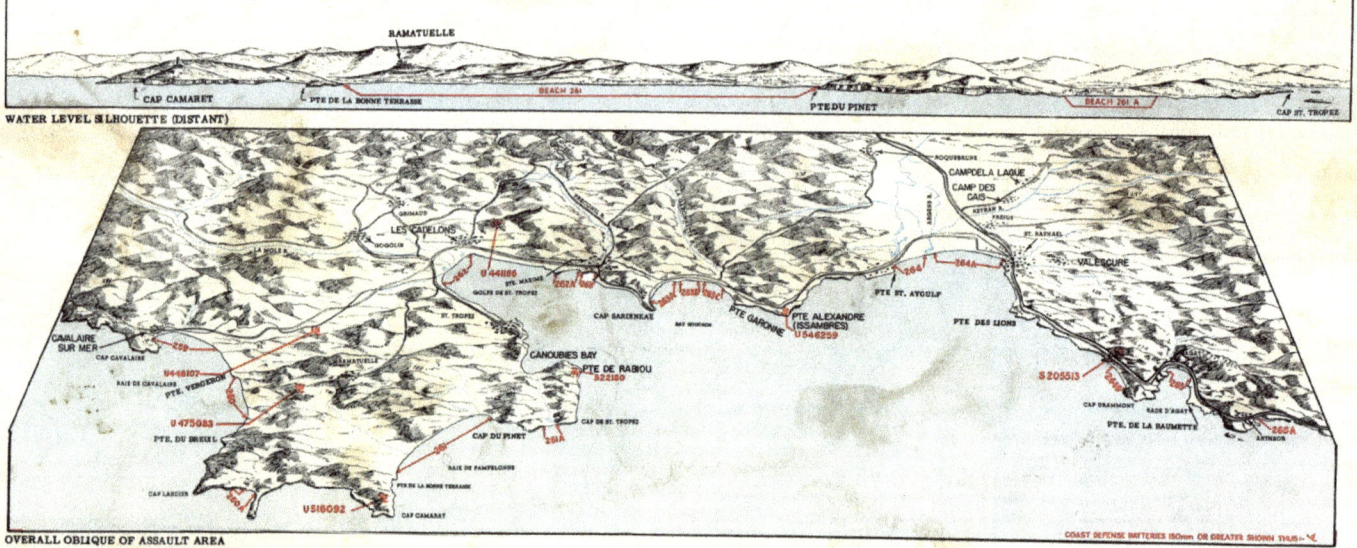

OVERALL OBLIQUE OF ASSAULT AREA

BEACH No. 261 (North)
CENTER OF BEACH: LAT. 43° 14' N, LONG. 06° 40' E.
COORDINATES: U-517105 – U-518144
NATURE OF SEA BOTTOM: SAND AND WEED; WEED BANK ALONG EXTREME NORTH END.
ANCHORAGE: 400 TO 600 YARDS OFFSHORE IN 6 FATHOMS; BOTTOM OF SAND.
LENGTH OF BEACH: 4,500 YARDS
WIDTH: 15 YARDS
SUITABILITY FOR CRAFT: LCA's, LCV's, LCM's, AND LCT (5)s (SOME WET LANDINGS); PONTOONS FOR LARGER LCT's AND LST's EXCEPT AT EXTREME NORTH END; RECONNAISSANCE DESIRABLE. OBSTACLES ALONG NORTHERN 1/3 OF BEACH MUST BE REMOVED.

LEGEND OF ROADS
MAIN TRAFFIC
SECONDARY
OTHER ROADS
TRACKS

Defense information as of July 20 1944.
LEGEND OF SYMBOLS ON REVERSE SIDE OF THIS SHEET

TOP SECRET – BIGOT
(Until departure for combat operation when this sheet becomes Restricted)

PREPARED BY COMMANDER U.S. EIGHTH FLEET
N-2 SECTION

A.F. 4466   Printed by 19th. Field Survey Coy., R.E., July 1944

FRANKLIN P. CURTISS, PVT

83rd Infantry Division, E/329, European Theater

Submitted by Paul Penfield, Nephew

WHEN PRIVATE FRANKLIN CURTISS stepped into an open field in Normandy on the morning of July 4, 1944, this moment was, for him and his buddies, the real beginning of World War II. Early though it was, the men had woken earlier still. Since 3:00 a.m. they had groped their way down dark, narrow footpaths outside the village of Sainteny, a small crossroads community in France.

On either side of them rose hedgerows twelve feet or higher, composed of tangled shrubs and thorn bushes. Hedgerows are among the oldest man-made structures in Europe, and have, from the dawn of agriculture, served as living fences, keeping cattle and horses from wandering free. As the centuries passed, they grew ever thicker and higher while the pathways between them eroded until the top of a man's head was barely level with the surrounding fields. In war, these made for ideal defensive positions.

It was still dark when Company E reached their point of departure for the attack. Mist rose from the field ahead, although it was less of a field and more of a marsh, or *marais* as the French called it. In ordinary summers, the soil dried just enough to support a few dairy cows, but this summer was not ordinary: the Germans had opened every spillway they could find in order to flood the Normandy fields, turning them into swamps. Under a lightening sky, Company E waited.

In those days, an American infantryman carried his entire life expectancy on his back—shaving gear, steel pocket mirror, toothbrush, mess kit, enough C-rations for four days, chewing gum, instant coffee, toilet paper, dog tags, photos and letters from home, one half of a pup tent, a canteen, a pocket knife, solid fuel for cooking, a rain poncho—all just to start with. Add to that the job-related gear—an M1 Garand rifle and bayonet, several clips of ammunition and a pocketful of loose rounds, a medical kit, at least four grenades, a steel helmet and liner—and together this added up to well over fifty pounds. Now, as E company advanced across the field, this extra weight sucked their boots deeper into the mud. Running anywhere was out of the question.

The day before aerial reconnaissance photos revealed a lightly defended German position 300 yards across the *marais*. This, in the opinion of the inexperienced officers, could be taken by frontal assault. What they could not know was that during the night, German paratroopers reinforced by the 17th Waffen SS had infiltrated the hedgerow just opposite. They were able to do so undetected because of a skill Company E had yet to acquire—noise discipline. As they slipped quietly into position, their American counterparts could clearly be heard moving forward through the mist. The paratroopers and SS, experienced veterans with four years of combat behind them, waited until Company E was halfway across before opening fire.

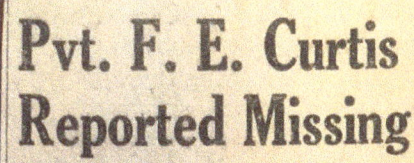

Pvt. F. E. Curtis Reported Missing

Mrs. Franklin E. Curtis, Shawandassee dr., Willoughby township, has been notified by the war department that her husband, Pvt. Franklin E. Curtis, had been missing in France since July 4.

The son of Mr. and Mrs. Frank Super, River rd., Willoughby township, Pvt. Curtis enlisted as a paratrooper in March, 1943, but was disqualified as a paratrooper after having successfully made his fifth jump because of a foot injury which he had received as a child.

He was then transferred to the 329 infantry, and was sent overseas about two months ago. Although not with the troops participating in the actual D-Day invasion, Pvt. Curtis was sent to France a short time later as a replacement.

It was over in minutes. When the shooting died away, an American medic yelled for a cease-fire. With German help, he gathered the few desperately wounded survivors, but for most, it was too late. On that morning, Company E ceased to exist. Franklin Curtiss, who had graduated from Willoughby High School only months earlier, was dead. He was nineteen years old. He was my uncle.

Defeat carries no laurels. I somehow sensed this, even as an adolescent, when I looked for his name on every war memorial I passed. Once, at St. Paul's Cathedral in London where an open ledger is kept on a gilded podium honoring the names of every American who died liberating Europe, I asked an attendant to look up his name. It wasn't there. So Grandma became a gold star mother and for the remainder of her life received $25 a month from the U.S. Government. Apart from that, an enlistment photo and yellowed newspaper obituary, Franklin Curtiss might never have passed through this world.

In 2014, my cousin George finally talked me into visiting what he calls "the battlefields of Europe." Europe has countless battlefields, but for Americans, there's usually only one: Omaha Beach. Prior to booking our flights, I went online to see what information I could find. There I was flabbergasted to discover an organization devoted entirely to the 83rd Division. On their expansive website, I not only found Franklin's name, the date, and place of his death but even more incredibly, the combat map used to plan the attack which took his life. I immediately downloaded a Google Earth aerial photo of Sainteny and superimposed the combat map over it. There it was. The *marais*. The hedgerows were in the same place. The farms, streams, and cattle paths were precisely where they were in 1944. It hadn't changed.

Two months later, together with Jean-Paul Pitou, the 83rd Infantry Division's French historian, we stood on the very spot where Company E had its first tragic day of the war. The sun was out; the day was warm, and apart from the cawing of a distant crow, it was absolutely still. There was no hint a slaughter had occurred here. We were accompanied by Glyn, an Englishman who owned a nearby vacation home. A few years earlier he had unearthed an American machine gun nest in his backyard, and since then had become a passionate devotee of battlefield archaeology. With powerful metal detectors, we began to sweep the hedgerows for any metal objects buried beneath the leaf litter. And there was no lack of them. Within minutes, we had dug up brass M1 cartridge casings, shrapnel, and unexploded mortar rounds. After July 4th, the fighting had continued for a week before the Germans withdrew.

"Look there," said Jean-Paul, pointing to a series of puddles along the hedgerow. "Those are 329th foxholes." We dug through them, uncovering more spent casings and tin foil fragments from instant coffee sachets. The detector buzzed again, louder this time.

"That's got to be a grenade," Glyn said, and so it proved to be. Next to it was an unfired M1 round. Glyn explained, "Garands give off a loud ping when the last casing is ejected from the clip. The Germans would listen for that and would know you were out of ammunition. The G.I.'s got in the habit of never firing the last round. Just a little bit of battlefield psychology you can learn by poking around in the dirt."

They say one man's trash is another man's treasure. As I slipped the live round into my pocket, my thoughts went back to that morning when we'd been introduced to the mayor of Sainteny. In his office at city hall, he uncorked a bottle of champagne to celebrate our visit. He raised his glass in a toast to Private Franklin Curtiss.

"Your uncle died to set us free."

Across the hall from the mayor's office is the city council chamber. It's a small room but nevertheless crowded with flags. Fifty, to be exact. One for every state in the union. In the center of

them all, in a place of honor directly over the podium, hangs the pennant of the State of Ohio. Anonymous though it might seem, that tribute has been placed there by those who received the most from E Company's sacrifice, the villagers of Sainteny themselves.

Our last day in Normandy was spent at Omaha Beach. It was August. We had missed the 70th year anniversary of the landing. It had been attended by heads of state from around the world including Presidents Sarkozy and Obama. Even now, the American Cemetery was jammed, but—with few exceptions—the tourists were all French, here to pay their respects to the American fallen.

George and I stood at the top of the cliff which overlooked Omaha Beach.

"I'm going down there," I said.

"Bring me back some sand," he said.

On the beach below, I traced the following words:

PVT FRANKLIN CURTISS
CO. E 329TH INFANTRY
KIA JULY 4TH 1944

As I stood with sand-filled pockets, the incoming tide washed his name out to sea, his only memorial. It may not have been much, but to me, it felt like more than enough.

Combats de rues dans Paramé
Rue de la Gardelle.

MYRON H. MILLER, S SGT

83rd Infantry Division, K/331st, European Theater

Submitted by Ken Miller, Son

THEY MET IN SAINTENY, France, on July 21, 1944, when my dad, Myron H. Miller, was a 26-year-old Pfc. He was assigned as a replacement soldier to the 83rd Infantry Divison, 331st Batallion, Company K. Raymond Barnes had been assigned just a few days before on July 17. When my Dad arrived, he announced he was from Dixon, Missouri, and asked if anyone else in Company K was from Missouri. Raymond, nineteen years old, raised his hand and said he was from Albany. They buddied right up that very first day.

During their first few weeks together many fellow soldiers were wounded or killed. Both young men from Missouri were scared to death, which made their bond even stronger as they fought tough battles among the hedgerows trying to advance. Three weeks later, on August 8, 1944, they made it to St. Malo. Used by the Germans as a fortified port, St. Malo was known for some of the fiercest street fighting that the Army had engaged in since the invasion.

On August 9, Company K was on the right of a three-prong attack, fighting door-to-door, in the northeastern section of the suburb called Paramé. My Dad and Raymond were in the same squad of twelve men at a street intersection when the squad leader ordered Raymond to cross the street. The German snipers had a high vantage point, shooting from the windows. Raymond reluctantly obeyed and was shot by a sniper as he ran across the street. As we remember the story, my Dad charged across the street, grabbed Raymond by the shirt and without slowing down, picked him up and carried him to cover on the other side. Raymond's wounds were so severe that my Dad thought he would surely die. The squad had to keep moving forward, and he had to leave Raymond behind with the medics while carrying the burden that he would never see his Missouri buddy alive again.

Dad survived the war and returned home to Dixon. Five years later, in the summer of 1950, he was a married man with a wife and two children, ages three and one. Our mom's grandparents lived in Clay Center, Kansas, and that summer, our parents decided to drive to see them. My Dad suggested a detour to Albany so he could find Raymond's parents and tell them what had happened to him in St. Malo.

As Albany is the county seat of Gentry County, there is a war memorial at the courthouse. It listed the names of Gentry County soldiers who had served in the war. Those who had died were identified with a star by their names. Raymond's name was there—and there was no star. My dad asked a man standing near him about Raymond Barnes. The man pointed down the street and replied, "I just saw Raymond a few minutes ago down at the garage."

Our mother waited in the car with my brother and sister, and my Dad took off down the street to the garage. Sure enough, there was Raymond in a mechanic's uniform smoking a cigarette. Overjoyed and amazed, Raymond left work and took my family to his house to meet his wife, June, and their two small children, Terry and Sherry.

They ended up staying overnight, and Raymond and my Dad sat outside on the porch all night long talking. Raymond had nearly died of his wounds, yet he survived. He showed my Dad the metal-backed Bible that he had carried in his fatigue shirt left breast pocket. It had been given to him by his sister Elizabeth. It had a deep indentation in the metal cover. When the sniper's bullet hit him, the Bible deflected the trajectory just enough to save his life.

The next day, as my family prepared to head to Kansas, they agreed that the families would take turns visiting each other every summer in either Dixon or Albany. They kept that promise.

I remember our trips to Albany were the closest thing our family had to a vacation it was like visiting family to be with the Barnes'. These visits continued until 1972 when Raymond was killed in a car accident. By the time I was born, in 1958, the older kids were good buddies. As they became teenagers, they would go off to do things together, leaving me to play in the backyard or the Barnes's cool attic with my brother and little sister.

Our fathers are no longer with us, but the two families remain close and have an incredible bond as the next generation of WWII buddies.

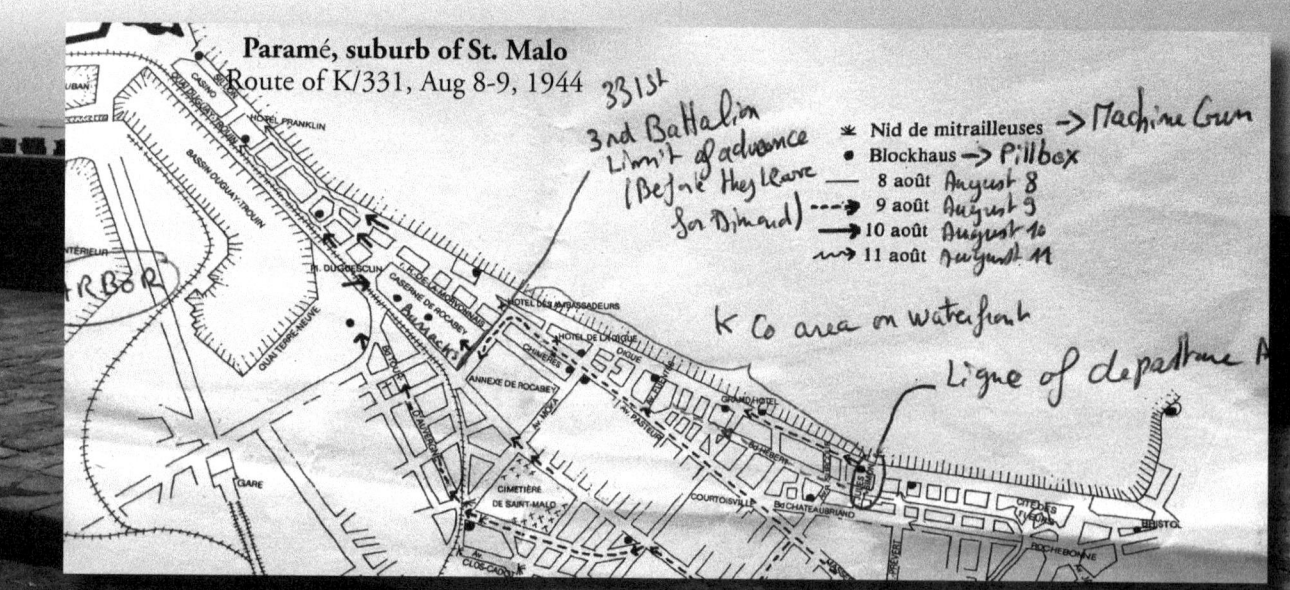

JOSEPH B. JENKINS

NEW GUINEA CAMPAIGN, U.S. NAVY, PACIFIC THEATER
*SUBMITTED BY BOYD MILLER, BROTHER,
AND PAULA MILLER LINDENLAUB, SISTER*

OUR BROTHER, JOE JENKINS, served in the U.S. Navy. During the New Guinea campaign, he was working as a fuel truck driver hauling a load of fuel in the company of a couple of natives who were supposedly helping the Americans against the Japanese. During the drive, the natives were speaking to each other in their native language, which Joe had learned enough of to realize they were actually working for the Japanese and were planning to kill him and take the fuel he was carrying when they got to their destination.

Joseph Jenkins was the stepbrother of Myron H. Miller, S/Sgt.

As they were crossing a mountain, Joe decided to take his chance and aimed the truck off a cliff and jumped out at the last minute leaving the schemers to perish in the crash. As far as we know, he was not injured from the jump and made it safely back to his unit. After the war, he returned home to California and married and had a child. He was killed in an automobile accident in 1950.

JOHN C. CREWS, PFC

12TH ARMORED DIVISION, "HELLCATS", EUROPEAN THEATER

Submitted by David Crews, Nancy Hance, Judy Brown, Children

I WAS INDUCTED INTO the Army from my home in Oklahoma City in 1944. I took my boot camp training at Fort Joseph T. Robinson in Arkansas and then was assigned to the 12th Armored Division, known as the "Hellcats," based out of Camp Barkley in Abilene, Texas, where I debarked for the European Theater of War on September 4, 1944. I told my new wife, Joelmae, "Goodbye" and boarded a train that took the new soldiers to our POE (Point of Embarkation) at New York City.

Our group was honored with a huge ticker-tape parade in New York City—a real patriotic sendoff! I was thrilled with the parade, but also scared, knowing I was going off to war—into combat. I was nineteen years old.

I crossed the Atlantic on the troopship *HMT Empress* out of Australia and landed in England for training and preparation ahead of moving into the theater of war in France.

In Britain, I was camped near London and was billeted in the home of some friends of my wife's British pen-pal, Mary White, whom I was able to meet. The friends who boarded me were extremely thankful for the United States' help and they treated me to breakfast in bed. I also met my Army friend, Gerald Daniels, with whom I'm still friends with today. During that October, we were able to see some of the sights in London before we crossed into the war in France.

We GI's did not know what the top secret plans were, of course, so we did not know exactly where or when we would be going, but when November came, we crossed the English Channel to Le Havre, France. Here, we became part of the Seventh Army under Generals Allen and Patch. We made our way across the French countryside to join our D-Day survivor buddies. I saw the church steeple where our fellow paratrooper landed—the tangled chute still on the steeple.

We joined up with the main battle lines near Weisslingen, Germany by December 7th. My occupation was as a radio operator. Our signals could not get over hills and mountains well. My radio shack was my half-track vehicle with a driver and machine gunner on the top turret (a .50 caliber gun) to help keep us safe! We changed our code machine several times daily to keep ahead of the Germans who were reading our codes. If I couldn't maintain constant communications, I would strap my 40-pound radio on my back and send and receive messages at the same time I was fighting the Germans, so I did earn my Combat Infantry Badge legally and proudly.

Unfortunately, I was a great target for snipers—me with my important radio communications and its long, 4-foot antennae. I heard lots of Nazi bullets zinging by my ears!

My memories of fighting across Germany are not good, but all bad—seeing friends of mine killed or injured. Fighting the Hitler Germans was intense. During the time of the Battle of the Bulge, we went through the famous battle at Herrlisheim and then cleared the Colmar Pocket. This was one of the worst winters in anyone's memory, at least in the last fourteen years—fierce winter snow up to our belts. We were well supplied with winter woolen coats and gloves, food, C-Rations and later, improvised K-Rations which we warmed up. We enjoyed the instant coffee. Many, many times, I would make my coffee in my metal cup, and right then, we would receive Kraut artillery 88s, which had an awful screaming whine coming in, and I would run for cover, losing all my hot coffee! I was sure mad at the Germans!

During this time, our enemy was the fierce winter snow and the German tanks. We could hear them coming from miles away because Hitler was running low on fuel. So, lots of "crack, crack, boom" to announce they were coming. We got our bazookas and destroyed them.

On January 7th, somewhere on the front lines, I suddenly came across a German foxhole. Emerging from the hole was a German Colonel. Fortunately for me, he was alone, but we were both startled and frightened. Facing my rifle, he knew he was captured, and I motioned to him to drop his weapon belt and move away, with his hands on his head. I was so nervous; I told him to "Stick 'em up!" He obeyed, and I retrieved his handgun. I remember that the Colonel was smiling as I delivered him to the MPs—the war was over for him. I received a Bronze Star for this capture.

The handgun I took from him was a Walther 7.65mm, which I still own. This gun saved my life many times during the fighting to follow, especially in Munich. This weapon was the best for clearing houses and basements and was very handy in street fighting. Shooting from a window or doorway, you are better hidden with a handgun. The Nazis would wonder, "Where did that shot come from?" A rifle sticks out, and if you shoot them with it, you get a live grenade in return.

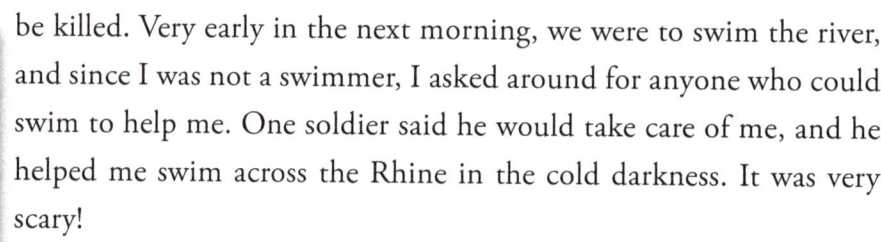

On March 17, 1945, our entire 12th Armored Division was transferred or "loaned" to General George Patton's Third Army. We became known as the "Mystery Division." This was because we were to be used as a secret tool to confuse the enemy. Patton would often pull us from the front, and being very mobile; we would be set up miles down the front. Perhaps Hitler would think, "Where did that army come from?" Or "How many armies do the Americans have?" It worked to our advantage.

We always did our quick moves at night. We would form a convoy using "cat eyes" for the vehicle's lights. These were light covers with slits about three inches long. Drivers had to very carefully follow the cat eyes of the vehicle in front of him. He usually could not see the road or anything else. On one of the mountains, one of the half-tracks missed a curve, and we lost that vehicle and the soldiers in it.

On March 27, 1945, we reached the Rhine River at Worms, Germany. The bridge was still standing with a fortified tower that had circling windows, perhaps four stories high. The bridge had been wired for explosives by the Germans. The only way for us to cross was to swim, or else be killed. Very early in the next morning, we were to swim the river, and since I was not a swimmer, I asked around for anyone who could swim to help me. One soldier said he would take care of me, and he helped me swim across the Rhine in the cold darkness. It was very scary!

We received a lot of fire from the tower sharpshooters and lots of our men were wounded or killed. We brought up tanks afterward, though, and blew the whole top off of the tower! Mission successful.

Our armies were superior to the Nazis. We were clothed better and fed better. We had rest periods several times. My first one was to Nancy, France, and the second one was to Paris. Of course, this was a morale builder. We were furnished free cigarettes, although I don't smoke and never have.

Hitler had brainwashed his army and the civilians, warning them that the Americans would rape the citizens and then kill them. When we captured a town, we first cleared all the houses, then the basements with guns drawn. The house that I cleared first, I'll never, never forget. In the basement was a family of four. A grandfather, mother, and children, with their hands folded in prayer. They begged us not to be raped and killed. They found out right away that we were good humans like they were. They were so relieved that they offered us food and milk. We could not accept the milk, though, because it is the easiest thing to be poisoned.

On April 22nd we reached the Danube river. The 12th Armored Division captured the bridge at Dillingen and erected a famous sign which stated, "You are crossing the beautiful blue Danube through the courtesy of the 12th Armored Division."

On April 26th we were at Burgau, just south of the Danube, when I realized that the arms fire we were under was coming from our own forces on the other side of the town. They thought we were escaping Nazis! I could not raise them on the radio, so I decided to run across the town with my radio pack until I could get the signal to them to stop the friendly fire. Burgau had not yet been cleared of the enemy, so I was under intense sniper fire the entire time. I remember the sound of the German bullets whizzing by my head all the way through the town. I also remember running very fast! Finally, our troops on the other side answered my radio message and stopped the firing, which saved many of our lives. I received my second Bronze Star with Oak Clusters for this action.

After this, we entered Munich, where I experienced very fierce street fighting.

On May 8th Germany surrendered unconditionally, and we halted fighting and waited for our time to go home. We shipped out from Bavaria on troop trains that were really just livestock boxcars with bare floors and thick hay to rest and sleep on. We traveled all the way across Germany and France in these boxcars to Camp Lucky Strike, near Le Havre. There, we would board ships for our thirty-day leave at home before heading to the Pacific Theater to fight again in the ongoing war with Japan.

Before the war, I had played guitar and sung professionally in Oklahoma City on KOMA radio, so before boarding the troop train, I bought a German guitar to take home. Unfortunately, the train lurched one day, causing one of the soldiers to fall over onto my guitar, which was ruined.

At Camp Lucky Strike, we spent several weeks until the trip back to the United States. I worked as a Company Clerk during that time and learned to play ping-pong. In August, I boarded the *S.S. Marine Devil*, one of the many troop ships taking us back across the Atlantic. The ship was very crowded and there was a lot of seasickness, especially below decks. I took a chance and slept on the deck to avoid it.

Just after leaving Le Havre, destination Boston Harbor, we received news over the ship radio that the atomic bomb had been dropped on Japan. About mid-Atlantic, we heard that the second bomb had been dropped and that the Japanese had surrendered, ending the war! Of course, we had a very big celebration on the ship, jumping, and hollering. I'm surprised the boat didn't sink! We were going home for good.

I believe that our troop ship was the very first ship to arrive in Boston after the war was over—perhaps the first one to arrive in the U.S.A. When we reached the harbor, we were met with fireboats shooting their jets of water into the air and a flat-top aircraft carrier with a Broadway musical being performed on deck for us to see all the way into the landing!

I'll never forget when we put our foot for the first time on good ole U.S.A. soil; the Red Cross handed us a tall glass of ice-cold *milk*. This was a treat because we were not allowed to have milk overseas due to the danger of poisoning.

I was bedded down at Camp Miles Standish in Massachusetts until I could return home.

I'd like to say that I am very grateful to the United States Government for the G. I. Bill, which allowed me to get an education and have a professional career that I otherwise may not have had the opportunity to enjoy. ©2011 David P. Crews, http://www.newrational.com/veteran/

Written by John C. Crews
Georgetown, Texas
May, 2005

EUGENE HARMACK, T5 CPL

83rd Infantry Division, HQ/329th, European Theater

Submitted by Marshall Miller quoting Gene Harmack

I MET GENE AT the Elk's Club in Affton, Missouri at a Battle of the Bulge meeting. Gene had been with the 83rd Infantry, 329th Regiment, HQ Company, working in communications during the war. After the meeting, someone asked Gene if he had known about German soldiers who tried to infiltrate American lines by wearing stolen American uniforms and claiming they had been separated from their units. This was Gene's reply:

"Sure that happened. We had all these passwords to see if everyone was an American, asking baseball questions and such—but they didn't really work. We just told them to drop their pants. If they were wearing German underwear we knew they didn't belong."

- Gene Harmack

**VETERANS of the BATTLE OF THE BULGE - St. Louis Gateway Chapter
8 May 2007, 62nd Anniversary of VE DAY - 8 May 1945**

TRIBUTE TEAM – WESTERN EUROPE

Bringing Honor, Dignity, and Respect to Fallen Soldiers

Special Tribute from The Miller Family

FRANK RUDDER'S LIFE MISSION: "To remember the brave soldiers; the ones who never made it home, who never had the chance to grow old and have a family. I want to honor those who returned home broken and with war traumas because they fought to free our countries from tyranny."

For years, he has lead a group of dedicated people who have been properly trained and certified in order to provide the proper protocol in honoring fallen servicemen and soldiers from WWI and WWII who fought with the Allies in the Western European Theatre. This is a serious matter; therefore, he and his passionate team make sure that the highest standards in representing colors and executing details are met.

The main goals of their team are performing details at memorial services and representing associations in honoring the memory in those who gave the Europeans their freedom, including veterans who are still alive. They feel it is their duty to bring honor, dignity, and respect to the fallen soldier for the families who lost their loved one on European soil.

Why do they do this? Because Frank feels strongly that they owe it to all soldiers. "We never can pay them back for what they did for us."

The Eternal Watch: Honor is served by ceremonial rest for 21 minutes, on the site where a soldier died. This "Eternal Watch" is dedicated to the fallen who spent their last minutes alone, to tell them, *"Don't be afraid, you are not alone, we will make sure you will never be forgotten."*

HARRY J. KIRBY, SGT

83rd Infantry Division, C/308th Engineer Combat Bn, European Theater

Submitted by Marianne Kirby Rhodes, Daughter

NOVEMBER 1944. THE ALLIED armies continued to take Europe back from Hitler's iron-fisted grip. Success followed success and the Americans had pushed from the beaches of Normandy all the way to Holland, Belgium, and Luxembourg. Hopes were high that the end of the war was near.

In Luxembourg, the 83rd Infantry Division continued to patrol east of the Moselle and Sauer Rivers between Bollindorf and Sierch Les Sains. The 308th Engineer Combat Battalion supported the infantry regiments with mine removal, obstacle removal, road reconnaissance, bridge construction, ferry operation, road repair, and instruction in booby traps and mines.

Company C, 308th, was stationed in the little town of Steinsel. To the G.I.s, it was a little slice of heaven. Neat, clean, friendly, with a bakery that turned out the freshest, most delicious bread they could imagine. Sure beat the heck out of K-rations.

The fellas patronized the bakery so frequently, in fact, that the lieutenant had to order them to cut it out. There wasn't enough bread for the townspeople when the G.I.s bought it all up.

The people liked the young, friendly American boys and when they discovered that November marked the celebration of that most American of holidays, Thanksgiving, they wanted to do something to show their appreciation to the soldiers far away from home. So the Steinsel folks invited individual G.I.s to share a Thanksgiving meal at their homes.

My dad, Sergeant Harry J. Kirby, was off duty, hanging out with some of the other engineers in the town center. Some young boys approached and with a few words in English and German, plus lots of gestures, the fellows understood that they were invited to dinner. One of the boys tugged at Harry's arm. "Come with me," he urged. "My home. Please, eat."

That was how Dad spent Thanksgiving 1944, at the home of the Pleimling family, feasting on rabbit with all the trimmings Luxembourg could manage. He never forgot that kind gesture and talked of it often to us when we were kids. Luxembourg was his favorite memory.

In 1994, we took Dad to Europe to mark the 50th anniversary of the D-Day Invasion. On the itinerary was a visit to Luxembourg and well, it's not very big, so why not go back to Steinsel? With two other engineer vets who had been in Steinsel in '44, he found the town, not much changed in fifty years, still neat, friendly, beautiful.

He also found the Pleimling family. And again, they invited the G.I.s into their home. Josef Pleimling, descendant of those other generous Pleimlings, had not been born yet in 1944, but he, his wife, and son served coffee and cakes from that long-remembered bakery to three old soldiers who still were surprised at the warm welcome they received.

Thank you, Pleimling family, and all the liberated citizens of Luxembourg who made it a Happy Thanksgiving in 1944 for the 83rd Infantry.

You gave these engineers from the 83rd some warm and pleasant memories they were able to take with them when, only a few weeks later, they took part in the Battle of the Bulge.

At the Pleimlings' home in Steinsel, June 1994: my dad, Harry Kirby, Mrs. Pleimling, Josef Pleimling, their son; Al Silverio and Quinto DiAntoni, also engineers from the 308th.

DELMER R. BEAM, CPL

6TH INFANTRY DIVISION, C/1ST REGIMENT, PACIFIC THEATER

Written by Marshall Miller as told by Roger Beam, Son, and Lana Beam Sloan, Daughter

WAR STORIES DON'T ALWAYS end when the shooting stops and soldiers return to civilian life. The family of former Army Corporal Delmer R. Beam can tell you all about the horrors of Post-Traumatic Stress Disorder.

Corporal Beam's separation papers list him as a "Combat Infantryman" in the Army's 6th Division, 1st Infantry Regiment, Company C. His World War II experiences started in 1939, as a 17-year-old, at Fort Jackson near Columbia, South Carolina and stretched into August 1945. This was after several years of bitter fighting in the South Pacific against Japanese forces at New Guinea and the Philippines.

Delmer's wife, Gladys, told her children, Lonnie, Roger, and Lana, that the father they came to know after the war was nothing like the "joyful, fun guy" who gave six and a half years of his life—and numerous difficult years beyond—to the cause of freedom.

Gladys said the war destroyed her husband, both mentally and physically. In the mid-1960s, Lana said he submitted to shock treatments at Mount Vernon Hospital to calm down his combat issues. The children couldn't understand why they weren't allowed to shoot fireworks on the Fourth of July. The few stories Beam told about his experiences were tough to hear.

Like the one where soldiers were ordered to shoot thirty rounds of ammunition every morning into the surrounding trees to protect the camp from Japanese snipers, who would climb high to get maximum angles on their targets. Once, Beam recalled, several soldiers were killed by a sniper, even after the morning strafing. After an exhaustive search, the sniper finally was located hiding in a water canvas bag hanging from a tree. He had crawled in, poked a small hole in the canvas and shot his victims with a pistol.

Japanese marksmen and fierce fighting weren't the only obstacles thrown in Beam's path. Malaria was a difficult burden, and an attack from scrub typhus mites nearly killed him. Delmer told his family he got so sick from the mites that he was presumed dead while lying on a stretcher on a beach. Someone saw him move, however, and he was transferred to a hospital ship.

His son, Roger, chronicled his memories of his Dad's experience in this excerpt:

> *AS A YOUNG BOY, I was always enamored with army war stories. I would ask him about the war many times. Only on very few occasions would he talk about it. It is strange how I can remember some of the stories he told me when I can't sometimes remember what I did yesterday. He told me about how terrible it was in the jungles of New Guinea, things that I, to this day, am in awe of.*
>
> *He said that he saw GI's almost kill each other over a piece of chicken wire. The reason is that they would stretch the wire over their foxholes so the Japanese hand grenades would hit the wire and bounce back from the foxholes before it exploded. It rained every day in the jungle and was very hot and humid. When they went out on missions at night, they always dug their own foxholes and had to sit in them and continually dump water out with their helmets all night long.*
>
> *He told me about his best friend, a young 19-year-old from Hope, Arkansas. While they were being attacked one day by Japanese, my Dad kept telling him to stop sticking his head up over the embankment they were behind, but the young man kept doing it until he got hit in the head and died in my dad's arms. This has always made a picturesque impression on me.*
>
> *There are a few other stories, but I would rather talk about the good things about my dad. I know he was haunted the rest of his life about what he went through, just like so many others. He was a good dad and even got better the older he got. He was talky to anybody about their salvation and studied the Bible every day. Dad never met a stranger; he would talk to anyone.*

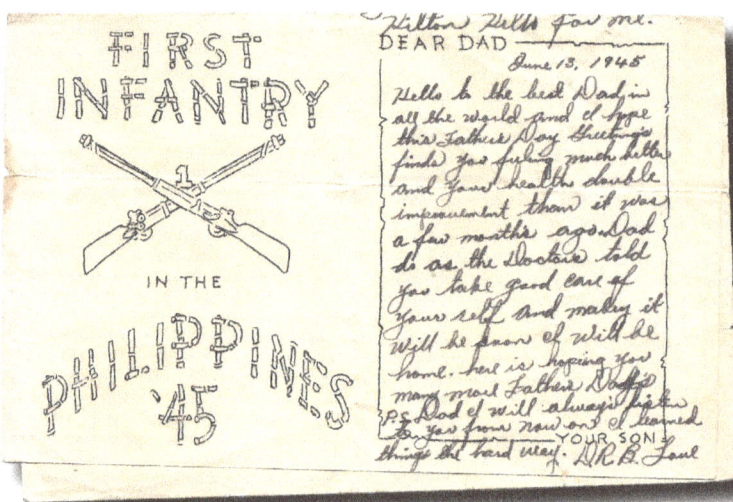

Despite his health issues, Delmer spent his post-war years in Dixon, Missouri, and worked at Fort Leonard Wood as a fire inspector. He died in 1991 at age 70. His daughter, Lana, had these words to remember her Dad: *I guess the most uplifting thing about my dad was…he really believed that he survived when others died because God wasn't done with him yet.*

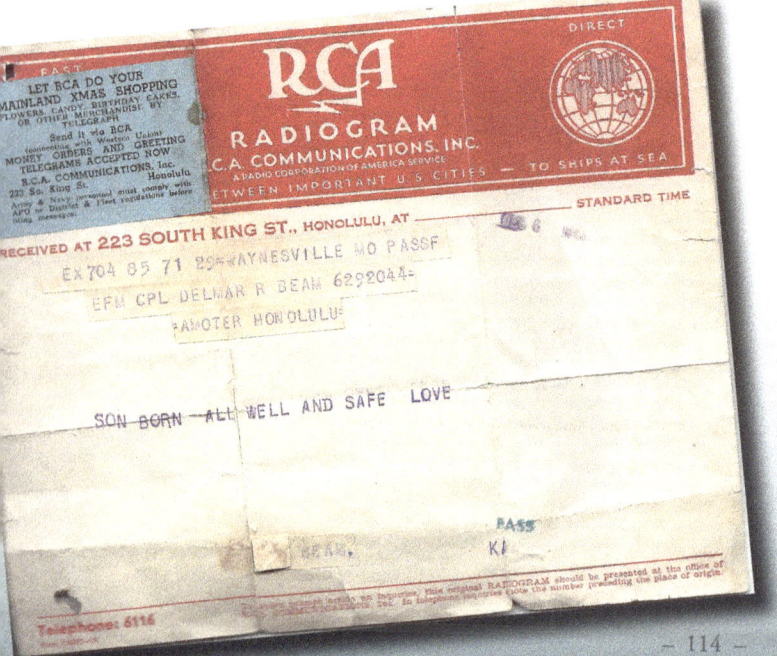

MY GRANDPA DELMAR TOLD me this story several times as a young boy. I think he always got a kick out of it and was probably one of his "better" memories of the war.

He told me of the time his squad was out one evening climbing around the sides of trees, collecting peppers that they used to flavor all of their food. They had rifles slung and arms full of peppers. As they came around a tree, to their shock and surprise they ran into a squad of Japanese soldiers, doing the exact thing! He said the resulting chaos was both terrifying and hilarious, as both groups scrambled away. Not a shot was fired and they saved their peppers!

In the midst of such a horrible time for my grandfather, it does make me smile a bit remembering how he smiled when telling this story.

Roger Beam, Jr.

Leather map case brought home by Cpl Beam after serving in the Pacific Theater.

Medals and ribbons earned by Cpl Delmer R. Beam for service from September 20, 1943 to August 20, 1945.

EVERETT E. 'BUD' WILKINSON, S1C

SS Cape Fear and SS Watson C. Squire, U.S. Naval Armed Guard, Pacific Theater

Submitted by Fran Wilkinson Beam, Daughter, Jim and Ned Wilkinson, Sons

EVERETT EUGENE (BUD) WILKINSON was born on July 15, 1925, and was raised in St. Joseph, Missouri. He was moved to join the Navy after the Pearl Harbor attack and did so as soon as he was old enough. He went to boot camp at the U.S. Naval Training Station in Farragut, Idaho in Company 738-43, Regiment 3, Battalion 11, graduating on October 16, 1943. Two weeks later, while home on leave, he married the love of his life, Roberta (Bobbie) Turpin and shortly after that shipped out for sea duty.

Bud was assigned to the U.S. Naval Armed Guard and served on Navy gun crews providing defensive firepower for Merchant Marine ships. Merchant Marine ships were a critical element in the Allied forces seagoing operations of World War II because they carried the bulk of all materials sent overseas, as well as many of the men who served there. A Merchant Marine ship was a target worth more than a destroyer escort or maybe even a destroyer. Sinking a Merchant Marine ship would deny the Allies much needed cargo for their combat theaters, so they were a main target of enemy submarines. The Merchant Marines suffered the highest rate of men killed in action of all of the Armed Services, even the U.S. Marine Corps.

In the South Pacific, Bud served aboard the *SS Cape Fear* for the February 1944 Occupation of Kwajalein and Majuro, the June—July Capture Occupation of Saipan, and later on the *SS Watson C. Squire* for the November Leyte Landings.

After the war he didn't talk a lot about his experiences, but youngest son, Ned, remembers stories about his initiation into the Order of Neptune, a ceremony commemorating a Sailors' first time crossing the Equator. "Pollywogs," as they were called, would be interrogated by a mock "King Neptune's Court" and made to endure increasingly embarrassing ordeals, such as crawling through tubs of rotten garbage and kissing the greased belly of "the Royal Baby." Elder son, Jim, remembers him talking about kamikaze planes encountered before official acknowledgment of their presence was released.

Daughter Fran: *Dad enjoyed life after his service years. He loved to hunt and fish and we spent lots of childhood weekends at the river, swimming pool or skating rink. He loved movies, especially war movies. I remember watching "Saving Private Ryan" with him. When it was over,*

I asked him what he thought about it and he said it was good, but one scene was too real for him. When the soldiers approached a bombed-out bunker while on patrol and the only sound you hear is buzzing flies. It reminded him of a similar experience he'd had in the Philippines.

In the mid-90s, I was fortunate enough to visit Hawaii and tour the Pearl Harbor Memorial. Dad had told me he was there during his service time, but he had never really expounded on it, so I vowed to make another trip there with him so he could explain the displays in the museum. He said he never wanted to see Pearl Harbor again, no matter how beautiful it might be today, as he was there in 1944, and it was still a sad sight he'd never forget.

Eldest Son Jim remembers some lighter incidents that happened. *While Dad was out to sea, Mom worked as a telephone operator in their home town of St. Joseph, Missouri. One day, she plugged into a call coming in from California and the long distance operator asked her to ring a number very familiar to her. It was her in-law's phone and she knew it was Dad on the other end of the line. She notified her supervisor, who took over her position so she could join in on the call. Later, after the war was over, Dad was back in St. Joseph on leave and was informed he was a few points shy of meeting the discharge requirement and he would have to be sent to Olathe, Kansas for a period of time. Back in those days, they didn't really know where that was so the family made their sad goodbyes and he boarded the train bound for Olathe. They all went home to await hearing from him in the future and were happily shocked when the phone rang about thirty minutes later and heard him say, "I'm here." He was close enough to come home on weekends until his time was fully served.*

All of his life, Bud was very close to his family and friends and he loved adventure in the great outdoors. Many, many hunting trips were made; elk and deer hunting in Wyoming and Colorado, wild boar hunting in Arkansas, fishing trips to Minnesota and Canada. Camp-outs on the White River, Gasconade River, Lake of the Ozarks, Truman Lake, and Lake Stockton. Annual deer camps with family and friends were some of the highlights of his life.

Bud had a great sense of humor and loved a good joke, even when it was on himself. Steve Adams, son of one of Bud's long-time friends, Bud Adams, recalls the following: Very early one morning, Bud and Bud headed up north for a duck hunt at Swan Lake. They began to notice a fog developing and wondered if they would even be able to see any ducks by the time they got there. They decided to stop at a truck stop to get something to eat and when they opened the truck doors realized the 'fog' was only inside the truck as they'd set the ashtray on fire.

Several of Bud's family members were musicians and he grew up singing and playing guitar and banjo. Family and friend get-togethers always had lots of singing and picking and having a good time. Bud and Bobbie were also proud members of the American Legion, and both served in various offices throughout the years at American Legion Post 69 in Springfield, Missouri.

After the war, Bud and Bobbie moved the family to Springfield, where he opened a photography business, Kordel Studio. After a fire damaged the studio, they moved to the Waynesville/Dixon area and he worked as a contract photographer at Ft. Leonard Wood for a few years before purchasing White Branch Marina in Warsaw, Missouri, and going to school to become a Mercury master marine mechanic. In later years, they sold the marina and moved back to Springfield, but he maintained a marine repair business at Lake Stockton for a few more years.

The last years of his career he worked for Sears Corporation assisting servicemen and delivering parts until health issues made that impossible. He was a beloved son, husband, father and grandfather, and he passed away peacefully at his home surrounded by his family in 2006. He was buried in the Springfield National Cemetery—his son, Ned, playing "Taps" on the trumpet as he'd requested.

FLOYD W. 'BILL' SHELY, JR

83RD INFANTRY DIVISION, K/331ST, EUROPEAN THEATER

Submitted by Martie Shely Chittum, Daughter

July 21, 1922 - August 1, 2016

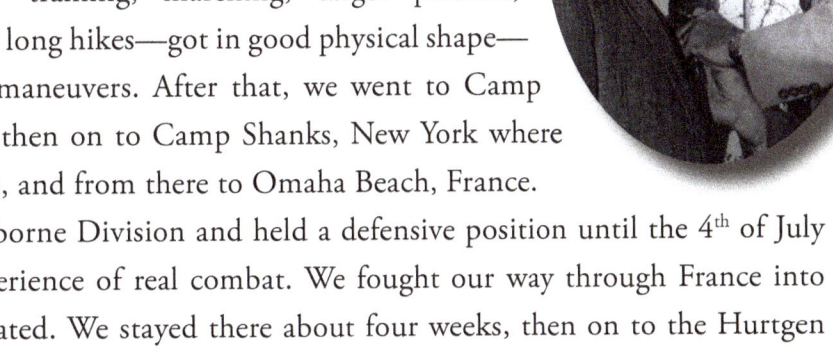

I STARTED MY ARMY adventure in October of 1942. I went to Camp Atterbury, Indiana which was the home of the 83rd Division. We did our training, marching, target practice, long hikes—got in good physical shape—then went to Tennessee for maneuvers. After that, we went to Camp Breckenridge, Kentucky and then on to Camp Shanks, New York where we boarded a ship to England, and from there to Omaha Beach, France.

We relieved the 101st Airborne Division and held a defensive position until the 4th of July 1944. That was our first experience of real combat. We fought our way through France into Luxembourg, which we liberated. We stayed there about four weeks, then on to the Hurtgen Forest, where we had a rough time. The weather was cold and we suffered from frost bite. We stayed in the Roer Valley several days and then received orders to move out.

One morning, we hiked to our trucks near a house. There were big shrubs and we decorated the biggest one for a Christmas tree—we hung anything we could find on it—it looked so good to us. As soon as we were loaded, the Germans shelled our tree. I believe they could have killed a lot of us, but they waited until we got out of the way—after all, it was December 25th. We were headed for the Battle of the Bulge in Belgium and on the way, we had Christmas dinner. Sure tasted good to a country boy far from home.

The invasion of France was the beginning of the end of World War II in Europe. I was a part of the Division that participated in five campaigns—Normandy, Northern France, Ardennes, Rhineland and Central Europe. Our route took us from Omaha Beach through France, Luxembourg, Belgium and across the Elbe River into Germany—a total of 1,500 miles in distance and more in casualties.

I'll never forget what we did.

CONNECTIONS

Special Tribute to David Curry

Written by Ken Miller on behalf of The Miller Family

THIS BOOK IS A personal historical adventure that recalls to me the television series "Connections," presented by British science historian, James Burke in the 1970's, wherein he discusses how the interconnected actions of people weave together to create unexpected and astonishing results. The amazing past of the World War of over seventy years ago is revealed to us by the efforts of so many historians, descendants, and friends across the world and is made possible by new ways of communicating. Our newfound knowledge and appreciation of the experiences of our fathers and grandfathers and the special bonds of new friendships are the result of this astounding connectivity.

A special word about a great connector, David Curry, is therefore appropriate. I have not met David myself but did speak to him on the phone several years ago when I made a few tentative steps in learning about my father's role in the war. I did not know until recently that David's father, Thomas D. Curry, who served in the 331st Regiment of the 83rd Infantry Division, along with my father, Myron H. Miller, was killed in action in Gey, Germany on December 10, 1944, just six days before my dad was wounded. David never had a chance to grow up knowing his dad, yet his efforts to learn about him, begun in the early days of the internet, was to be crucial in connecting so many others with their fathers and grandfathers. We all owe David Curry our gratitude and appreciation.

David's website, Brothers-in-Arms, is a wonderful and well-written source of information about the exploits of the 83rd, Company F, and the 331st in particular, and was for a long time the only place for veterans and descendants to connect with each other. It is well worth visiting at kb8tt.net/brothers/. Now with Facebook, David admits that his method of communication is a bit outdated and has decided to not actively update the site anymore. However, his labor of love will remain an important research tool to help more descendants of WWII.

In David's memorial to Thomas D. Curry, we learn that David's son, Mike, and Bob "Sarge" Parsons, were also key connectors. Excerpts from Thomas' letters home tell a story of their own and are a touching reminder of everyday life in a crucible of fire.

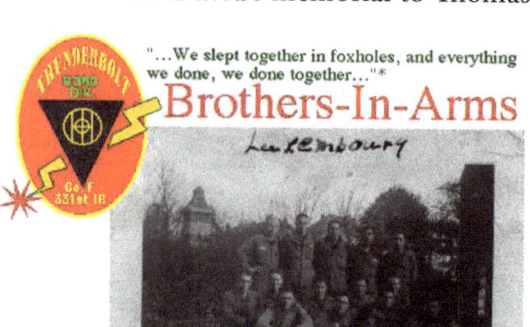

Thank you, David, for being there and leading the way. We salute your father, Private First Class Thomas D. Curry, for his sacrifice. It is great to know both of you.

THOMAS D. CURRY, PFC

83rd Infantry Division, F/331st, European Theater

Submitted by David Curry, Son

I GREW UP AND lived most of my adult life without ever knowing very much about my father. "He was killed in the war" is what I told anyone who asked about him. My mother kept his picture on her dresser. I would often look at it and wonder about the man in the uniform. How was I like him? How was I different? Questions I could not answer. Life went on, and he was never more than that picture on my mother's dresser.

Then, my mom gave me some keepsakes she had saved from that time. My sons and I poured over them and then we put them back in their box. That probably would have been the end of it, but my son Mike found Bob Parsons on the Internet. "Sarge" was in the same company as my father and remembered him. Our correspondence with Sarge mushroomed into an explosion of old memories. We still have much to learn. If we learn nothing more, I have answered those questions about the man in the photograph. Now, years later, I have found the father I never knew. A day does not pass that I don't think of him.

Although he was a young man, my father was ancient by Army standards. He was thirty years old when called to active duty, and thirty-one when killed in action. He was probably referred to as an "old man" by most of the other men in his company. He was not a large man, but my mother said the Army "built him up," and he never looked better. Even so, his ETO Enlisted Man's Identification Card lists his weight at 139 pounds. At the height of 5 ft. 7.5 in., he probably didn't have an ounce of fat on his body. He had brown hair and brown eyes, and a ruddy complexion attributable to his Scotch-Irish ancestry.

He was called to active duty on 26 October 1943 and, after seventeen weeks of training, he was sent overseas to became part of F Company/331st Infantry Regiment on 17 July 1944. He was moved to the front lines, 2 and 3/4 miles south of the town of Sainteny, along with 45 other GIs from the 41st Replacement Battalion that was stationed at Treviers, south of Omaha Beach. He arrived just as the 83rd had regrouped along the Ays River. Operation COBRA began the morning of 25 July. Over 1,500 heavy bombers dropped 3,300 tons of bombs to saturate the entire target area. Then, more than 380 medium bombers dropped 650 tons of high-explosive and fragmentation bombs, while 550 fighter-bombers dropped more than 200 tons of high-explosive and napalm. The 3.5-by-1.5 mile target area was only 1,500 yards in front of the American line. There was fear that this was too close for heavy bombing, in fact, many GIs were killed that day by short bombing runs.

On 26 July, the 83rd entered the pursuit, and in heavy combat crossed the Taute River the next day. They cut the St. Lo-Periers road and forced their way into Le Mesnil Vigot. The drive carried them eight miles beyond their starting point. The 83rd Division then assembled near Feugeres, and on 3 through 5 August they moved out of the Cotentin Peninsula and turned west into Brittany. The roads were strewn with German tanks, trucks and staff cars, and often with dead Germans. On the coast near Mont St. Michel, Pontorson, and Dol-de-Bretagne they received orders to capture the port towns of St. Malo and Dinard.

St. Malo was the main port on the northern coast of Brittany. Because of its turbulent past as a privateer stronghold, the town was protected by stone walls. It would take two weeks of street fighting to raze St. Malo. On 6 August, the Germans demolished all the quays, locks, breakwaters and harbor machinery and set fire to the city. On 9 August, the enemy defenders were forced back to the Citadel at St. Servan and to Dinard on the west bank of the river just opposite St. Malo. On

16 August my father was awarded the Combat Infantryman Badge for displaying exemplary conduct in action against the enemy in France.

The 83rd Division then moved on to Luxembourg. Most Luxembourgers spoke several languages, and many spoke some English. Cafes were opened where the GIs could enjoy good Luxembourg beer, music, and dancing. The men of the 83rd finally had some breathing space, and they began to forget about the formidable Siegfried Line waiting for them across the Moselle. The 83rd spent Thanksgiving in that tiny country. Although it was not the same as being at home, the people of Luxembourg opened their homes to the GIs.

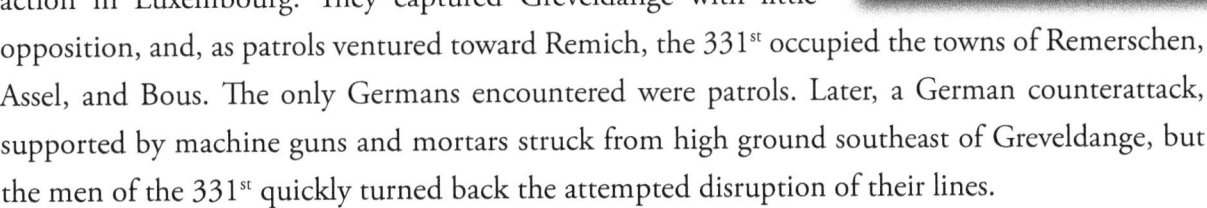

The 331st was the first regiment in the 83rd Division to see action in Luxembourg. They captured Greveldange with little opposition, and, as patrols ventured toward Remich, the 331st occupied the towns of Remerschen, Assel, and Bous. The only Germans encountered were patrols. Later, a German counterattack, supported by machine guns and mortars struck from high ground southeast of Greveldange, but the men of the 331st quickly turned back the attempted disruption of their lines.

As the 2nd Battalion advanced further toward Remich, they knocked out machine guns that the enemy had emplaced in concrete. It took the direct fire of the attached 774th tank battalion to accomplish this. After taking the towns of Wallenstein, Bech and Kleinmacher, they captured Schengen. For the first time in more than a month, they faced heavy artillery fire. German guns in the Siegfried Line east of the Moselle poured salvos into the lines, resulting in thirty casualties, the heaviest losses in over a month. They continued the mission and took Remich on 28 September. The 3rd Battalion captured the high ground northwest of Ehnen, but had to fight through heavy machine-gun and mortar fire to do it.

From the 1 through 5 of October, the 83rd advanced in heavy combat to the West Wall across the Sauer as the 329th fought the battle for Grevenmacher. On the 7th, the 329th took the city of Echternach on the Sauer River.

> *October 8: "There isn't a lot to write about over here. I sure wouldn't want to live the way they do. The barn and the house are all built together and the front yard is the stable yard. Doesn't seem to be very sanitary but most of the people seem to be healthy as hell, in fact they seem to thrive on it." TDC*
>
> *October 29: "We had quite a little treat the other day--the first real hot bath I've had since I left England (quite a topic for correspondence)." TDC*
>
> *November 14: "It looks like we not only will have to lick these supermen, but will have to go in and knock their heads off." TDC*

November 19: "I just got my ballot the other day, so threw it away. I see by the returns that the election didn't amount to much this time. I guess the people must be used to voting for F.D.R. All I hope is that he puts these Germans in their place, when this is over. Someone will have to fix them, so they won't start another war in a few more years, and I think he is the man that can do it. I'd hate to think of our son having to grow up to fight." *TDC*

November 22: "Here it is, another Thanksgiving Day that I won't be home. I hope it is the last one this way. We still have a lot to be thankful for; some of the things that happen over here don't seem possible … The mail situation is bad again, probably due to the Christmas rush. I got a half-dozen packs of cigarettes from Mom the other day and they just got here in time—we didn't get any for a few days, so you can see that we are having the same trouble over here as the people back home." *TDC*

November 26: "I was reading an old paper today and the people over there must be nuts. According to this paper, the war was practically over and the people were just waiting to celebrate. It's funny how good the news sounds, but anyway, I hope it ends soon—the sooner the better. It is beginning to look as if they really want to get totally destroyed, and if that's what they want, they are going to get it." *TDC*

By 29 November the First Army had just about cleared the Hurtgen Forest and was overlooking the Roer Valley. The process had reduced two more divisions, the 4th and 8th, to tatters. The 9th Army had also been slowly advancing north of Aachen towards the Roer.

December 2: "These shoes we wear are quite the thing—sometimes I think my feet would be warmer without shoes. In one of your letters you wanted to know how things were over here. I should be asking you. We hardly ever hear anything except rumors, and some of these are fantastic. About a month ago, someone over here had a paper, and there was a piece in it about some German prisoners in the States going on a strike for something or other. What the hell is wrong with the people over there? Do they think we are over here for our health? Then there are those who are quitting their jobs and going to better-paying ones. I still can't see why they can't be held to their jobs like we are." *TDC*

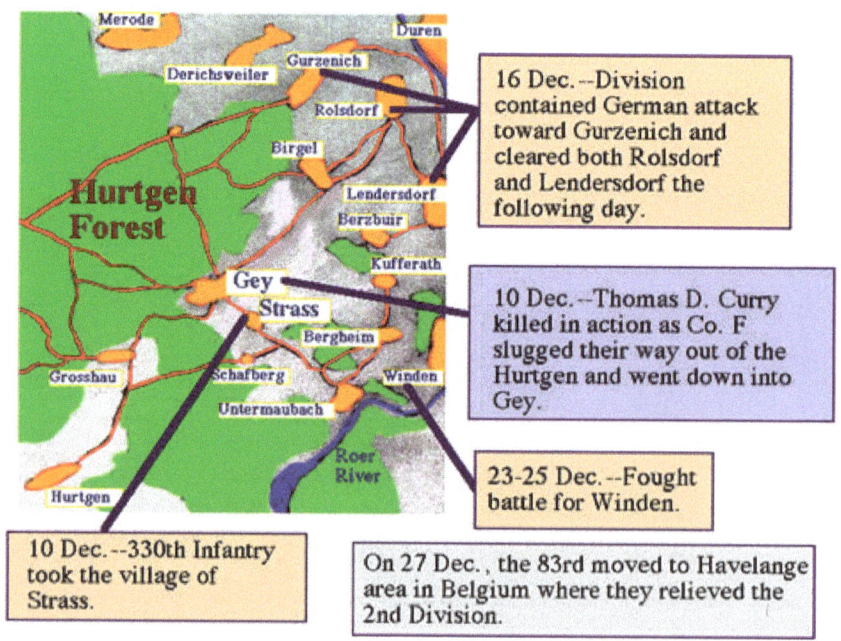

This story about Thomas D. Curry was reprinted from the Brothers-in-Arms website with permission from David Curry, http://kb8tt.net/brothers/.

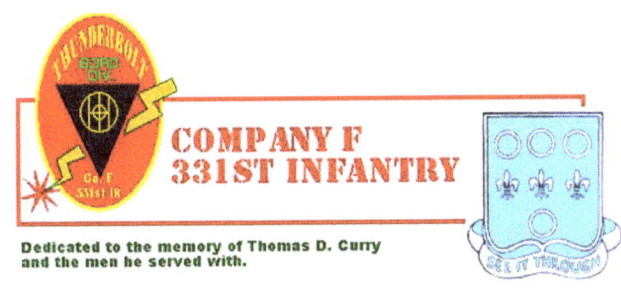

December 3: "Here it is another Christmas away from home—I hope it is the last one like this. There isn't much that I can send, except the same love that I have had ever since I've known you." TDC

December 6: "Tell people not to mention 'good luck.' There isn't any such thing over here. God takes care of us one way or the other." TDC

On 7 December, the 83rd Division relieved the 4th Infantry Division and attacked to clear the west bank of the Roer on 10 December. My dad was killed in action that morning as the GIs slugged their way out of the Hurtgen and advanced to the villages of Strass and Gey. John Helms said that my dad was taken out by an 88-mm artillery shell. My dad's Individual Deceased Personnel File indicates the cause of death as "Shrap. Chest."—confirming John's recollection.

My dad's story ends here, but the 83rd Infantry Division's does not. They fought through the Ardennes in the bitter cold and snow to beat back the German Bulge. Then they raced through Germany. The 329th lead the way most of the time and gained fame as the "Rag-Tag Circus" as they rode through the German provinces on tanks, motorcycles, jalopies, and any other means of transportation they could find. The 331st sped along not far behind on the flank. They raced across the German countryside until they were ordered to stop less than 60 miles from Berlin.

The GIs of the 83rd Division were awarded one Medal of Honor, one Distinguished Service Medal, five Legions of Merit, 798 Silver Stars, 34 Soldier's Medals, 7,776 Bronze Star Medals, 4,747 Purple Hearts, 271 Medical Badges, 20 Meritorious Service Unit Plaques, and 106 Air Medals. They were honored with 18 British Awards and 65 French Awards. They destroyed 480 enemy tanks, 61 enemy planes, 29 enemy supply trains, and 966 enemy artillery pieces. In the end, the 83rd Division, born in war, was disbanded and all its men reassigned to other units. There were no welcoming home parades for the Thunderbolt Division, but the GIs of the 83rd would carry its memory home with them.

DAVID V. FOLEY, 1ST LT

8TH AIR FORCE, 466TH BOMB GROUP, 787TH BOMB SQUADRON, EUROPEAN THEATER

Written by Marshall Miller, Submitted by Dennis Foley and Jim Foley, Sons

DAVID FOLEY WAS BORN in 1917, the son of David Sr. and Virginia Foley. He never talked about his war experiences to his wife, May Gray Foley, and his three sons, Dave, Dennis, and James. When Dave died several years ago, Jim found some old photos of their dad that he had never seen. One was a picture of the crew with the aircraft in the background, and stenciled under the window at the navigator's station were the words "Red Nose Foley." The plane was a B-24 with the name "Glad to See Ya" emblazoned on her nose. That's all it took for Jim to start his search. He got on the web and looked for the aircraft's name and came up with a lot of new information. Jim remembered seeing a bunch of medals in a drawer as a kid but didn't know what happened to them. He was able to order duplicates of the medals from the records center and his mother-in-law made a display that sits on his mantel today.

David's unit, the 466th Bombardment Group, was activated at Alamogordo, New Mexico in September 1943 and received combat training at various locations in the Southwest. The Group was dubbed the "Flying Deck" after a naming contest, with each squadron named after a different card suit. David's squadron was the 787th, or White Squadron, dubbed the Spades.

First Lieutenant Foley was the navigator on a B-24H Liberator named the "Glad To See Ya." The crew was designated as Crew #726 and consisted of the pilot (Frank Walcot for eleven missions and Dean Roser for the remaining twenty-two missions), co-pilot (William W. Hurt), navigator (David V. Foley), bombardier (Joseph B. Hayes), radio operator (Howard Lewis), flight engineer (Jack Reynolds), nose gunner (Joseph Whitaker), tail gunner (Bernard Johnson), waist gunner (Arthur Camacho), and ball turret gunner (John Kraeger).

In March of 1944, the ground support components left New York on the Queen Mary for Scotland. The air echelon with sixty-two aircraft left soon after and the two groups joined up at Attlebridge and AAF Station #120 on the east coast of England. Wasting no time, the group flew its first combat mission on March 22, 1944. Target—Berlin. It was the longest initial assault ever flown by any unit in the history of the European Theater and one of the heaviest bombardments on record of the German capital.

The Group participated in bombing pillboxes in support of the D-Day landing on June 6th. On July 25, 1944, the 466th led the entire 8th U.S. Air Force in Operation Cobra, the bombing of the German lines around St. Lo and Periers. The Allies sent 2,500 aircraft to bomb an area four miles long by two miles wide. After nearly two months of fierce ground fighting, the Allied forces were able to breakout from the Normandy beachhead.

Lieutenant Foley finished his thirty-three missions on August 25, 1944, and was able to return home. We know that from March 22 until August 25 David participated in some of the most dangerous missions of the war. After he left the crew on September 16th of that year, the "Glad to See Ya" was involved in a mid-air collision with another B-24 in a training mission over England. There were no survivors.

David's war story is still incomplete. He didn't leave us any personal stories about his time in the Army Air Corps. We can piece together a lot of the history of his exploits, but his personal stories are gone. David passed away in 1973, but his dedication and sacrifice make him a true American hero.

1st Lt. Dave Foley taking a nap on an English train coming over from Ireland to England. 1944

Taken over seas E.T.O. 1944

WILLIAM 'BILL' SPRIGGS, S SGT

83RD INFANTRY DIVISION, C/329TH, EUROPEAN THEATER

Submitted by Paula Spriggs Nezezon, Daughter

I WAS 17-YEARS OLD when my friend Bob Dishaw said he was joining the Navy and asked if I wanted to go with him to enlist. We arrived at the Navy Recruiter's office, but after my physical examination, I was not accepted because I was colorblind. I turned around and walked across the hall to join the Army. They had no problem accepting me—I was a warm body!

I went to Fort Dix for reception and to Fort McLellan, Alabama for basic training. After that, I traveled back up north, where I shipped out of New York City on June 16, 1944, to a port in Great Britain. I believe we arrived there around June 27, 1944, and were brought by train to a repo-depo where we set up. That first night they brought us into a Quonset hut that was dimly lit with only low voltage hanging lights. As I sat there, I heard a deep, booming voice that sounded strangely familiar. Turning around, I asked if that was Howard Edwards, and he answered, "Yes, who's that?" I answered, "It's your cousin Bill!" Howard had clerk-like duties; logging the soldiers in, doing the paperwork, and making sure we were all accounted for. After the usual greetings, I told him I had a three-day pass but wasn't able to go because I had no shoes. He offered to let me wear his, and I was happy to use them for my pass to the city.

OMAHA BEACH - We came across to Omaha Beach as replacements not assigned to any division or unit yet. I believe it was around the 7th or 8th of July. The weather was terrible while going across the channel. Waves were high, water was choppy, and winds were strong. On the landing craft coming into Omaha Beach, we were packed like sardines, and most guys were overcome with seasickness because of the rolling seas and the boat rocking. There were many, many ships all around fighting for the space to get in.

Mulberries had been fabricated in England and were then floated across. They looked like cement tanks and were to be used as floating wharfs that would allow them to off-load men and supplies. Unfortunately, we couldn't dock because the mulberries had been either blown up or sunk by the weather, so we had to jump over the side and into the water. Now I was 5'2" tall, and 125 pounds carrying an 80-pound pack because we were carrying supplies in addition to our own gear. When I jumped over the side I dropped completely under water, but a tall guy grabbed me by the scruff of my neck and pulled me to my feet. When we made it to the beach, a Buck Sergeant met us at the bottom of the hill that appeared to me to be about a mile high, and ordered us to ascend to the top. As we were climbing, we heard the sound of loud booming gunfire. We hit the dirt. He said, "Get up! That mail is going in. It's not for you!"

NORMANDY - When we arrived at the top, we were escorted into an apple orchard and got our assigned foxholes. We were offered dinner, which I took back to my foxhole, but unfortunately, it was located right next to a bloated, dead cow. I couldn't eat much that night because of the smell.

The next day we were brought to the front and were assigned to a Staff Sergeant. From there we advanced through the hedgerows of Normandy. Sometimes the hedgerows would take two days to get through. British troops were supposed to be on our flank but didn't move up on time, so we were coming under heavy fire. One of the guys and I found ourselves caught between two hedgerows with machine guns cross-firing over us. We found an empty machine gun foxhole and crawled in. It was a bright moonlit night and my buddy and I were stuck in the middle of the gunfire. I said to him, "A cloud is going to go across that moon, and when it does, be prepared to run like hell back to where we started." When we got back to our troops, there was supposed to be a password challenge in order for them to let you into the foxholes. Neither my buddy nor I knew the password, but I used the universal language of swearing, so they let us in.

BRITTANY - Then it was on to Brittany, where fierce fighting continued. We would fight until 10:00 or 11:00 p.m., and then jump off again at 3:00-4:00 a.m., hoping to surprise the Germans. On August 7, 1944, we moved onward, only to encounter a mine field. Three of us decided that we were not going through the mine field, so we went to a crossroad that was under machine gun fire by the Germans. As we got across, it was a dead end, and we saw the Buck Sergeant get shot. His last words were, "Oh, Ma." These were the last words of most of my buddies as they died.

We decided we had to get down the minefield one way or another. At that time, one of our soldiers came across the mine field holding his right arm. As he got closer to us, he dropped that arm, and we saw that he had been shot through the shoulder. When he dropped the good arm, he had been shot in that one as well. He kept telling us, "Don't go down there! Don't go down there!" But we had to keep going. I had watched where he came from, and decided that we would try to follow that line to the front. It was late in the evening, and the sun was going down. By the time we got to the battle front many of our soldiers had either been killed or wounded, mostly because of the tree bursts that showered down. The area was tree-lined with concrete bridges from meadow to meadow. A lot of the wounded crawled underneath the bridges. We carried dead and wounded out to a road some distance away. For some reason I became the triage officer tasked with organizing necessary movements and acquiring supplies. We were in need of blankets and stretchers. At one point I heard a soft voice ask me "Is there anything I can do?" In my best vernacular, I answered: "Get your ass somewhere and get more blankets and stretchers out to the road!" Then I realized that the captain I said that to was actually Chaplain Captain Halloran. I don't know if my face turned red, but it sure felt like it.

The next day, I was ordered to retrieve dog tags from the deceased soldiers. Of course, I had never done that before and didn't know what I was supposed to do, so I took both tags from the men, one of which was my good friend from Vermont, Raymond Sanville. I agonized for sixty-five years that those men I took the tags from ended up as missing in action because of what I had done. However, thanks to the European Chapter of the 83rd Infantry Group, I found out that Raymond was buried in Vermont, so it appears that those men were reunited with their families after all.

On August 8, 1944, I was wounded in the knee by shrapnel but went back to the line shortly after. Sometime after that, I mailed my cousin's shoes back (the ones I had borrowed in Great

Britain on my first day) to my aunt in New York City. She had heard that I had been wounded in action, and when she received the package, there was only one shoe left in the box. She sent my mother a letter telling her how sorry she was because she assumed the one shoe meant that I had lost a leg. We've had lots of laughs over that one!

Our objective was the area of St. Servan Sur Mer and St. Malo. Our information from U.S. intelligence was that there were only around three thousand to six thousand German troops there, and Colonel Crabill's orders were to have us go in and clean it up since there weren't many troops there. There were twelve thousand, and the battle was intense, lasting two weeks. The Germans were vowing not to give up. They were forced back to the Citadel, where they fought from underground bunkers, but were finally forced to surrender. We then made our way to Luxembourg where we spent Thanksgiving.

BATTLE OF THE HURTGEN FOREST - The whole division was committed to relieving the 4th Division on December 3rd through the 8th, when all regiments were on the line. I, being in the 1st Battalion of the 329th Regiment, entered the forest in the middle, at a position from Gey to Hof Hardt on the 8th of December.

The forest must be described as complete devastation with tree tops looking like toothpicks, and the ground was mud twelve inches deep in the tire tracks. As infantry soldiers, we endured the rain from early October which kept us at least accustomed to the conditions. Even the Jeeps needed pushing as they transported food and supplies. Charlie Company moved forward through the woods under heavy machine gun fire and also with direct 88mm mortars used as anti-personnel weapons against us. The loss of our troops took its toll. I must state that as infantry soldiers, we never knew the day, the hour and for the most part, we didn't even know the place we were in. What we did know is that the "Jerrys" had the total woods zeroed in and were shelling the hell out of us. The condition of the ground prevented us from digging a "foxhole" (shallow grave), which would have allowed us to take cover from mortars and high-velocity

tree bursts that rained down shrapnel (small nail-like steel). This is what did the killing and injured many of the troops.

As winter came on, we were on the offense. It was intense—moving forward under fire from machine guns, small arms, and mortars. We had to try to knock out the machine guns to get to the mortars, which were behind, sometimes over a mile or so. We never considered the conditions. Rain, snow, sleet, or knee-deep mud, we fought. We went without food all the time. Our meals consisted of K-rations for breakfast, lunch, and dinner. Breakfast was canned eggs. For lunch, a packet of bouillon powder for soup, cheese, crackers, and a D-bar, which was chocolate so hard you had to scrape it on your teeth to eat it. For dinner, it was spam. Sometimes we didn't receive three meals, and sometimes we didn't get any. There were also instances where we had the meals but didn't have the time to eat them. Instant coffee was available, but a fire was needed to heat the water, and we couldn't make a fire as it would be seen, so we didn't have coffee very often. Even soup bouillon mixed with water had to be eaten cold.

Our mission was to move to the Roer River at a town called Rolsdorf, directly across from the large German city of Duren. My company moved through our sector in ten days, culminating in a terrible fight. When we finally broke out of the forest, we had approximately ten clips of ammo left, which would be only one hundred rounds for all that was left of "C" Company, so we used rifle grenades against buildings.

We were the furthest most American Army into Germany on December 18, 1944. We sent patrols across the river from the city of Duren and found nothing. We were relieved around the 23rd (my guess) and we thought we would rest and build our squads, platoons, and company.

No! General George Patton decided we were needed in Belgium and we didn't know why. However, we moved seventy-five miles overnight to the totally destroyed city of Aachen, which was nothing but a pile of rubble. They did somehow offer a "Christmas dinner," served in a mess kit which we ate on top of the rubble prior to going to the line at the point of German penetration in a town called Rochefort.

BATTLE OF THE BULGE - The fighting was fierce with our tanks and infantry impeding any further penetration of the German Army. "B" Company, 83rd, 329th Regiment became surrounded within the village/city. It was imperative for the rest of the

regiment to extricate them. After three days and three nights of constant pressure, the loss of many tanks and troops, and the radio of "B" Company finally failing, we thought they had been taken prisoner. But we continued to press on and luckily relieved them as the "Jerrys" took flight.

It was there that I lost one of the bravest men I had the privilege to serve with. Staff Sergeant Emmett Beason was shot with what I believe was a 50-caliber bullet through the lower jaw. As I had to continue on, I tried to make him comfortable. Believing that a person who would lie down with such a wound to the face would surely die, I tied him upright to the tree with his belt. It was sheer hell to leave him. However, I hoped that he now had a chance to make it to the aid station if found. I cannot say enough about Emmett. In the battles we were in, this being number three, he was the first to volunteer for the risky requirements imposed on the company known as Charlie Company. He was a six-foot-four-inch warrior (I found out his height sixty years later), and as his assistant sergeant we dug our foxholes together—normally two-feet wide by six feet long, and thirty inches deep. They were like graves and were dug so that if we got shelled we were beneath ground level and the shrapnel would fly over. Because I am five-feet-two-inches tall, I would tell him, "You big so-and-so @#, if it weren't for you, I could dig half a hole and crawl in it in no time." You may ask, why foxholes? In order to survive, each time you moved forward, you would immediately (when stopped) start to dig a hole for cover. More often than not, you dug alone when you might be taking fire.

The fighting continued through Belgium, and in February we were ordered to go to Ekelrade, Holland, which put us about 15 miles from Aachen. From there, we made our way across the Roer River to the vicinity of Gusten and then continued to Neuss, the Rhine River, and across Germany. The 1st and 2nd Battalions completed the liberation of Halberstadt, and we were tasked with cleaning and mopping up any resistance. Some of us were told to stay there and catch up with our company later. It was there that I met a young girl named Alice Hidden. She had come to Germany from the U.S. to visit her grandparents in Halberstadt. When the war broke out the Nazis took her passport, so she was unable to return to the U.S. Her grandfather had been killed in the basement of their house when it was bombed. They had lost everything and had no food. I got a truck, loaded it with food, and delivered it to her and her grandmother. After the war was over, she wrote twice to my aunt in New York City, stating that she made it back to New York and asking if I had made it through. She said that after we had left, the stuff I gave them had been stolen from them. Unfortunately, I never returned an answer to her letters, and to this day, I still wonder what happened to her after she came back to the U.S.

We caught up with the troops on the push to Barby and the Elbe River. Our battalion crossed the Elbe in assault boats under cover of a smoke screen. The enemy fought fiercely like continental soldiers, running towards the gunfire, and dropping like dominos. I believe this should have been considered our sixth battle, but because there had been an agreement that we would not go beyond the Elbe River, we didn't get credit for being there. At Zerbst, the Germans were asked to surrender but refused. They wanted us to pretend we were fighting with them so they would be captured and would save face. At the beginning of May, the gunfire stopped, the sun came out, and we stayed in our foxholes for a couple of days before we heard that the war was over.

I left Europe on November 22, 1945, and arrived in the U.S. on November 28, 1945. It was just a job, and my job was done.

ERNEST JOHN CARROLL

USS Quincy (CA-39), U.S. Navy, Pacific Theater

Submitted by Sharon Barnett Sooter, Niece

ERNEST JOHN CARROLL WAS MY uncle whom I never met. He was born April 3, 1922, in Miller County, Missouri to John and Emma Carroll, the oldest son of twelve children. All six of the Carroll sons served in the military: Ernest, Harold, and Sidney in WWII; Ralph in Korea; and Bob and David in the U.S. Army.

Ernest John served on the heavy cruiser, *USS Quincy*. The *Quincy* was part of the American naval force that supported the landings in the Guadalcanal invasion in August of 1942. Prior to the Marine assault on Guadalcanal on the 7th of August, the *Quincy* destroyed several Japanese installations and an oil depot during her bombardment of Lunga Point. She later provided close fire support for the Marines during the landing. Along with the heavy cruiser *USS Vincennes*, the *USS Quincy* was sunk in the Battle of Savo Island in the early morning of August 9, 1942. Ernest John was one of 529 men who was lost with his ship.

My grandparents were very proud of all of their sons, but it was very hard for them to watch each son leave home to serve in the military after losing Ernest John in WWII.

MYRON H. MILLER, S SGT

83rd Infantry Division, K/331st, European Theater

Written by Del Miller, Son, as told by Boyd Miller, Brother

I WAS JUST A little boy when my big brother came home from the war. He was tall and strong and a real life hero, and I sat at his knee to hear the details of life and death. I asked him if he knew anything about P47s. His answer was, "Let me tell you what I know about P47s." And we settled down in a big chair, just the two of us, and he gave me the story.

They were fighting from a trench, he said, outnumbered and running low on ammunition, enemy machine guns pinning them down in the trench with no way out.

And then a Panzer came roaring out of the woods and sped straight toward the trench. The tank's guns could not point downward, so the danger was not being blown up. Instead, the tank drove up to the edge of the trench and ran its giant tracks over the edge pushing a ton of dirt into the trench. The tank backed up and ran over the edge again and again. The tank sawed back and forth, making its way up the trench line forcing my brother and his men further down the line.

But they were running out of trench and in just a few minutes they would either have to climb out of the trench into the face of murderous machine gun fire, or else be crushed beneath tons of dirt and steel. They had just minutes left to live.

Then two small dots in the sky grew into two P-47 fighter-bombers screaming out of the sky until they were louder than the tank directly above them. Suddenly, gigantic explosions and a huge fireball spouted from where the tank had been, and the tree line where the machine guns had fired upon them now erupted in a geyser of fire and splintered trees.

The planes flew over them, waggled their wings and flew away, leaving them huddled in the trench in the eerie stillness. After a few minutes, they climbed out and walked away. Alive.

My brother really liked P47s.

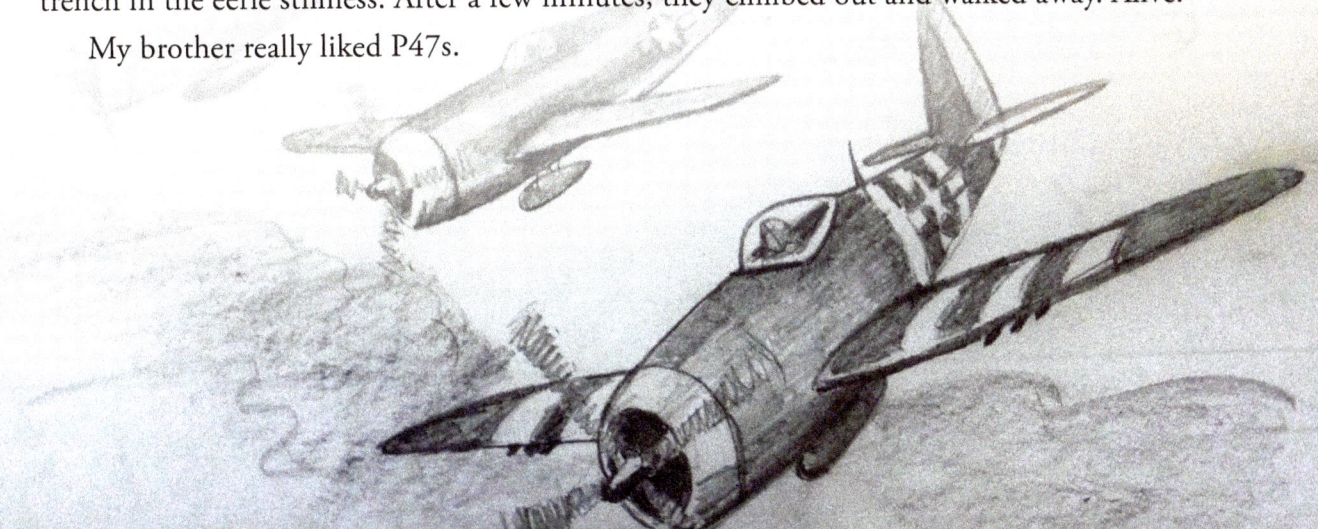

VIRGIL W. SLADE, S SGT

B-17 Waist Gunner, U.S. Air Force, European Theater

Submitted by Dayna Linton, Grand-Niece

The following is taken from Virgil Slade's biography in the Slade Family Book, *Slade Family Stories* and edited by his grand-niece, Dayna L. Linton.

I WAS BORN ON DECEMBER 12, 1923 in the small farming community of Redmesa, which is about 20 miles Southwest of Durango, Colorado to James Clarence Slade and Catherine Arabelle (Belle) Willden. I was born at our home, which was the common practice in those times, as most people could not afford the luxury of a hospital. This was in the days of the Model T Ford. It was also during the Big Depression—jobs were scarce, and money was almost non-existent.

When I was in high school, Pearl Harbor was bombed on December 7, 1941. Everyone was joining up to go fight, including our brother, Ralph. All my friends were going into the service, so I decided to go. I went into the Air Force because I had always wanted to fly planes, so I thought this was my chance. I managed to get into cadet training, but before I could really get into flying, they decided they had enough pilots, so I was sent to gunnery school.

I ended up on a B-17 bomber as a waist gunner. I was stationed in Southeastern Italy, where we flew from there to Germany, Austria, Northern Italy, and other places in that area bombing train depots, factories, and anything military. Of course, that was the plan, but we flew so high to keep from being hit by flack, that we missed most of the targets, so they started what they called "saturation bombing." They would fill the sky with bombers covering a wide area. The lead plane would drop his bombs; then all the rest would follow. That would cover quite an area, as we would have several hundred planes with each dropping twenty bombs. Even then, we would have to go back the next day to get what we missed the first time.

When we first got to Italy, the whole area was covered with clouds and we couldn't see to drop bombs, so we didn't fly missions for almost a month. The radar wasn't that good at the time to be able to see through the clouds.

I spent most of my time out on the line working with the line crews learning all about the planes. I became good friends with the line crews and really found out what made those planes work. It paid off later, as I got advanced to an Engineer and became a Staff Sergeant, which made more money. Besides, as a Staff Sergeant, I didn't have to draw KP (Kitchen Patrol) or guard duty, and when I did, I got to ride around in a Jeep and check on the other guards.

We were all put in big tents—from six to ten people to the tent. Being a dumb farm boy from the sticks, and seeing all those crates that the wing tanks for the fighter planes were shipped in going to waste, I took some of the crates and made me a nice cabin with windows, doors, and everything. I even had running water—hot and cold. I put in a tank from a scrapped plane up in a tree, then had the water truck pump water into it. I then ran a cold water line, then with another line, I ran into our heating stove and coiled the copper tube around inside the stove and had hot water. My sister, Doris, even sent me some curtains for the windows. Others saw how comfortable I was, and they built cabins similar, but none as nice as mine. I let our radio operator move in with me as there was plenty of room, then our tail gunner wanted to add a lean-to on the back, so I let him. He was an artist, so I let him paint the ceiling. He painted it light blue with stars all over it. Our squadron was stationed in an olive orchard.

As soon as the weather cleared, they started bombing missions again. The first two times out, they broke up our crew and sent us with older, more experienced crews. The first bombing mission, I really found our how deadly the enemy's anti-aircraft guns were. Several of our planes were shot down. You could be looking out the window watching a plane flying along side of you, then a ball of fire, with only pieces falling through the air. Nothing left—no parachutes. Nothing.

When we flew a mission, we had to get up early, around 2:00 or 3:00 in the morning, so we could eat and go to a briefing on the mission we were to fly on. The weather didn't look too favorable, so I didn't think we would be going, but we did. It was a mission over Vienna, Austria, which was one of our toughest targets.

We took off about daylight. I was flying with another crew, so I didn't know any of the other crew members. I flew as a waist gunner, as that was what I was assigned to on our crew. It took several hours to get into enemy territory, so I went to sleep. When we got into enemy territory, we loaded our guns and test fired them. Then we watched for enemy fighters.

Nothing happened until we were almost there. Then they opened up with their anti-aircraft guns. We got some flack that knocked out one of our motors and damaged another, so we had to drop our bombs and turn back. I was quite disappointed, as I had heard so much about how rough a target Vienna was. Besides, when you had to leave the formation, you were sort of like a sitting duck, and much more subject to enemy fighters.

We kept a sharp lookout for fighters, but none showed up. We were about to get into a fairly safe territory, when we came out of a cloud bank right over a small town and, boy, did the anti-aircraft guns open up on us!

One shell burst right on our wing, fire everywhere. All I remember is grabbing my parachute and jumping. The plane exploded almost immediately. I must have been mostly out of the plane when it blew as I don't remember falling, it was more like just floating in the air.

I finally got my chute fastened to my harness that I had on, then I pulled the rip cord. I remember it was jerking me like crazy, then I hit the ground. There was quite a bit of snow on the ground, but it still knocked the wind out of me. I was dazed, but I still had my senses about me enough to quickly get out of my chute, gather it up and hide it in some brush nearby, as I knew I was close to a town of some kind.

I thought of the plane and looked up to see three chutes coming down. It seemed like it took them forever to reach the ground and by the time they did, there was quite a crowd of people gathered around, armed with pitchforks and knives. There were also some German soldiers there trying to keep the crowd back. Our three guys owe their lives to those soldiers. The civilians would have killed them.

We always carried a gun in our flight suits, but we were told not to use them against soldiers, but to protect us from the civilians. I guess after having their homes and loved ones blown up and having a chance to get a little revenge, who could blame them?

I thought one of our guys was going to land where I was hiding, but he didn't. By that time, I was sure glad that I had been so slow in pulling my rip cord, as that is all that saved me.

With the ground being covered with snow, I was afraid they would discover my tracks, but my luck held out. The civilians and soldiers soon left with our three guys and I felt much better. I'd lost my gun, so I was pretty much helpless.

I decided to get as far away from there as possible, so I started to crawl down a ditch that was close, which I thought would take me away from town. I crawled for quite some time, then decided to look around and see where I was. I had crawled right into town. Right at the time I looked out, a small boy saw me and went away yelling like crazy. I knew I had to find somewhere to hide; there was a well close by and I crawled down inside it and got back under the cement covering. I had just got out of sight when it sounded like the whole town was there yelling like crazy. They soon left, I suppose they thought the kid was seeing things.

We had been instructed to stay out of sight for at least twelve to twenty-four hours, before trying to make our way back, so I decided to stay in the well until dark.

While I was waiting for things to quiet down, I fell asleep and didn't wake up until morning when they started to use the well again, so I was stuck there until night again.

My legs were numb and cramped, even though I did have room to lay down. It was fairly warm for such cold weather, but I was still half frozen. Of course, the clothes we wore on those flights were supposed to keep us from freezing to death at thirty below, and I'm grateful for them.

That night, about the time things were starting to quiet down, I was thinking about trying to get out, when all hell broke loose. I then heard the anti-aircraft guns going like crazy, so I knew the Limeys—that is, the British—were doing their night bombing. We bombed in the daytime, and they did at night. This was done to break the morale of the German people. Soon, I could feel the earth shaking from the bombs. I thought this is my chance to get out; then one bomb landed very close to where I was and it must have started a fire because the townspeople stuck a hose down the well and started pumping water out of the well, which went on for the rest of the night.

I almost wished I was dead by the next morning. I was cold, hungry, dog-tired and ached all over. I knew if I didn't get out soon, I wouldn't be able to. I never prayed so hard in my life, as I did then.

That afternoon, the guns started going again, so I decided to make a break for it, as I knew it would be our guys this time. When I heard the first bomb explode, I took off. I ran until I couldn't go another step, then I hid in a clump of bushes and waited for dark. I was able to partly quench my thirst with snow.

That night, I started my long trip back to our lines. I walked all night without any mishap. I found a nice sheltered spot and spent the day. I was weak, hungry, and getting very desperate. Our escape packets were actually two packets. One had a map, a compass, matches, some first aid stuff, and twenty dollars in U.S. one dollar bills. Then in the other packet, were K-rations (food). My trouble was, the packet with the food had fallen out. Someone didn't button the flap to keep it in.

I felt I was going to faint if I didn't get something to eat, so I decided to chance a farmhouse. I was at that stage; I didn't care if I got caught. There was only an old couple at the farmhouse. They were half scared to death, but I let them know I was hungry, so they gave me some food, then wanted me to leave. I took some bread with me and left. I paid them from my escape kit.

I found a place to hide that day, then set out again that night. I tried to make that bread stretch, but it didn't last long. I walked that night and the next with only a few scares when a car or something would come down the road. The snow was too deep to walk any place else.

I decided to chance a farmhouse again, and this time I really was lucky. I made it out of Austria and was in the partisan country. They treated me swell and fed me. I slept there all day and I felt a hundred percent better. I gave them the rest of my money for a horse and started out for a partisan army camp. I had also covered my uniform with some local clothes, as they indicated there were still some Germans in the area.

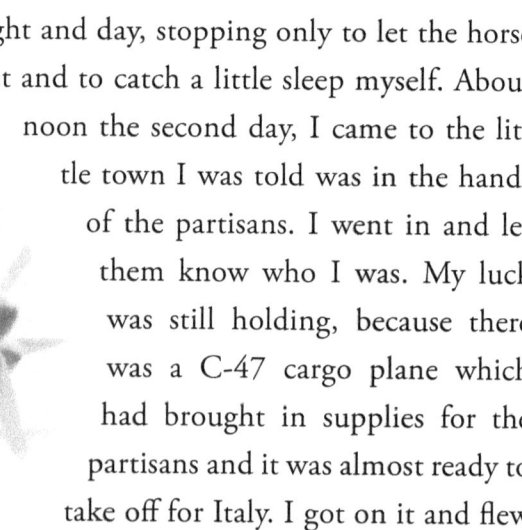

I rode night and day, stopping only to let the horse rest and to catch a little sleep myself. About noon the second day, I came to the little town I was told was in the hands of the partisans. I went in and let them know who I was. My luck was still holding, because there was a C-47 cargo plane which had brought in supplies for the partisans and it was almost ready to take off for Italy. I got on it and flew back to an airfield in Northern Italy. They then flew me back to dear, old Foggia the next day.

It seemed like I had been gone months, not days. I wasn't even gone long enough to get on the missing-in-action list.

They sent me right back up the next day on another mission, which was the way they did it so a person didn't have time to stew about being shot down. I was with my crew this time and it wasn't a rough mission. It soon became old hat flying missions. On some, we ran into a lot of flack (anti-aircraft fire), but we didn't see any enemy fighters, and that's what I was supposed to be there for.

We all wanted to get in as many missions as we could, because as soon as we got thirty missions in, we got to go home on a furlough. I was able to fly more than any of my crew did, as I always flew when they did, and every once in awhile I got to fly with another crew when they needed a flight engineer, as I was a spare in that category. I had been promoted to engineer but was still assigned to our crew as a gunner as well.

Mostly, it was rather boring flying up so high, with clouds covering most of the ground below. One mission they sent us on was a support mission for the ground troops. We went in at less than ten thousand feet to bomb bridges in front of the retreating Germans in Northern Italy. We could see the fighting going on, the smoke from the big guns, and what looked like small ants moving around. Even with several hundred big bombers dropping twenty bombs apiece, we still missed one of the big bridges. We were sent back the next day to get that bridge. This time, just ten planes were sent. We went in early, just daylight, and went in very low. We got the bridge and also lots of holes in our plane from ground fire.

When Germany surrendered, I had twenty-four missions in. Those that had twenty-five were sent home on a furlough. All I wanted to do was just get out of the service, so I really thought my luck had run out.

We thought we were going to be sent to the Pacific Theater of war. However, we just stayed in dear, old Foggia, Italy, as an occupation force. Those that got to go home on furlough spent thirty days at home then were re-assigned to B-29s and sent to fight Japan. So I guess someone was looking out for me.

I have no complaints about my part in the war. I came back whole—physically and mentally. I never had to kill one person. Oh, I'm sure the bombs we dropped killed many people, but I didn't do the dropping, nor did I fly the plane. I was just there to shoot at any fighter plane that tried to shoot us down. All the time I was over there, I didn't even see one enemy fighter plane that was in the air, or shoot one bullet, except in practice or just to test the guns each day to be sure they were working.

I can't even say I helped win the war, much less say that I won it. However, I did do one good thing; I kept some other poor guy from having to fill that spot. If I hadn't been there, someone else would have.

After Japan had surrendered, they started discharging everyone by the point system. Again, I was just a few points short of having enough to head home. So there we stayed.

One day out of the blue, they made an announcement that we were all flying home. We were flying our planes back to the U.S. About a week later, we were on our way home.

CARROLL O. TURNER, LT COL

Maj, 909th Signal Co., Aviation Unit, 9th Air Force, European Theater

Submitted by Carol L. Turner, Granddaughter

THE BOMBER CAN'T RELEASE its payload without a target. Generals can't move troops without coordination and strategy. Beaches can't be stormed, Allied forces integrated, or tactical movements communicated without specialized technical services essential to efficiency and success.

For the Allied Command during World War II, nothing was more invaluable than various Signal units.

Meet Major Carroll O. Turner, who had a front-row seat and important hand in the June 6, 1944, D-Day invasion of Normandy and a role in the eventual victory.

His career started as a reserve officer upon graduation from ROTC in college. In 1942, he was called into service and assigned to the Middle East Air Force in India, commanded by General Brererton. It was renamed the 9th Air Force and moved to Egypt where Captain Turner was promoted to Major and assigned as Deputy Signal Officer. Their air support was critical as the Allied forces matched wits with German Field Marshall Erwin Rommel, the Desert Fox.

In 1943, General Brererton was chosen to set up the 9th Air Force in England as a Tactical Air Corps to parallel the 8th Strategic Air Force. Turner was among the nuclei of experienced headquarter staff officers accompanying the General to England. Major Turner was deeply engaged in staffing, equipping, training, and organizing the signal functions of the 9th Air Force in England. As D-Day approached, he was assigned Commander of the 909th Signal Company Depot Aviation unit stationed at Stansted, England to prepare for the invasion of the Continent.

The 909th was integral in the mobile Super Headquarters which would advance rapidly between forward Army bases and the 9th Air Force tactical groups. After the invasion, the 909th set up and maintained wireless communications to ensure close and effective ground-air cooperation as it dashed across France and Belgium. When a combat unit needed air support, it was the 9th Air Force plane(s) he would see overhead.

The 909th was heavily involved in the tactical engagements of the Battle of the Bulge, then moved Eastward as part of the Western Allied Invasion of Germany. The Company was deep in the heart of Germany on VE Day.

How important were Turner and his company to the success of the Allied troops in Europe? Turner was promoted to Lieutenant Colonel and received six Battle Stars and the 909th awarded a Meritorious Unit Award for outstanding devotion to duty in the performance of an exceptionally difficult task, superior performance, and a high standard of discipline.

Turner served his final year of military duty in the Pentagon before returning to civilian life in Fairview Heights, Illinois, with his wife, Hazel, and his four children.

STANLEY P. BIELEN, PFC

83RD INFANTRY DIVISION, HQ/331ST, EUROPEAN THEATER
*SUBMITTED BY JOYCE BIELEN MCNALLY,
JUDY BIELEN SMITH, AND KEN BIELEN, CHILDREN*

My Recollections Before, During and After the Battle of Sainteny in Normandy
written in April, 1996, by PFC Stanley P. Bielen
(October 18, 1924 – January 30, 2015)

WHEN THE GERMANS INVADED France, I was 14-years old. I sympathized with the French and English as they were friendly toward the United States and were our allies in World War I. As many American youth then, I was very patriotic and wanted to help rid the world of the dictators who were oppressing other people and nations.

In August 1943, at the age of eighteen, I joined the American Army. I was sent to Camp Van Dorn in Mississippi to join the 63rd Infantry Division for Basic Training. In January 1944, I was transferred to the 83rd Infantry Division at Camp Breckenridge, Kentucky and assigned to 1st Battalion Headquarters, 331st Infantry Regiment. I was made a Battalion Scout with the Intelligence Section (S-2 Section). I was trained to become an expert at reading maps and the compass. This would be useful in performing my duties which were reconnaissance patrolling, manning the battalion observation post (OP), getting information from enemy prisoners, and picking up information on the battlefield, such as enemy plans, maps, and the units they belonged. This was important for the American Army when planning their actions for battle.

The training also consisted of much physical exercise and strengthening programs, including marching long distances, calisthenics, ranger training and maneuvers. One training exercise was marching fire which required the infantry to advance behind an artillery barrage. This was my first exposure to the horrors of war and I still had not even left the States. Two shells fell into my company, killing six and wounding twenty. I was one of the wounded. When the 83rd was getting ready to sail to England in April 1944, I was still being treated for my wound and was given the choice of staying in the Camp and joining another outfit, and maybe going overseas later, or staying with the 83rd. I chose to stay with the 83rd.

We crossed the Atlantic to England in the largest convoy to ever go up to that date. The 331st was on the troopship *George Washington*. It was the command ship of the convoy with many warships and other ships around us. One night, a German submarine fired a torpedo which just missed hitting our ship. We docked in Liverpool, England and were taken by rail to the area around Chester. In this area, we continued our training. Still more training for us was in the mountains of Wales. I enjoyed my stay in England, visiting Chester and the Welsh towns. The people were very friendly and the country was very beautiful. While we were in the Chester area, we lived in pup-tents in Tarpoley on some farmland.

When the invasion of Normandy started, we were put on alert and moved to the south of England. We boarded ship in Southhampton and sailed to the Normandy Coast facing Omaha Beach. That morning, a terrific storm had developed and we couldn't disembark and make our landing. The storm kept us on the ship for four days. When we left the ship, the waves were still twenty feet high. I went over the side of the ship on a cargo net into a small British Landing Craft.

We landed just east of Vierville-Sur-Mer, where the monument is now standing, and where the first American cemetery was at Omaha Beach. My battalion assembled around the town of Bricqueville. The 83rd then moved to Carentan to relieve the 101st Airborne Division. My battalion went to Cantepie. I started to go on patrols at night, keeping to our own front lines. On one patrol, we were almost ambushed by a German machine gun. A 101st paratrooper stopped us at the moment just before we would have moved into the machine gunner's sight.

I also set up the battalion observation post at a farm house watching the Germans across the marshland. This activity continued until the 4th of July. It was then that we made our first major attack, a drive on the right of the Carentan-to-Perier Road until we were almost to Sainteny.

Then we crossed the road to take Sainteny. The fighting was very difficult in the hedgerows. The Germans had tanks, the infamous 88mm artillery gun, rockets, "Screaming Mimi's," mines, machine guns, and riflemen, all well-dug-in and well-camouflaged. We lost many men to wounds and death. They also had snipers hidden in the trees and buildings. When returning to my company area, I saw a sniper in a tree who had been shooting at our company and pinning the men down. I, along with my buddy, fired at him, killing him.

It was difficult getting high enough to observe the enemy. Our artillery had a small Piper Cub airplane which was a godsend. This plane directed fire and kept the German artillery silent whenever the plane was in the air, for the Germans feared counter-battery fire from our artillery.

The Germans would use the church steeple to observe us. For that reason, the church steeple in Sainteny was destroyed by our big guns. The Germans were using the steeple as an observation post. We also fired many artillery shells into Sainteny to hinder the movement of enemy troops and supplies. The town suffered a tremendous amount of destruction from both the American and German guns. After we captured the town, the German artillery continued to blast away at Sainteny making it a very dangerous place to be.

The first time I went into Sainteny, I was looking to get some prisoners and to search the German dead for information. I then went to an area on the south side of Sainteny to set up an observation post. You never get accustomed to the horrors of war, but after a while, you become battle hardened. When I first touched a dead man to move him off a path, I was repelled by it. But after a while, I would use the dead to shield me from harm. Once I jumped into a German foxhole with a dead German in it, this saved my life as a mortar shell landed a few feet from the hole while I was in it.

In Normandy, the German, Russian, and other prisoners we took were very frightened. They went through hell with all the shelling, bombing, and other deadly fire we sent their way. Most of the Germans I saw in Normandy were dead. (We took many German prisoners later on in the war.) Our artillery was so rapid and deadly that the Germans thought we had automatic artillery. The truth is we had many artillery guns. They would fire day and night.

To escape the deadly fire from the German artillery, I had to dig a hole in the ground. Wherever you would stop, you had to dig. I sometimes wonder today about the number of holes I dug from Omaha Beach to St. Lo. It seems like a thousand. The foxhole was not entirely safe, as you could still get hit by a direct hit on your hole. Or, a mortar or artillery shell that hit a tree above you could explode and rain shrapnel down on you. Shrapnel accounted for more deaths and wounds during our battles. Of course, I could not stay in my hole, as I had duties to perform. This is when an infantryman is most likely to get hit.

In Normandy, very seldom were we fed hot food. Every morning, we received our food rations for that day. The rations were called K-Rations. They came in three small boxes which I carried in my pockets. Water was taken from the streams and purified with a tablet that was issued to me.

The American infantry soldier carried everything he needed for battle and to survive. Weapons carried included a rifle, bayonet, trench knife, hand grenades, and TNT explosives. Additionally, the infantryman carried a shovel to dig foxholes, a canteen for water, a medical pack, a mess kit, a gas mask, and a backpack to hold a raincoat and a shelter-half. All of these items weighed about 40 pounds.

When we arrived in Normandy, very few of us had any idea what the battles would be like. In training, we would perform our missions without an enemy firing back with deadly intent. It was frightening to most of us to see so many casualties when we arrived in France. After climbing the bluff at Omaha Beach, I came upon a tragic scene of many dead American soldiers piled up temporarily and waiting to be buried in bed sacks.

In war, there are many soldiers who suffer from the horrors of battle. They would go into battle fatigue, or, as it is also known, shell shock. I had the experience of seeing a soldier in the next foxhole shoot himself in the foot. He felt so sure that if he stayed, he would be killed. In all the battles I was in, this was the only soldier who did this to himself.

The battles are so horrible, that no one can imagine what it is like, unless they have experienced the terrible struggle that goes on twenty-four hours a day, every day. The only way that one is relieved of this horror is when he is killed or wounded. Many of the wounded were permanently disabled, losing arms or legs, or suffering from other injuries. We had an expression, the "Million Dollar Wound." This was a wound that was not disabling, but it would take you away from the battlefield. I was fortunate, as I was slightly wounded and did not require evacuation from the front lines.

There were times in Normandy when I felt I would not see my family again. Above all, I wanted to survive so that my family would not suffer the loss of a son and brother. We were a very close and loving family. I contribute my going through the war unharmed to the prayers and love of my family. Every day, my mother went to church to pray that I would be safe.

The American Army and its soldiers were never taught any other way. They were to win every war, and the history of America at that time was that they had never lost a war. This feeling was felt by all the men even through all the hardships. We entered France confident of victory over the enemy.

The German soldier had much experience in battle. Being battle-tested and bloodied, he was a tough fighter and an expert in defensive strategy. This experience has to come about before a soldier can become battle-hardened. The bloodying of an army unit tests the officers and men. Those that fail are weeded out and replaced by those capable of leadership. Then, the men are able to withstand the rigors of battle.

After the battle for Sainteny, we drove the Germans back through the town of Auxais, and then to the La Varde Peninsula. The marsh and the Taute River stopped us. The terrain, the deepness of the river, and the fire of the Germans kept us from crossing this open area. On the 25th of July, three thousand American planes bombed the German lines. We were pulled back about a quarter of a mile from the front so we would not be hit by our own bombs. Where I stood during the bombing, the ground shook up and down like it was jelly. The blast from the bombs could even be felt at that distance.

The bombing destroyed the German defenses, and we started our advance. We started walking and chasing the Germans at 1100 hours on the 25th, and we did not stop until 2200 hours that night. The next day, we started at 0600 and advanced until 1500 hours. It was then that we were pinched out of the line by other divisions, and the Battle of Normandy was over for us.

Some thoughts of Normandy:
- The American paratroopers that adopted me when I set up an observation post in their area. The sign of adoption was presenting me with a silk scarf made from a parachute.
- Sleeping in foxholes with three to four inches of water and being bitten by hoards of mosquitoes.
- The bloated dead cows that smelled so bad.
- Watching the German soldiers from my observation posts on a warm sunny day cooking their meals over an open fire, as if they were on a picnic.
- Never seeing a young French girl during my entire time in Normandy. The truth was, we saw no French people on the front lines.
- Drinking the apple cider from the huge barrels in the barns.
- "Bed Check Charlie," the German plane that came over at midnight to drop his one bomb.

After Normandy, we were assigned to the Third Army under General Patton. We moved through Avranches to Brittany where we fought from Mont St. Michel to Dinan, Cancale, St. Malo, Dinard, St. Lunaire, St. Breic, and other small towns. The fighting was difficult in Brittany, especially at St. Malo.

After Brittany, we were sent to guard the south flank of the Third Army along the Loire River from Nantes to Orleans. Here, I patrolled many times at night into No Man's Land looking for the enemy.

After three weeks on the Loire, we were sent to Luxembourg. We fought to drive the Germans over to the other side of the Moselle River and out of Luxembourg.

On December 6th, we were sent to the Hurtgen Forest around Aachen, Germany. The battle in the forest was brutal and was second only to the Battle of Normandy in its intensity. After clearing the enemy all the way to the Ruhr River, on the 25th of December, we were sent to the Ardennes to stop the German drive into Belgium. This was also a very difficult battle because of the immensely cold weather and the very deep snow. Many men froze to death after being wounded.

After the Ardennes, we went to Holland to rest and refit for our next battle, over the Ruhr River at Julich to the Rhine River at Dusseldorf. Next, we went to the town of Wesel to cross the Rhine River to help surround the 300,000 strong German Army in the Ruhr industrial area. Then, it was a race to Berlin. We covered 220 miles in nine days going day and night. We crossed the Elbe River, and were but 40 miles from Berlin. We were the closest American division to Berlin when we were ordered to stop and let the Russians take the capital of Germany.

We then went to the Hartz Mountains for Occupation Duty for a month, and were sent next to Bavaria and Austria for the same. While in Bavaria, I was stationed across the river from Hitler's home town, Braunau am Inn, in Austria.

Some of our men were being sent home, as they had the required eighty-five points. Points were figured on amount of time in the army, number of months overseas, number of battle stars, and number of battle decorations. In September 1945, I had seventy-one points and was slated to go to Japan for the invasion of the home island. We started training at a former German SS Camp and were there when the atom bomb was dropped on Japan. With that, our training ended and we were sent back to Simbach am Inn in Germany. The number of points necessary for discharge was reduced to seventy points, and I was sent to Camp Chicago near Reims, France to await a ship for passage to the good old U.S.A. I stayed at Camp Chicago for eight weeks during which time I visited Paris and Reims many times. I had no duty at the camp because all combat veterans were exempt and could leave the camp anytime they wished.

In the middle of November, we boarded the troopship *General E.B. Alexander* at Le Havre. After thirteen days of stormy seas, we landed in New York Harbor. We went to Camp Kilmer for a few days, and then on to Fort Dix, New Jersey, where, on December 4, 1945, I received my Honorable Discharge, and was on my way home to my family.

What a wonderful feeling it was. Even today, tears come to my eyes when I think of that day. Thank God I made it home!

- *Two Bronze Stars*
- *Good Conduct Medal*
- *World War II Victory Medal*
- *Five Battle Stars entitling receipt of a Silver Star*
- *World War II Victory Medal*
- *Army of Occupation Medal with Germany Clasp*
- *French Commemoration Medal, Sainteny, France, 50th Anniversary of D-Day*
- *The Town of Sainteny Medal, given to the 83rd Infantry Division, 50th Anniversary of D-Day*
- *New Jersey Distinguished Service Medal*
- *Combat Infantry Badge, the most cherished medal of all*
- *French Legion of Honour Medal, July 2014*

JOANNES JOSEPHUS OP DE BEECK, 'SEPPE'

Partizanenkorps Leuven 4th Company 'Schreurs' Detachment Putte, Belgium

Submitted by Jelle Thys, Cousin

JOANNES JOSEPHUS OP DE BEECK, better known as Seppe, was my grandfather's cousin, making him my first cousin, twice removed. He was born November 18, 1921 and lived in the village centre of Putte until the Germans invaded Belgium. After Belgium capitulated on May 28, 1940, some of the citizens decided to collaborate with the Germans. These kind of people quickly became known as the *Blacks* (or *Black Brigade*), while the resistance fighters were named the *Whites* (or *White Brigade*).

Even before the war, Seppe had one very close friend, A l f o n s "Fons" Camps. Both of them being young (twenty years old), they were known to frequent the cafes in the village. During one of these nights in early 1941, they got into a heated conversation with one of the Blacks and called him out in front of everyone. This made them outlaws very early during the occupation.

Alfons Camps ended up leading Detachment Putte and the unit evolved into an armed resistance group that, by May 1944, had an impressive resume: (armed) robberies, sabotage of trains and power stations, secret printing, demolition of a factory and liquidations. Company "Schreurs" and Detachment Putte did it all. One of their actions stands out, however, the famous "robbery of the church bells" on September 11, 1943. Despite the name, this "robbery"' wasn't really a robbery. Because of shortages in Germany, the German government ordered all Belgian church bells to be taken down, brought to Germany and melted down for ammunition. The resistance got the news and decided something needed to be done. In any case, it would be extremely dangerous for Seppe and the other resistance fighters to undertake an action in the village centre, where several *Blacks* were known to live.

On September 10, 1943, the Germans arrived, together with a Belgian contractor and worked all day to remove the floors in the Church Tower and install all the equipment and pulleys to bring down the bells. They only finished late in the afternoon and, because of the dark (of course no light could be made), they decided to come back the next day and finish their job. The resistance group had obtained a spare key of the church and went in that night after dark. Using the German equipment, they brought down two out of three church bells and loaded them onto a wooden cart equipped with rubber wheels. After that, the resistance fighters brought them to a small cabbage patch about 200 yards away from the church. There they buried the bells and replanted the cabbage so no one would notice someone had been digging there. Despite this not being a big military victory, it was a big humiliation for the Germans, and they reacted fiercely. The pastor, his sexton and several villagers (among them some of the men that brought down the bells) were captured. The third bell (the smallest) was taken away and never seen again. One of the resistance members was tortured until he gave up the location of the church bells. When the Germans came to collect them, they brought him in the bed of a truck. One of the few villagers that dared go to the scene commented later, "It was someone else they brought, I did not recognize him because of the wounds all over his face and body."

The Germans took the church bells away but when the Port of Antwerp was liberated, they were still there in one of the warehouses. Both bells are still in use in the church of Putte today.

By May 1944, many of the other resistance units had been eliminated and Detachment Putte was the last of its original outfit still operational. However, on May 23, 1944, the German government decided to organize a bike race, a social event which was (and still is) very popular in Belgium. Frans Storms, one of the leading figures in the group, advised them not to go— to him, it was a clear trap. However, the pressure had been extremely high on the group for the past

Putte Kerk

months and they got reckless. They decided to go, against the advice of Storms, and lay themselves down in the grass along the track. The Germans had two trucks and several collaborators following the race and after two laps they pulled up to the group. About ten armed Germans jump out and start firing on them. After a brief firefight, Seppe Op de Beeck lies dead on the ground, his best friend Fons Camps is wounded and surrenders along with three others, only one manages to get away through a nearby field.

The events of May 23, 1944, effectively put an end to the actions of Detachment Putte. For three full years the men had lived in hiding, striking at the Germans and the collaborators at every possible chance. The pressure on them got too high, being in hiding for years made them reckless and they made one very costly mistake. Fons Camps, Seppe's best friend, spent the rest of his life in captivity and after a short trial, was sentenced to three times death penalty. He was executed by a gun squad on August 14, 1944. The last letter he ever wrote to his parents reads as follows:

> *Do not weep for me, parents and sisters, do not weep for I loved you all very much. Find comfort knowing I die for a good cause. If you ever find me, please, bury me next to Seppe, goodbye! Never forget me!*

Joannes Josephus "Seppe" Op De Beeck and Desiré Alfons Camps were buried side-by-side in the cemetery in Putte on May 19, 1945. They have been there together for the past 72 years.

FRANK A. KLEPPER, PFC

494th AAA Gun Bn, Coast Artillery Corps, KIA, Putte, Belgium

Special Tribute from The Miller Family, written by Jelle Thys

ON NOVEMBER 2, 1944, the 494th Anti-Aircraft Artillery Gun Battalion arrived in Putte and set up their batteries as a part of Operation Antwerp X. Four days later, Frank Klepper, a member of D Battery was Killed In Action by a U.S. 40mm shell that came down and hit his 90mm gun. The explosion and shrapnel killed Frank Klepper and injured six others: William Stireman, William Bassi, Martin Mueller, Herbert Barnard, Adam Valuchivich and James Swanson. Ironically, the battery was leaving the gunsite because they had found themselves to be in the line of fire of other gun sites. Three out of four guns were already gone and gun n°4, manned by Frank Klepper and his buddies, was waiting in a traveling position for the transport trucks to return.

In 2013, Frank was honored with the unveiling of a monument by the WWII collectors association of Putte named "Kamp44." They are a group of friends from Putte and surrounding villages with the goal of keeping the memory of the WWII veterans alive. One year later, in attendance of Frank Klepper's nieces and the grandson of William Stireman, the monument for Frank Klepper and the men of the 494th AAA was installed at its current position.

MARVIN J. SCHAEFFER

USS GEORGE F. ELLIOT (AP-105), U.S. NAVY, PACIFIC THEATER

Submitted by Barbara Schaeffer Pritchard, Daughter

MARVIN JOHN SCHAEFFER WAS born June 30, 1927, in the small family living quarters over his parent's butcher shop in Pollock, South Dakota. Pollock was a small farming community of about four hundred people. During his youth, Marvin attended school, worked in the family store, helped his father cut ice from the Missouri River in the winter to store and cool the meat during the hot summer months, and worked threshing the South Dakota wheat during the harvest months. The depression hit the small community hard, but the proud people of Pollock worked to keep their town together. During his high school years, he played the trumpet, six-man football, and basketball.

After graduating from high school in 1945, at the age of 17, Marvin enlisted in the Navy, as did many of his peers. He wrote, "I was sent to Minneapolis for my physical, arrived there June 5, 1945 and passed my physical and was sworn into the Navy all in the same day. The same night, we left by train for the Great Lakes Naval Station and I started my first day of Navy life on June 6, 1945." He completed boot camp at Great Lakes, Illinois. From there, he went to San Bruno, California where, as an enlisted Navy Sailor, he was issued an Army Uniform, Army Springfield rifle, and gear, and was trained for the invasion and occupation of Japan.

Marvin's unit was assigned to the *George F. Elliot*, a merchant ship used as a troop transport ship. The original mission was to invade Japan, but before they left California on August 6, 1945, President Truman authorized the dropping of the atomic bomb on Hiroshima, Japan, changing Marvin's mission and, more than likely, his future. The transport ship went on to the Marshall Islands and then to Tokyo Harbor on October 13, 1945, where they sat for thirty days on board their ship while their mission was changed.

Marvin landed on the shores of Yokosuka as part of the occupation force. He was put in charge of a Japanese warehouse where he had many Japanese soldiers under his command. He lived in a Japanese officer's home along with six other Navy men. One particular friend, Paul Eibdo, was in

charge of the motor pool. On weekends, he would borrow a truck and the six would go exploring. On one particular weekend, they visited the beaches where their invasion was to have taken place. It was a beautiful sand beach about a half a block deep and several blocks long, encircled with tall bluffs. Inside the bluffs, they could see caves that had housed large machine guns. They discovered later that the expected casualty rate of their mission was one-hundred percent.

Upon returning to the states, Marvin used his GI bill to attend South Dakota State University, where he earned a Civil Engineering degree. An interesting note: out of his high school graduating class of six young men, five of them went on to earn degrees in Engineering, crediting it to a good math teacher. Marvin went on to work for the Wisconsin Department of Transportation and helped plan and build the massive interstate system we all take for granted. He spent his life serving the citizens of the State of Wisconsin, eventually becoming the Administrator of the Division of Highways and Transportation Services and Deputy Secretary, Department of Transportation, State of Wisconsin.

Like so many WWII veterans, Marvin shared very little of his experience with his family. He said he made friends with his Japanese counterparts and they were a gracious people. He did what was expected of him as a young American and never thought twice about it. He lost friends and family in the war and was grateful and humbled by their sacrifice. In his basement he had a Japanese sword given to him by a Japanese soldier, his Army-issued rifle, and a few sailor whites. Most of what was learned about his service came from his friend and former service man, Paul Eibdo. Paul contacted the family and visited with Marvin's son-in-law, who told Paul that Marvin had shared very little about his Navy Service. Paul replied that he too had just spoken more about it than he ever had to his own family.

Marvin died on June 24, 2016, surrounded by all of his children. It is with pride and sadness that we are saying goodbye to a proud and humble generation of Americans.

ANDRÉ G. BEAUMONT, PVT

83RD INFANTRY DIVISION, F/331ST, EUROPEAN THEATER

Submitted by André Beaumont, Self

OUR UNIT HAD MOVED beyond the Roer River into Germany in February 1945, when one afternoon, the entire Company F, 331st Infantry Regiment, 83rd Division, was assembled for a briefing. It was to be the only pre-attack briefing that I had in my entire infantry career!

We learned that our company had the mission of capturing the town of Loveling, which was astride several roads leading to the Rhine River—a key target of the Army at that phase of the war. Our Captain, Thomas Mitchell, told us the Regimental G-2 Officer (Military Intelligence) informed him that Loveling would be heavily defended with lines of barbed wire, minefields, and trenches. We were to eat an early breakfast and be awakened at 3:00 a.m. for a pre-dawn attack. Bandoliers of extra ammunition were distributed, and we were checked to see we each had at least two hand grenades. Also, while we ate dinner, the Mess Sergeant issued us each three K-Ration boxes to stuff under our field jackets, informing us that we may not have any hot meals after breakfast.

This was the most serious combat preparation that many of us had experienced and anxieties ran high. I barely slept that night and found myself trembling in fear. I looked at my watch and it was 3:00 a.m., but no one awoke us. 4:00 a.m., 5:00 a.m. passed. At 6:00 a.m., we were summoned for breakfast and then marched off in two files for about a mile.

There in a field, were about twenty tanks of a design none of us had ever seen before. These were Chaffee tanks, the Army's new light tank that featured a low silhouette, whole new track, bogie system and a rotating turret with a 75mm gun. They replaced the pre-war light tanks that were annihilated by the Germans. (These were of high silhouette, thin armor, narrow tracks and a 37mm "pop" gun.) Each squad was ordered to climb on the backs of the tanks and they would take us into the attack. This was a different experience for most of us. It was even pleasant for those of us on the rear of the tank because we sat atop the motor's grill and enjoyed the warm air that mellowed the cold morning breezes.

As we moved up, we passed a battery of self-propelled 105mm howitzers that were

shelling our objective. We moved to the edge of a large prairie and could see the town in the distance. Gray puffs of smoke accentuated by red/orange flashes marked the howitzer shells as they landed in and around the town. Our tanks spread out to form a line across the edge of the prairie. The finale of the artillery barrage was a score of white phosphorus shells that exploded in great white plumes. When the artillery stopped, the tanks opened up with their 75mm cannons and once again the town was speckled with gray puffs and red/orange flashes. Now we could see buildings start to crumble and fires breaking out in the town.

Simultaneously, the tanks revved up their engines and began to move forward. The line of tanks not only continued firing their cannons, but their machine gunners popped out of the tank turret and began firing their .50 caliber machine guns, spraying bullets spiced with red tracers (every 5th bullet was a tracer) all over the town. As the tank moved forward, there was a sudden explosion and I was thrown off the tank. I figured this was it! But I was the only one thrown from the tank and I felt no pain anywhere. It felt like someone had kicked me in the rear. I reached around and felt the area of the "kick" and found that my first-aid pouch was shredded. (The pouch was hanging on the right rear of my cartridge belt). I deduced what happened: we had been told to keep the fulminate of mercury detonator and fuse far apart from the ¼ pound block of TNT we carried and I had placed the TNT in front of my cartridge belt—taped on by the buckle—and had placed the fulminate of mercury detonator in my first-aid pouch.

The detonator consisted of a six-inch fuse with a small copper tube containing the detonator chemical. The heat from the motor's grill had set off the detonator. (In the future I would keep my detonator and fuse entwined in the camouflage netting of my steel helmet.) I ran to catch up with the tank and climbed back on board. Everyone had a good laugh when I told them what happened.

Soon, the tanks stopped about five hundred yards from the edge of town. We were ordered to dismount and form a

skirmish line and move toward the town. As we advanced, we began to receive small arms and machine gun fire from the village. One bullet came so close to me; I heard it whizzing by me and could feel its heat on my left cheek. Missed me by less than an inch! My buddy Verlin Twedt and I spotted the flashes of the guns that were firing at us coming from a long wooden shed on the edge of town. We each unloaded a clip of M1 ammunition in the direction of the flashes and directed our squad's BAR (Browning automatic rifle) man to spray the building with his .30 caliber bullets. Firing ceased, and we moved on into the town. Later, we found three dead Germans and four wounded inside the shed.

In pairs, we went from house-to-house and cleared each to make sure there were no soldiers or armed civilians within. Several times, we threw hand grenades through cellar windows as that would have been the most likely place for anyone to hide. Our squad came upon a small sauerkraut factory which had cement coffin-like bins full of moldering cabbage. Several German soldiers were hiding among these bins and opened fire on us. We responded with hand grenades and rifle grenades (a type of grenade launched from an attachment on the barrel of an M1, it was a lethal short-range projectile). We moved through the building and found several dead Germans—one body was in a sauerkraut vat! A sour Kraut indeed (pardon the pun)! Other soldiers came out and surrendered. Verlin took them to a detention area that had been set up in a town square. Soon the town had been secured and we set up defensive positions.

There had been no barbed wire, no mines, no trenches, and no "heavy" defense. This is why military intelligence is an oxymoron. Also, in all other attacks, we would be marching in two single files and suddenly be ordered to form a skirmish line—no briefing, no "intelligence"—just move out and attack what was in front of you.

ALOYSIUS 'AL' KLUGIEWICZ, M SGT

83rd Infantry Division, HQ/331st, European Theater

Submitted by Tim Klugiewicz, Son

ALOYSIUS "AL" KLUGIEWICZ, FORMALLY joined the U.S Cavalry Corps in 1934. Discharged in 1938, he rejoined the service prior to the United States entering WWII. He entered active duty February 1941.

During the war, he served as a Master Sergeant with 331st Infantry Regiment in the 83rd Infantry Division where he was Communications Chief. Al landed at Omaha Beach on D-Day +17. On July 4th, his division engaged in its very first battle in the village of Sainteny after relieving the 101st Airborne Division near Carentan. That day, the 83rd lost 1,500 men in combat. He participated in all subsequent battles through Normandy, Northern France, the Rhineland, the Ardennes and Central Europe.

Normandy

My dad celebrated his 100th birthday in June of 2016. On August 20th, 2016, he joined six other WWII veterans who were awarded the French Legion of Honor, France's highest distinction at Conneaut Township Park, Ohio. What a proud moment.

ROBERT F. KAUFFMAN, PFC

"D" Co., 36th Armored Infantry Regiment, 3AD, European Theater

Submitted by Bob Konings, Friend

IT WAS ON MAY 9, 2009 that I met Bob Kauffman for the first time. He was visiting the area where I now live (Grandmenil, Belgium) and he fought during Christmas 1944. I read a lot about him, saw his interviews and speeches on the internet, and he was about to publish his own book, *The Replacement: The Maturing of an 18-year old in WWII*.

And finally I had the chance to meet this remarkable man.

We clicked from the beginning and became close friends during the following years.

Bob (born August 7, 1925, Emmaus, PA) fought his way through Europe from the beaches of Normandy, all the way up to the hamlets in the Belgium Ardennes, where he was wounded for the third time and was finally sent of home.

Since the passing of his beloved wife Gertrude, he came back to Europe each year, visiting all those places which were engraved in his memory.

That first time we met, we ended up in the garden with his son and his son-in-law and a couple of Belgian and German friends who were with him. It was during that first meeting that I asked him a question I never asked again to a veteran. I asked him if he still hated the Germans because of what he had experienced. He looked at me, with that funny twinkle in his eyes, "Why should I? At that time, we were imposed enemies. After the war, I wanted to know who my former enemies were. So I started to contact them and visited reunions of German soldiers. It turned out they were ordinary men, just like me."

Bob visited us six times. After his first visit in 2009, he came twice a year, bringing several people to Europe. He brought his kids, grandsons Jay and Eric, son-in-law Alan, and good friend, David.

Each time, we'd drive for a couple of days through the Ardennes looking for all the places where he fought and discovered new things. There were many, many moments I had to park the car on the side of the road because we were laughing so hard I couldn't drive anymore and my stomach was hurting. Not only was he a great storyteller, he was also a great lecturer and very wise man. His memories were vivid and he could lead us through all his memories and to all the places where he survived the war. His memories lead us to a big surprise: On October 23,

2010, we found the foxhole that Bob dug on January 9, 1945, just outside the hamlet of Ottré and which he shared with his best buddy, George Sampson. Of course, we visited the foxhole on every occasion that Bob was in Europe. It was as if we connected those dark days in January of 1945 with the nowadays, filled with joy and laughter.

Bob saw himself only as a soldier who was always afraid to get seriously wounded, which could affect his future life. He didn't see himself as a war hero. Once we were standing at a barn, in the hamlet of Hebronval. We walked into the hall and he showed me a cellar door. In that cellar, sixteen German soldiers were hiding in January 1945, and Bob captured them all. The story is not in his book, *The Replacement;* I asked him why it was not in his book. His words were priceless, "I did not want to look like a show-off."

One thing kept Bob busy: In January 1945, he lost the top of his pinky during a one-on-one fight with a German officer who tried to shoot Bob. Luckily for Bob, he only lost the top of his pinky and the German officer his life. Till the last visit, Bob tried to locate the exact place and the village where this incident had happened. But we could not find it, which made him sad and frustrated.

During the last day of his last visit to Europe, Bob played the organ of the Grandmenil church. This was the church he had shot at with his bazooka because of a German sniper who was hiding there.

Seeing this old man, playing his music (he played "Amazing Grace") gave me goosebumps. With his dark eyes and most serious look, he played the organ, sometimes missing a note, because he lost the top of his pinky finger and could not reach the key.

On June 2, 2013, I got a call from his grandson, Jay, that Bob passed away. I was in shock. Bob would never visit us and the former battle fields again. I would never have pain in my stomach from laughing with this old man. I had lost a great friend.

On the other hand, I instantly knew that his stories, his lessons, and his hilarious humour would never be forgotten by me, my wife, and my two sons.

Each time I travel through the Ardennes, looking for stories and looking for traces, I carry Bob with me and still laugh about all the fun we had together.

MYRON H. MILLER, S SGT

83rd Infantry Division, K/331st, European Theater

Submitted by Jane Ballard Roth, Granddaughter

"COME KISS YOUR GRANDPA'S scratchy face!" My dominant memory of my grandpa, Myron Miller, was climbing onto his lap to kiss his sandpapery cheek. I can still smell the fields that clung to him and feel the weight of his arm around me as he bent his cheek towards my little face. Since I was only six years old when he died, my memories, as I consider them now, are all sensory in nature. After all, we take in life through our senses: what we see (the crinkles around his eyes as he smiled down at me), what we hear (the sound of his harmonica as he played "Red River Valley"), what we smell (the scent of the outdoors), what we taste (the chocolate-chip cookies that he taught me to dunk in cold milk), what we feel (my tiny hand inside his big calloused one). As I have reached adulthood, though, and my understanding of his life has filled out, I feel something else: an intense pride in what he gave of himself to fight for our country. Because it had to involve giving.

I'm an English teacher, and so WWII poetry has been a lens through which I've tried to understand my grandpa's experience. Poetry often relies on the use of imagery—the evoking of sensory experience through language—and in many ways, it remains to us the only means of "feeling" what our fathers and grandfathers felt. Poets like Henry Reed, Randall Jarrell, John Ciardi, and William Meredith capture the sights and sounds and smells; they wrestle with the hard why of war; they describe a longing for home and for the familiar; and they show us that beauty and ugliness can coexist.

While the poetry of war gives us insight into our loved ones' struggles, I believe it offers another, larger gift as well. In a world in which human conflict is (unfortunately) inevitable, it demands that we remember the human element, the true cost of war. My grandpa was just a young man—not yet married, not yet a father—when he left to fight for our country. His whole adult life was then colored by what his senses took in as he marched through Europe. No one who participated in our victory over evil came back unchanged. Randall Jarrell wrote, "You know what I was, / You see what I am ... " Poetry helps me glimpse the part of my grandpa that he gave, that he traded, so that we could be free. If I could kiss his scratchy cheek today, it would be more than a perfunctory gesture; it would contain my endless, wordless gratitude.

LETTERS FROM MY UNCLES

Excerpts Featuring Authentic Letters

Submitted by Mark Palasek, Author

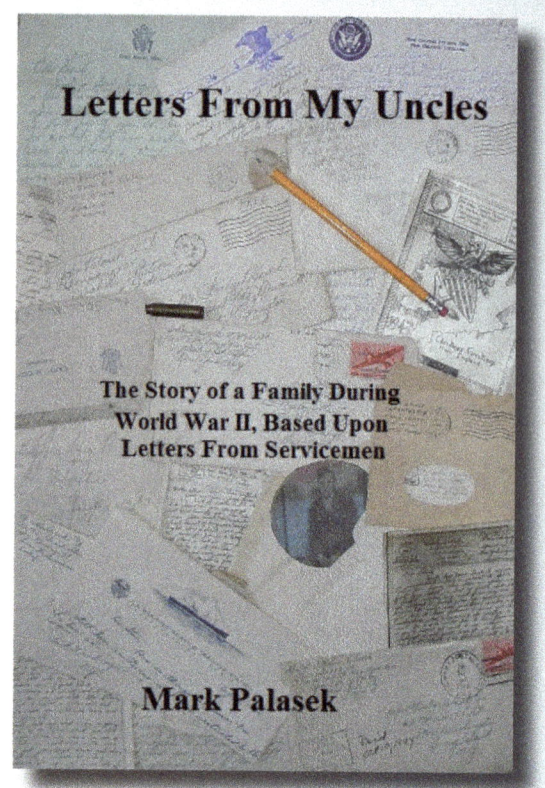

LETTERS FROM MY UNCLES: The Story of a Family During World War II, Based Upon Letters From Servicemen by Mark Palasek is the story of a family during World War II, based on actual letters from his uncles who served their country. The letters are reprinted as they were written by the soldiers, with permission from Mark Palasek.

This fascinating book is available at Amazon in the U.S. and Europe, Barnes & Noble and Kindle

Here are a few excerpts:

From Joe, "Somewhere in Italy," January 26, 1944:

Hello Stanley,

how are you? I hope this letter finds you in the best of health as I am.

I'm sorry I couldn't write sooner but you know how it is up on the front lines. The Jerry's keep us to busy, ducking things they through at us. So a fellow has little time on his hands. And they were giving up plenty of trouble you probably read about it in the papers. Every day. Well while you are reading about the news were sweating out another attacked, and making the news. Its a tough road for some and those dirty rats know there beat but are too damn stubborn.

I was taken to some of the prisoners we captured one day and they were talkin in polish to me. They say there polish but most of the Nazis can speak polish. And they told me different things which I don't believe. For they think if they say there polish they will get better break. But none of them are no good for they keep shooting till they have no more ammunition then get up with there hands up and yell unarmed. But some of the boys are hasty on the trigger and squeeze the trigger and ask quextions latter.

Ive got some souvenirs from a few Jerrys which I hope I don't lose. Well Stanley there isn't much to write for I said about all I can and I hpe the censor don't scratch some of it out. For I could tell you things which I now you wouldn't believe, and I myself nont like to write about it for I want to forget everything that goes on every day, and try to see the bright side of the picture but its going to be hard for the war is going on and were fighting it. So I just think I'll cut it short and I'll write as much as I can.

Your pal Brother Joe.

From Steve, France, October 3, 1944:

Dear Stan,

Here I am once again, scribbling a few lines to inform you that I am to date feeling fine just getting along. I have received your few lines which have deeply touched me. I am sorry to hear about Johnny, Mary's brother, may his soul rest in peace. I sympathize with you in the our of distress, Here's hoping that god give your wifey the strength and health to carry on where he left off, Johnny. He was a swell kid and a darn good soldier, gave his best for his country and loved ones. No one knows who goes next, for the going is slow and hard. We are all in it, carrying on where other left off. Your grip, you curse your luck, then again your at ease taking it on the chin. I will only say this much, to go through all I have to date, to witness all this destruction and pulverization of cities towns and village, the children and the great majority of people, homeless, not knowing where there next meal is coming from, If I onl did one great deed over here, I know my time was well spent regardless of what the conditions were. For I do now that while I am here no harm will come to my dear ones back in the states. That if I pull out in one piece I will only have a faint memory of all this hell which has brought only grief and sorrow to many a home. A job that has been done well so as to not have a repeater such as we had after the last war.

Fritzy as we know is really tough and don't let anyone tell you otherwise. He is now being kicked around on his own soil. How long he can take it no one knows although it's a gain yard by yard he fights on. I have slept under open skies in abandoned buildings a college and now a one time mansion where some big shot lived. We have followed the paper hangars trail, he also has lived here, all ear marks show it. I have constantly been on the go. This letter I have just received is the first one in ages. I haven't had a letter from my wife as yet. I have been writing every one as much as time permitted. Back in the states, I used to write very often, here the scene has completely changed. I am sorry I can't name cities or towns do to the strict censorship but the day shall come when don't have to write letters.

I hope by the time this letter reaches you, it may find your wife Mary in best of health and spirit. Tell her she must be a soldier, you all must be for I realize this may come to the unexpected, we must fight on, preserve and take care of ourselves, to the best of our ability. God bless you and guide you through thick and thin, keep in step with the millions who are with you fighting on to victory and the safe return to our homes, so help us god.

I remain your pal and brother Steve.

From Eddie Kasper, "Somewhere in Germany," January 26, 1945:

Dear Stan,
Received your letter today and was glad to hear from you.
I'm on the front line now and have a few minutes to write. boy its really hell here and no place for a civilian because we mow down anything in front of us. I have a german pistol, its called a luger, what a pistol. I bet you would like to have it. It comes in handy where I am but when I get home I'll show it to you. Well boy I never thought I'd see war but here I am creepin up and crawling. I'm all shaken up and jumpy it really knocks the hell out of a guy.
be good and I'll be waiting for a few lines from you.
your pal, Eddie.

JAMES F. FABER, LT COL

83rd Infantry Division, 2nd Bn, 331st Reg, European Theater

Submitted by Elizabeth Faber Brusa and Lila Faber Smith, Daughters

LIEUTENANT COLONEL JAMES F. FABER was the commanding officer of the Second Battalion 331st Infantry when the 83rd Division landed in Normandy near the end of June 1944. When the Division began its attack on the 4th of July, Faber led the Second Battalion southward, from the village of Meautis, in a deadly battle through the swamps and hedgerows along the Carentan-Periers road. By the 9th of July, they had advanced to a position just north of the town of Sainteny. There, the battalion was stopped in its advance by German tanks and counter-attacking infantry units. Faber personally led American tanks in an effort to knock out the German armor and take the town of Sainteny.

The following account of this action is from the "Recommendation to Award the Congressional Medal of Honor (Posthumously)," which was submitted by Lieutenant Colonel Leniel McDonald:

"About 1130, 9 July 1944, the attack of the Second Battalion 331st Infantry, was temporarily halted by the sudden appearance of four (4) German tanks in the Battalion sector of advance. Led by these tanks, the German Infantry launched a counter-attack against the Second Battalion behind a heavy artillery and mortar barrage. Lt. Col. FABER realizing the seriousness of the situation, personally led two (2) tanks into position to engage the enemy tanks.

To reach this position, it was necessary for Lt. Col. FABER to expose himself to heavy direct fire from the enemy lines. This he did with utter disregard for his own safety to bring fire on the enemy tanks. His action resulted in one (1) German tank being set afire, the crew being burned to death. Lt. Col FABER continued to direct fire on the enemy position until the lead American tank was hit and it was necessary for the supporting tank to withdraw. Prior to this action, casualties had reduced our companies to only half strength. Two companies had lost their company commanders. "G" Company was pinned down on the left of the Battalion sector, suffering heavy casualties and unable to further their attack, as well as continue the attack of the Second Battalion. Lt. Col. FABER organized "E" and "F" Companies to assault. Again, Lt. Col. FABER went to an exposed position, crawling forward to lead a bazooka team to within seventy-five (75) yards of the German tanks. His aggressiveness resulted in the destruction of another enemy tank and the damage of a third.

Now assured that his battalion would not be assaulting armor, Lt. Col. FABER ordered his men to follow him and led a charge against the enemy position. Through a hail of withering machine gun fire, and under heavy mortar and artillery fire, Lt. Col. FABER personally led his troops toward the objective. Going from point to point in the battalion sector, he encouraged the men to press the attack. The surprise and fury of the assault shocked the enemy into leaving covered and concealed positions. The German counter-attack had been slowed down by the destruction of their armor and now, due to Lt. Col FABER's attack, it was halted and turned into a disorganized rout. As the Germans retreated in disorder, sixty-five (65) were killed by rifle and mortar fire of our own rushing troops.

So furious was the charge, our troops stormed into the town of Sainteny before it could be organized for resistance and the enemy were driven from the town. As soon as the objective had been reached, the town was subjected to heavy shelling from enemy artillery, heavy mortars and direct weapons fire from three (3) sides, for not only had Lt. Col. FABER led his battalion to the Corps objective, but he now occupied a salient into the German lines, with strong enemy forces to the South, East and West. Continuing, without hesitation, to expose himself to the heavy fire falling on the position, Lt. Col. FABER personally organized the defense of the objective. Placing his command group in the center of the area, Lt. Col. FABER occupied a command post in the town itself.

The shelling continued during the night at intervals. At daylight, German artillery began a terrific pounding of the Second Battalion position and tanks on both sides of the town poured in rapid fire from 88mm and 75mm guns.

As relief units were now moving up to relieve his battalion, Lt. Col. FABER ordered his command group to displace to the North of the town. While his troops were moving to their new assembly area, he remained behind to personally supervise the evacuation of the wounded. Responding to a call for help that came from an isolated building, Lt. Col. FABER was killed by a direct hit from a high velocity weapon.

Highly respected and greatly admired by every Officer and Enlisted Man in his battalion, Lt. Col. FABER's every action under fire and in the face of the enemy was courageous and inspirational to his entire command. His deeds of personal bravery and self-sacrifice conspicuously demonstrated that he considered successful completion of his assigned missions more valuable than his own life."

*FABER, JAMES F. (KIA)
Synopsis:
The President of the United States takes pride in presenting the Distinguished Service Cross (Posthumously) to James F. Faber (0-920829), Lieutenant Colonel, U.S. Army, for extraordinary heroism in connection with military operations against an armed enemy while serving with the 2d Battalion, 331st Infantry Regiment, 83d Infantry Division, in action against enemy forces on 9 and 10 July 1944. Lieutenant Colonel Faber's intrepid actions, personal bravery and zealous devotion to duty at the cost of his life, exemplify the highest traditions of the military forces of the United States and reflect great credit upon himself, the 83d Infantry Division, and the United States Army.
Headquarters, European Theater of Operations, U.S. Army, General Orders No. 122 (1945)
Home Town: Fresno, California

RICHARD J. 'DICK' COYLE, PFC

28TH INFANTRY DIVISION, 109TH REGIMENT, EUROPEAN THEATER

Submitted by Stephen Blaes, Brother-In-Law

RICHARD JOHN COYLE WAS born October 27, 1922, in Paterson, New Jersey, the second son of James and Dorothy Coyle. The family soon moved to Clifton, New Jersey, where Dick grew up. After his father passed away in 1940, Dick graduated from high-school and found a job at Curtiss Propeller manufacturing propellers for fighter planes. The job provided money for a home for his mother and himself but not enough to fund a college education.

Dick stayed at the factory until his draft notice arrived in December of 1943. Dick recalled how he went to the draft board and they told him it was either him or his older brother Jim. Jim was eight years older than he, married, and had just had a child, so the draft board picked Dick.

On February 15, 1944, Dick Coyle traveled by bus to Fort Dix, New Jersey where he was inducted into the United States Army. He was sent to Camp Wheeler in Georgia for his basic training and was selected to specialize in communications, specifically as a lineman. His job was a dangerous one … to string wire from H.Q. to the units on the front lines.

Dick arrived in England in August of 1944 and waited several weeks before receiving orders sending him to Omaha Beach. From there, he traveled by rail across France and Belgium until he arrived in Germany, near the town of Aachen.

Fresh troops were badly needed on the front lines in the Hurtgen Forest. In late October, Dick was assigned as a replacement soldier to the 28th Infantry Division, 109th Regiment. It was here that Dick got his first taste of combat. Being a lineman, he didn't face rifle fire but was all too aware of artillery rounds that the Germans lobbed into American support units situated behind the lines. He remembers the profound cold more than anything and recalls how he "had it bad, but not as bad as the riflemen." At least he got to sleep in a tent and had hot meals.

After four or five weeks, the 28th was pulled back into Luxembourg, near the town of Diekirch, for a little rest. Flanked by the 106th Infantry Division and the 9th Armored Division, they were seemingly safe from the worst of the war.

Dick remembered he was on guard duty outside a small hotel where his fellow soldiers were sleeping. In the early morning hours before dawn, he heard artillery fire. Suddenly the shells began raining in, lighting up the village. He rushed in and yelled to his buddies, "We're zeroed in! Get out!" The troops scrambled out into the winter snow, some without their coats or boots. The Battle of the Bulge had begun.

Shortly, German troops were within rifle range and the 28th was fighting for their lives. He recalled how he and others had to hide for several days until they could rejoin their units. One of his vivid memories was when he was sent to string wire to a forward unit. When he had finished, the officer asked him to wait and watch. The officer then called back on that very line he had just strung and called in an artillery strike on a German position. From their vantage point on a ledge above the target area, Dick told how he "watched the shells flying overhead and the German's scattering."

Once the German offensive was stopped and pushed back, the 28th was relocated to Colmar, France. Their job was to replace the 3rd Infantry Division and clear out what was to be called the Colmar Pocket. With that mission accomplished, Dick's unit was again sent to Northern Germany, with the anticipation of crossing the Rhine and heading for Berlin. Instead, the 28th ended the war near Bonn, Germany in early May 1945.

With the war finished in Europe, the 28th was sent home in July for a 30-day leave with orders to report to Camp Shelby in Mississippi for amphibious landing training. They all knew what that meant—the Pacific. About halfway through his leave, the atomic bombs dropped on Hiroshima and Nagasaki and the war was over. Finally, in January, Dick was returned to Fort Dix, New Jersey and received his honorable discharge.

After the war, Dick took advantage of the G.I. Bill and attended St. Peters College in New Jersey, and graduating after thirty-six months, with a degree from Uppsala College in economics and a minor in Spanish. Dick retired in 2008 at the ripe young age of 86. He said he didn't want to retire until he was sure "he had enough to do to keep him busy."

ALPHONSE MONFORT

Little Boy during Battle of the Bulge, Malempré, Belgium

Written by Eddy Monfort, Son, as told by Alphonse Monfort

IN 1944, I WAS ten years old. I lived in a village of seventy houses called Malempré, near Manhay, where a big battle took place during the Battle of the Bulge in the Ardenne forest.

After four years of German occupation, we were so happy to be liberated by the American troops. It was the first liberation on September 10th. For us children, we discovered chewing gum, cola, orange, etc. We also admired the soldiers and their vehicles, especially the Willy's Jeep.

So our happiness was short-lived. Three months later, the noise of the battle was more and more intense. We saw the first refugees who told us, "They've come back! They've come back!" The young boys of the village, from 18-25-year-olds, prepared to leave their house. We cannot imagine the return of the Germans. So, on 23rd of December 1944, the American troops present in the village took a prisoner in the forest near Malempré. He was probably from a patrol. That forebode nothing good! My parents decided to stay in the cellar. The first shells start to fall …

On Christmas Eve, 1944, around midnight, we saw the Germans coming back, listened to their studded boots on the street. They were in poor condition. Some of them transported their ammunition with a dogcart we used for transporting milk and such. When they entered the home, they took first the food and when they found a good cellar, they did not hesitate to put out the civilian people. Malempré was taken very easy by the German troops. We never understood why the American troops with their Sherman left the town a few moments before the arrival of the enemy. We will learn later that the American troops received the order to form a new position in Manhay and the area. From this new line, they will stop definitively the advance of the German army.

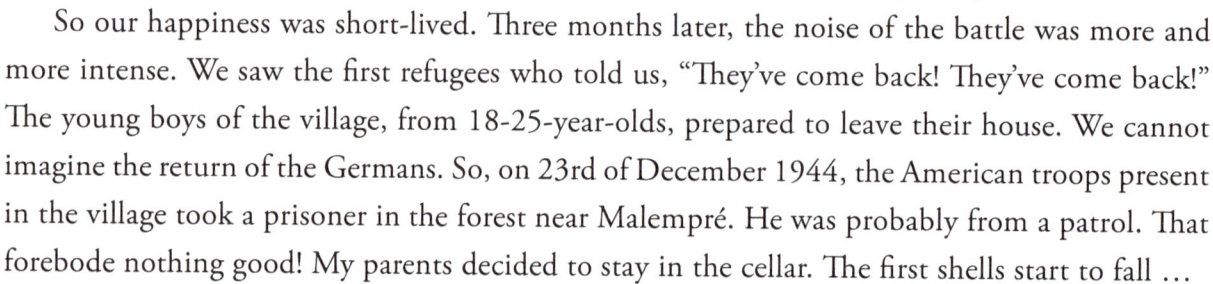

Malempré was occupied by the Germans, not the good ones, but the soldiers with their black uniform with a double flash of lightning situated on the neck. The SS troops! The front line was situated at a few hundred meters from Malempré and stayed there for several days. It was a period of fear, especially for our parents because as children we could not understand the magnitude of the events.

I remember very well moving from our home to walk across the streets of the village. We were searching for another cellar, better than ours because our roof was only in wood. During our walk, my family, including parents, grandparents, my three sisters and I, had to fall on the ground, as the bombing began to fall on the village. After a long moment, we finally found a cellar on the top of the village. Many other families were present including some German soldiers. We stay in it for a week.

The children were installed on a pile of potatoes. To pass the time, some people told stories, but most of our discussion were the prayers, especially when the bombing started to fall on the town. For food, we had the potatoes, when we could cook. We had some bread or cake, baked for the Christmas Season, that we saved before the Germans took it. My father and my sister of 20-years-old, went back every day, during a calm, to the home to take care of the cattle and milk the cows when it was possible.

One day, we saw the Germans were more excited, the battle took a new direction. On the 3rd of January, 1945, Malempré was liberated by the Americans troops. We were happy but sad to see the destruction in the village. Several houses burned, the church and all houses in the village lost their windows, broken by the artillery, the roofs, and the walls had holes everywhere. It was so sad. It was also the winter with a lot of snow and the temperature under the 0° Celsius. Ourself, we were in poor condition, no wash during a week in a cellar filled of persons … without talk about the toilet. At the exit, we were dirty, infected of lice and the Americans give

us powder to put on our head. In spite of the liberation, we stayed more few days in the cellar because of the artillery shells, German this time, continued to fall, but with less intensity.

When I left the cellar, I saw between two houses; a German soldier put on an American uniform. I told it to a GI, and some of them went to search for this soldier. I listened to some shoots and understood the German was killed. In the village, we can see everywhere, the bodies of soldiers. Most of them were German because their bodies were carried later. I remember the GI's put a cable on the feet of the dead soldiers and took off with the Jeeps. They were afraid to discover the booby traps under the corpses.

Today, I cannot imagine why we were not killed by our stupid games. The young children and some adults played with all the ammunitions after the war. We found it everywhere lost on the battlefield. We played with a rifle, hand grenades ,etc. … For example, with some friends, we put the powders of ammunitions, like the spaghetti, in Jerry cans. We lit the fire, ran in the back of a tree, before to see the Jerry can mounted at 25 meters and exploded. We destroyed several of them like that! After the war, some people and children died from these games or with some mines which had been forgotten in the ground.

In Malempré, during the battle, three people were killed by artillery and two others, young brothers of twenty-one and twenty-nine years old, were killed by the German SS troops. Without any reasons. With the bad conditions of this winter 1944/1945, many people were sick and died by the cold in the cellars.

A period we cannot forget!

Looking northwest from Malempre, where Alphonse lived. In this direction lies the city of Antwerp, the goal of the Germans in the Battle of the Bulge. But just on the other side of this ridge is the village of Manhay, which was where the US Army stopped the German thrust and pushed them back to Malempre and eventually back to Germany.

The land between Manhay and Malempre was a battlefield. From this location you would have seen soldiers fighting their way down the ridge and across the snow covered fields.

Malempré, Belgium

JENNINGS E. BARNETT, SGT

Tail Gunner, 1040th U.S. Army Air Force, European Theater

Submitted by Sharon Barnett Sooter, Daughter

My dad left for the Air Force when I was ten months old and returned home when I was two-and-a-half. My brother Donald was four-and-a-half at that time. I remember that my dad never talked to me about the war, but my mother told me he was a tail gunner and had a rough time for a while. I didn't understand until later in life how hard it had to be for him. Back then, they didn't have help for soldiers with Post Traumatic Stress Disorder. My family is very proud of the men that served their country, especially my father, Jennings, and his three brothers; Earl and Elzie in WWII, and Wayne, in Korea.

JENNINGS EUGENE BARNETT WAS born in Iberia, Missouri on May 3, 1918, to Owen and Idella Barnett. Before entering the service, he was a farmer. He was ordered to report for his physical exam in St. Louis on April 4, 1944, and was inducted June 16, 1944. Private First Class Jennings E. Barnett received his diploma in flexible gunnery at Kingman Army Airfield near Kingman, Arizona on October 28, 1944. He served as an Armorer/Gunner in Central Europe and Northern France as a member of the 1040th U.S. Army Air Force Base Unit from March to September in 1945. He was honorably discharged on December 6, 1945, in Santa Ana, California with the rank of Sergeant.

His certification of filing for an honorable discharge from the U.S. Army was recorded on October 7, 1946, at the Miller County Courthouse (the deputy recorder that signed it was non-other than Lee Mace of Ozark Opry fame). His decorations and citations include EAME Theatre Ribbon, American Theatre Ribbon, Good Conduct Medal, and Victory Medal.

WILLIAM A. 'BILL' GEPPERT, JR
83rd Infantry Division, A/331st, European Theater

Submitted by Annamarie Geppert Hellebusch, Daughter

ON SEPTEMBER 15, 1923, William A. Geppert, Jr. entered this world. He was the first-born child to Anna and William Geppert. They would call him Bill. Over time, four sisters and three brothers would join the family. Bill became part of American culture in the 1930s and 1940s, where "the watch word of the day was "we" not "I," and the hero was the "common man" as described by Peter Jennings in his book *The Century*.

Bill was my dad and my hero. He occasionally shared his stories about World War II. During war time, many of his friends were being drafted, including his childhood friend, Jack McGettigan. When Dad received his draft notice and reported to the draft office, he was rejected because he did not have perfect vision. He later returned and asked to be reconsidered for the Army. They accepted him and told him that he would never be on the front line. He trained in Mississippi, before being shipped overseas. In July 1944, and at the young age of twenty, he was shipped to St. Malo, Brittany, France as part of the replacement troops from D-Day. Since he was one of the new guys when he arrived, many of the soldiers did not talk to him because the fatality numbers were so high that it was too painful to develop new friendships. He once told me that one Sunday morning in France he was offered the opportunity to be driven to another camp to take a shower. He said he was too tired and wanted to take a nap on his day off. Sadly, the army truck transporting those soldiers hit a land bomb, and all were killed.

On the battlefields in France, Bill stopped to help fallen soldiers. He would pierce the ground with the wounded soldiers' bayonets and place their helmets on top of the gun so that medics could locate and transport these brave men to the field hospital.

On August 12, 1944, Bill was shot by German snipers in his left femur and fell immediately to the ground. When he recalled this story, he said the German soldier shot him again in the right shoulder. He called out to the German, "You already got me once." He passed out on the field, after much blood loss and pain. He woke up three days later on the Feast of the Assumption at an Army Field Hospital in France. The American soldier who transported my dad to the hospital shared that he could not let him die on the battlefield after he had watched my dad try to save so many other injured men. Later, he was transferred to a hospital in England where his left leg was placed in pin traction. Not long after his arrival in England, most of the patients were discharged stateside. Bill knew something was going to happen if the military knew they needed all those beds. The Battle of the Bulge occurred the next month. The next four years of recovery would prove to be challenging, but Bill was so thankful to be alive.

Bill was hospitalized for forty-four months at McGuire Hospital in Richmond, Virginia and Valley Forge Medical Hospital in Pennsylvania. He endured multiple orthopedic surgeries and five bone grafts to his femur. He was placed in a body cast for many months. As a result of those injuries, his left leg was four inches shorter, and he was fitted for orthopedic shoes with a lift. He never regained complete range of motion in his right shoulder. The orthopedic doctors recommended amputation of his left leg after concerns about the success of the bone grafts to his hip. Fortunately, the last graft was successful.

My grandfather was running the family demolition business and in April of 1948 he suffered his fourth heart attack. He asked my dad if he could get a 30-day medical leave while he recovered from his heart attack. My grandmother picked up my dad on May 20, 1948, at Valley Forge Military Hospital after he was honorably discharged. My grandmother drove her son to the office. In an article from 2008 in the *Demolition* magazine, my dad recalls in the interview to the reporter that his dad "presented the idea of forming a new company for his four sons, Bill (24), Joe (22, recently discharged from the Navy), Jim (17), and his youngest brother

Dick (then just 10). So began Geppert, Bros., Inc." At the time, the company was demolishing houses in Philadelphia to create space for the construction of new homes for the return of war veterans. This would mark the beginning of the "Baby Boom."

This generation of men and women, epitomized the word resilience. They believed in America and were determined to make America a better place for future generations. Their hard work, determination, and ability to not let the adversities of the past hinder their future goals, allowed our country to grow and thrive.

My dad married A. Marie Blanche on June 1964. They had one daughter, Annamarie. Annamarie is married to Stroud Hellebusch, and they have two lovely daughters, Morgan Blanche and Grace Elizabeth.

My dad was awarded a Purple Heart and a Combat Infantry Badge. I never heard him speak a negative thought or word about his physical disabilities because of his war injuries. He was proud to have served his country. In an interview, my dad was asked what motivated him, and he replied that his war injuries to his leg and shoulder had the biggest impact on his life, and while they limited his activities in some ways, his disabilities drove him to strive harder for success in the industry he loves. He believed in kindness and compassion. His contributions helped conquer one of the evilest forces in the history of man.

God Bless America!

COMPANY K

A Special Tribute to the Men of the 83rd Inf Div, K/331st

Submitted by Robert McNabb, Son of James F. "Mac" McNabb

THE MEN OF COMPANY K/331st hold a special place in my heart. In collaborating with the Miller Siblings, we knew we must honor these men because of our fathers' shared service in Company K. I personally had the honor of meeting some of these men or their families when I attended 83rd Infantry Division Association reunions with my father. These are men who sacrificed and endured terrible hardship, and in so doing, they ensured that Company K would *See it Through*. They are men who shared foxholes together and who bravely fought shoulder to shoulder.

The list of names printed is not all-inclusive; these are only a few of the many who served in Company K. Some of them attended reunions where they reunited with each other and rekindled that unique and special bond of combat veterans. They were, and are, part of an esteemed brotherhood. This page is to honor them, and all who served, with a special remembrance for those who gave the supreme sacrifice to preserve our precious freedom. They have our heartfelt thanks and praise for their selfless service to our great nation.

Unfortunately, we were not able to gather stories of these special men, but would like to honor them here:

- George S. Baker
- Albert A. Belvedere
- Robert D. Boyer
- Franklin L. Chiampa
- Stanley C. Duff
- L. Paul Englund (KIA)
- Emmanuel "Manny" Epstein
- Robert Freesen
- Hugh "Hughie" Houser
- Wilbur Johnson
- Frank W. Morris
- Paul V. Ours
- Theodore Ritchie
- Everett E. Rogers
- Wilfred F. Zander

The K/331st men whose stories we are happy to share in this book:

- Raymond W. Barnes
- Captain Marion B. Cooper
- Captain Everett C. Deger
- Joseph E. Ehmet (KIA)
- Captain Daniel W. Halladay
- Frank J. Horvath
- Normand R. Malo
- Wilder O. Mathena
- James F. "Mac" McNabb
- Harold "Bud" Merrill
- Myron H. Miller
- Kenneth L. Moore
- Floyd W. "Bill" Shealy
- George R. Young

ROY 'BUD' MENSING, 1ST SGT

Driver, Land Craft, Vehicle, Personnel (LCVP), Pacific Theater

Submitted by Roxie Mensing Twaddell, Daughter

MY FATHER, ROY MENSING, was born in Fargo, North Dakota on September 4, 1915. He spent most of his youth in small rural towns in Montana, where at one time, he worked in a coal mine and on a horse ranch, until joining the army at the age of sixteen. Back in those days, you had to have your parent's permission or signatures of two citizens of the town you were living in. My dad always laughed and said he had the local minister and the town drunk sign for him, so he could leave Montana and see the world. I never did find out if that was true or not.

He was sent to Hawaii, where he took his basic training. I can't imagine how he felt being sixteen years old and going from the wheatlands of Montana to the tropical islands of Hawaii. Talk about a culture shock! My dad made the army his career. He was shipped to various army bases during his army days and ended up in the South Pacific during WWII, and then later he was sent to Korea to help with the restoration. It wasn't until after his death that I learned what part he had played in WWII.

My husband, my mother and I were touring a collection of the Associated Press pictures of WWII that were on display at the Truman Library, when my mother pointed to a picture and said, "That is what your father did during the war." I looked over, and it was a soldier driving a landing craft, called the LCVP (Land Craft, Vehicle, Personnel) or the Higgins Boat. These were

the vehicles that carried the soldiers from the ships to land on the beaches. I was stunned! The things my dad must have seen, heard and went through during that time! He never mentioned anything about the war. He kept everything inside and for that I am so sorry. What a burden that must have been to see such horrors and keep them to yourself.

My father was a fun-loving man who was the biggest kid out of all of his five kids. He taught us how to ride horses, ice skate, roller skate, taught us how to dance, and taught us how to truly enjoy life. He even built a cabin for his sons to camp out in and a picnic area on our farm for us to have picnics with neighbors and friends. In the small town of Dixon, where we lived, he was known for his Halloween costumes, which usually awarded him the prize for best costume. He and my mother were 4-H leaders for nearly twenty years, helped sponsor monthly dances for us local kids, and helped start a sheltered workshop in Pulaski County. He was always busy helping someone and making people laugh.

Overall, he spent nearly thirty years in the army, finally finishing his tour at Fort Leonard Wood, Missouri. He went on to work for the Forestry Service for a while and then later for Civil Service. I still to this day wonder how he was able to function and never let on what he had endured during the war. I honestly believe that the soldiers of WWII were the "Greatest Generation" and I have had the honor to know and become good friends with several of this "Great Generation."

My father passed away in October of 2004. He never said a word about his part in the war or his army days. He just pressed it down deep inside and carried on with his life. I'm thankful that he came home to his family and I pray that he knows how proud of him I am and how much he meant to me. I was a very lucky girl to have a father like Roy Mensing.

EUGENE J. GODIN, CPL

83rd Infantry Division, 322nd Field Artillery Bn, European Theater

Submitted by Gene Peloquin, Brother-In-Law

BORN IN WOONSOCKET, RHODE Island on October 19, 1917, Gene was one of eleven children (eight beautiful girls and three handsome boys) of French Canadian parents with ancestral roots in Canada and Normandy, France. In Woonsocket, Gene was raised in the Social District where about 95% of the populace spoke French at home, in the neighborhood, and in the schoolyard of Saint Anne School, the parish school. The Sisters of the Presentation of Mary staffed the school, with half of the day being instructed in French and the other half in English.

A child of the Great Depression, Gene left school at an early age to go to work in the textile mills, having been trained as a weaver by his father Philippe, a skilled weaver and good bread-winner. His mother, Marie, a diminutive woman, toiled day and night and was a fine homemaker—imagine daily meals for a family of thirteen!

During the Depression, Gene joined the Civilian Conservation Corps and was stationed in Vermont working on forestry and conservation projects. He earned $30 a month, with $5 paid to him and the balance of $25 being forwarded to his family to help put food on the table.

In April 1941, Gene married his sweetheart, Rita Peloquin; they were a great, loving couple. Shortly afterward on December 7, 1941, the Japanese attacked Pearl Harbor and America went to war. Rita and Gene's first child, Robert, was born on October 10, 1942, and less than six weeks later, Gene was off to serve his country, assigned to the 83rd Infantry Division, as a field artillery gun crew member, the 105 (mm) howitzer. Rita and Gene broke up their cozy apartment and Rita, with six-week-old Bobby, came to live with all the Peloquin family members at the family homestead. What a great blessing it was for all of us!

Gene fought with great distinction (Bronze Star and Combat Infantry Badge) in the five European campaigns—Normandy, Brittany, Northern France, Rhineland and Central Europe. After the war had ended, Gene, Rita, and Bobby were finally reunited as a family. Gene retuned to work as a weaver and loom fixer in countless mills of the area, and at one time he would even travel on a weekly basis to a mill in Quebec seeking to provide for his family.

Rita was a talented sewer/mender of woven cloth. In 1950, their second child was born, Dotti. Both parents saw to it that their two children received a great college education, an opportunity that evaded them.

To his nephews and nieces, Gene was known as "The Candyman." Gene was a devoted husband, father and pépère (grandfather) of Michelle, Ashleigh, Casey and Philippe— in all the roles he excelled, but as a pépère, he doubly excelled. After a long and well-lived life, Gene died on January 21, 2007, at the age of 89.

At the Mass of Christian Burial at All Saints Church, Michelle Mondoux, Pépère Gene's oldest grandchild, at that time a post-doctorate candidate at the National Institute of Health, gave a great eulogy that really shines the light on Pépères. Excerpts follow of Michelle's superb eulogy:

"As a child, I thought I had figured out a sort of Pépère checklist:

- *Pépères are retired loom fixers, which means they can pick you up from school every day.*

- *Pépères always have a lot of food at their house and it is always good. From the minute you walk in the door, they ask what you want—they have creamsicle, fudgesicle, ice cream sandwich, and ice cream stick, and that's just in the freezer.*

- *Pépères fought the Germans, and they have the medals to prove it.*

- *Pépères love to sing, sometimes with a microphone at parties, and sometimes just when you're pulling the car into the garage.*

- *Pépères love all their children exactly the same, and that's why, after the Easter egg hunt, Pépères go around and make sure everyone has exactly the same amount of money from their eggs—plus five dollars.*

- *It wasn't until I was older that I realized not all kids were lucky enough to have a Pépère, and older still when I realized how special it was to have my Pépère, Eugene Godin.*

- *Being a loom fixer didn't just mean he could fix our broken toys, it meant that he had worked very hard, for a very long time. It meant that he knew the value of the dollar bills—and ten-dollar bills—that magically appeared when you "shake hands with Pépère."*

- *He fought the Germans, so he knew the value of his time with his family.*

- *He loved to feed us—not just because kids love candy, but because he knew what it meant to be hungry, and did not want his family to share that knowledge. And although the chicken and the coconut cream pie were delicious, our Ma Glockner's visits were really recurring Thanksgivings, for each other and the strength of our family. And he had earned the right to pay the check and drink his carafe.*

- *He loved to sing—he sang at home, at weddings, and I've heard he even sang at the Stadium once. Maybe at one time, he had dreams of singing on an even bigger stage, but the stages he graced brought him obvious joy and he brought all of us together.*

- *I know only three other people here today were lucky enough to call Gene Godin their Pépère. And I know that there are stories I've never heard about things that made him special to you. But I am sure that the love and joy that made him a wonderful Pépère, made him your wonderful friend Godin, your wonderful Uncle Gene, your brother, your father, your husband.*

Thank you to everyone who has shared stories with me about what made him so special, and I hope that whenever we are together, we will try to capture his wonderful spirit and carry Pépère with us, always."

May Pépère Godin rest in peace!

Eugene Godin (L) and brother-in-law, Raymond Peloquin (R)

RAYMOND H. PELOQUIN, PFC

83rd Infantry Division, HQ/3bn/ATco/329th, European Theater

Submitted by Gene Peloquin, Brother

RAYMOND H. PELOQUIN OF Woonsocket, Rhode Island, entered the US Army on Armistice Day 1942. A large contingent of locals also answered the call to arms that day, including Ray's brother-in-law Eugene Godin and good friend Normand Malo.

The above trio were all assigned to the 83rd Infantry Division at Camp Atterbury, Indiana. On June 18, 1944, they landed on French soil at Omaha Beach in Normandy, where they helped play a decisive role in the European Theater. Commencing on July 4th, and for two hundred forty days, they helped liberate France, Luxembourg, Belgium, and Germany. Ray was a Private First Class and part of the antitank gun crew. He served heroically in five European Campaigns; Normandy, Northern France, Rhineland, Ardennes, and Central Europe. Ray was awarded the Combat Infantry Badge and the Bronze Star Medal (First Oak Leaf Cluster) for exemplary conduct in ground combat.

In life, Ray always said that serving as a soldier in the 83rd Infantry Division was what made him most proud. He was a good soldier, as were all of his buddies of the 83rd Thunderbolts.

Ray Peloquin walked on the sands of Omaha Beach in July 1944. A descendent of the Acadian and French Canadians, just like more than half of the men of Woonsocket in the small state of Rhode Island, he left the city of his birth to liberate the far away lands of his ancestors.

In 1944, I was a young American who had never left his hometown. The war in Europe, what a great adventure. In the beginning, I did not think of death, but later, I saw so much drama. So many of my friends killed. Too many scenes that cannot be erased in a lifetime.

Raymond Peloquin

Prior their entry in the Army, Gene (left) and Raymond (right) attended many family outings together.

A Message of Peace

IN 1990, RAYMOND PELOQUIN wrote the following words when his hometown newspaper, *The Journal*, asked people to share their Christmas memories. He wrote three vivid paragraphs which are as relevant today as they were in 1944.

During the Ardennes campaign—called "The Battle of the Bulge"—the Germans were making heroic and fantastic efforts to reach the Meuse River. Their plan: split the Allied Armies.

December 24, 1944: About 10:00 p.m., small Belgian village, deep snow, still snowing heavily. No moon. No stars. Very dark. No lighting of cigarettes. Kitchen crew arrives with chow: baked beans with a ladle of fruit cocktail thrown on top of the beans. Within a couple of minutes, both beans and fruit welded, frozen together. But I was hungry and scraped this mess into my mouth. God, it was cold—frozen hands, frozen feet, frozen legs, frozen everything.

December 25, 1944: My foxhole roommate from Alabama says, "Merry Christmas," The sun came out that day.

The younger Peloquin, Eugene, served several years in the Navy, he says, "If we remember the horrible conditions of war, we might strive harder for peace. My brother, brother-in-law, and good friend who fought in the 83rd Infantry Division, 'all went through hell.'"

ACTUALITÉS

NORMANDIE
Le retour des héros du jour J

Le 6 juin 1944, 150 000 jeunes Américains, Anglais et Canadiens se lançaient sous le feu ennemi à l'assaut des plages normandes. Ils avaient 20 ans et combattaient pour la liberté. Cinquante ans après, ils témoignent pour « Pèlerin Magazine ».

A Woonsocket (Rhode Island), les vétérans américains du jour J se préparent pour le Cinquantenaire.

LES VÉTÉRANS AMÉRICAINS
"Un peu de nous est resté là-bas"

Les GI's de juin 1944 n'ont pas oublié. Et les vétérans seront nombreux, cet été, sur les plages du Débarquement. Avec eux sont attendus près d'un demi-million d'Américains.

De notre envoyé spécial aux Etats-Unis
JEAN-FRANÇOIS LE TEXIER

Cinq juin 1944, 23 h 30. Les « paras » américains de la 82e Airborne survolent la Manche en direction de la Normandie. Parmi eux, Bob Murphy, un jeune homme du Massachusetts, n'a pas encore 18 ans. Et il a triché sur son âge pour parvenir à s'enrôler. « Nous n'avions jamais combattu, se souvient-il, mais nous étions volontaires, et sûrs d'être capables de faire le boulot. » L'objectif de la 82e, c'est Sainte-Mère-Eglise. La petite cité normande allait devenir le premier village libéré de France, après Ranville, au terme de terribles combats.

« Le 6 juin, peu après minuit, nous avons été largués très bas, à 300 pieds d'altitude. Je suis descendu sur le village et j'ai atterri dans le jardin de l'institutrice. A 4 h 45 Sainte-Mère-Eglise était libérée, mais nous avions perdu 35 % de notre compagnie. »

Le para Bob Murphy. Une rue porte son nom à Sainte-Mère-Eglise.

Aujourd'hui, Bob Murphy, l'ancien « para » du jour J, partage son temps entre sa propriété de Floride et son important cabinet d'avocats à Boston. Mais il est toujours resté en contact avec la population de Sainte-Mère-Eglise qui lui a offert le 6 juin pour fêter, avec 50 000 compatriotes, le cinquantième anniversaire du Débarquement : « C'est comme si une partie de moi-même était toujours là-bas. J'ai même sauté à nouveau avec quelques camarades en 1964, pour le vingtième anniversaire. Et cette année je reviendrai en Normandie en juin pour rendre hommage aux camarades qui sont tombés. »

UN PÈLERINAGE SUR LE SABLE D'OMAHA

Raymond « Ray » Peloquin, lui, était sur le sable d'Omaha en juin 1944. Descendant d'Acadiens et de Canadiens français, comme la moitié des habitants de Woonsocket, dans le petit Etat de Rhode-Island, il avait quitté sa ville natale pour libérer la lointaine terre de ses ancêtres. « En 1944, j'étais un jeune Américain qui n'était jamais sorti de chez lui. La guerre en Europe, c'était l'aventure. Au début, je ne pensais pas à la mort. Mais après, j'ai vu tellement de drames, d'amis tués. Trop de choses qu'une vie entière d'homme ne peut effacer. » C'est pour ces raisons que Raymond Peloquin, « jeune homme » dynamique et volubile de 72 ans, quittera à nouveau sa jolie maison de bois pour un périple de dix jours en France avec un voyagiste : « Ce sera un grand moment de souvenir. Quelque chose comme un pèlerinage. Car

en France, nous avons dû oublier la guerre, Hitler et le nazisme ; ici, c'est différent... » Assis dans l'une des grandes salles de la mairie de Woonsocket, avec d'autres anciens combattants de la ville qui préparent les festivités locales du 6 juin, l'ancien GI cherche l'approbation de ses amis, tels Benoît Brière, l'ancien artilleur, ou Arthur « Bones » Belair, ex-MP, policier militaire. Mais c'est Roger Petit, président du Comité du Cinquantenaire, qui résume l'avis général : « En Amérique, la plupart des jeunes ne savent pas que le souvenir doit servir à ne pas refaire ou laisser faire les mêmes erreurs. Aucun d'entre nous ne voudrait voir ses petits-enfants devoir prendre un fusil. »

UNE « BONNE AFFAIRE » POUR LES VOYAGISTES

Le voile d'oubli jeté sur la guerre du Viêt-nam par l'opinion américaine semble avoir rejailli sur les soldats de 1944. L'Amérique a des trous de mémoire que seuls les « vétérans », comme on appelle là-bas les anciens combattants, tentent encore de combler. Pourtant, cette année, ce sera différent. Chaque ville aura sa commémoration et, côté business, les voyagistes américains ont depuis longtemps les yeux tournés vers la vieille Europe. Depuis plus d'un an, les publicités abondent, proposant des séjours organisés en France et même sur tous les théâtres d'opération de la guerre en Europe. Pour 3 000 dollars (environ 18 000 F), les voyagistes organisent un parcours qui va de l'Angleterre où 1,2 million de GI's étaient rassemblés en 1944, jusqu'en Allemagne, en passant par les plages de Normandie, la Belgique et la Hollande. « Pour le 6 juin, nous emmènerons 400 personnes en Normandie, estime Bruce Epstein, responsable du Grand circle travel, un des principaux « tour operator » de Boston. Et encore ce nombre a dû être limité à cause du manque de chambres d'hôtel. » Bref, pour les voyagistes américains, le « Cinquantième » se révèle être « une bonne affaire ». D'autant que, pendant les mois d'été, c'est un demi-million de visiteurs d'outre-Atlantique qui devront se rendre sur les plages du jour J. « Il ne faut pas s'en étonner, considère Philip Jutrus, ancien du Débarquement installé en France depuis la fin de la guerre. Nous avons tous plus de 70 ans. Cet anniversaire est le dernier « Hourrah ! » pour la plupart d'entre nous. »

Pourtant un très grand nombre de vétérans devront suivre les festivités depuis les ▶▶

> **UNE PUISSANCE CONSIDÉRABLE**
>
> 57 500 Américains ont participé au premier jour de « la plus grande invasion de tous les temps ». Bien équipés, bien entraînés, la plupart n'avaient pourtant jamais combattu. Et au soir du 6 juin, 3 500 « boys » étaient morts sur la terre de France. Malgré le mur de l'Atlantique édifié par Rommel, l'infanterie avait pris pied sur les plages d'Omaha (la plus meurtrière du Débarquement : près de 3 000 tués sur 7 km) et d'Utah tandis que les paras des 82e et 101e divisions aéroportées établissaient une tête de pont dans le Cotentin. Bientôt, à partir de ces bases arrachées difficilement à l'ennemi, la puissance humaine et matérielle américaine fera la différence. Car, au total, plus de 1,2 million de GI's auront participé à la libération de l'Europe.

Cinquante ans après avoir débarqué, Raymond Pelloquin reviendra le 6 juin.

PÈLERIN MAGAZINE N° 5817 - 27 MAI 1994

MYRON H. MILLER, S SGT

83RD INFANTRY DIVISION, K/331ST, EUROPEAN THEATER

Submitted by Myra Miller, daughter

I REMEMBER LOOKING FOR the red glow outlining the tip of his cigarette burning in the dark summer night. I knew he was out there in the yard, sitting by himself quietly, in the white wooden rocker. I didn't realize he could see me against the light illuminating from the house, a seven-year-old, sneaking barefoot through the cool and tickly grass.

If I was lucky, he would have his harmonica with him. I remember listening for the soft wail of "Red River Valley," knowing he was cupping his hands around the mouthpiece to get just the right vibrato on certain notes. Then, he would launch into "Oh! Susanna" or "You Are My Sunshine" with a swift and lively beat ... probably, because he knew I was creeping just a few feet away! Then he would grin (it felt like he was grinning even though it was dark) and say, "Get up here on my lap!"

I would climb up, and he would start to softly sing;

She climbs upon my knee
She's all the world to me
To me, she'll always be
That little girl of mine

Two eyes that shine so bright
Two lips that kiss at night
Two arms that hold me tight
To me, she'll always be
That little girl of mine

Fast forward to 1979, my dad was president of the Dixon R1 School Board and I was a graduating senior. He was on stage to hand everyone in my class their diploma—I got an extra hug and a kiss with mine! Then off to college I went, leaving my mom and dad with an empty nest and his illness that nobody ever spoke about.

I was busy ... busy with classes, taking care of the volleyball team, working a part-time job, and enjoying my freedom. Too busy to go home much.

It was November of 1980, and he caught a cold. Due to his immune system being weak from leukemia, he couldn't fight the infection. A week later, right before Thanksgiving, he passed away. I was a 19-year-old college student without a daddy.

Thirty-five years later, in December of 2015, I was watching a WWII documentary. I called my brother to ask what unit my dad served in during WWII. He emailed me a page of information. At that moment, I realized that I didn't know anything about what he did in the war. The documentary scared me; *Was my dad one of those guys? How did I not know this?* I felt so ashamed for not knowing, not caring, not asking.

The rest of the story is kind of a blur. I started researching and felt a huge sense of pride and a rush of adrenaline when I would find a key piece of information that none of my siblings knew about our father. I think the common thread my siblings and I were feeling during this process was that we got closer to our dad, we finally understood what he went through, we got him back with us, and realized he truly was a "hero."

Once I found the United States Army 83rd Infantry Division Facebook page, things really started snowballing. The book idea, finding our book publisher, a trip to Europe with my brothers following our father's WWII footsteps, unbelievable tours led by seven experts from the 83rd Infantry Division Association European Chapter, attending the 83rd Infantry Division Association's 70th Reunion in Washington D.C., meeting more people whose fathers and grandfathers were in WWII and veterans still living, another trip to Europe with two families looking for footsteps, laying out the 140+ fabulous stories in this book, and now ... writing my own page about my Daddy.

I hope he is proud of his little girl.

JAMES F. 'MAC' MCNABB, S SGT

83rd Infantry Division, K/331st, European Theater

Submitted by Robert McNabb, Son

JAMES F. MCNABB WAS born February 9, 1914, in Bryn Mawr, Pennsylvania to James F. and Ellen McNabb. He was the third child with two older brothers and a step-sister. Life was good for the family as his father worked as a gardener on a private estate which afforded a comfortable upbringing. He and his brothers attended the local parochial elementary schools, and he followed his brothers through West Catholic High School in Philadelphia, graduating in 1932. Although college was not as popular as it is today, he attended Banks Business College for two years in preparation for a business career.

Unfortunately, jobs were not plentiful at the time, and he followed in his father's footsteps, becoming a gardener in Bryn Mawr. He maintained this career becoming the head gardener/foreman until being drafted into military service at the age of 28 in 1942. It was off to Camp Atterbury in Indiana, where he joined the 83rd Infantry for basic training. From there he went to Fort Breckenridge in Kentucky to Tennessee for maneuvers and eventually on to New York to depart for overseas. The remainder of the 83rd history is fairly well-documented from the Normandy landing on through to the Battle of the Bulge. He was with the 83rd from start to finish and fought in five campaigns in the European Theater.

While with the 83rd, my dad reached the rank of Staff Sargent, carrying the radio and running communication lines while within various villages. He was fortunate enough not to sustain

any serious wounds but witnessed many of his comrades' demises, including some close friends within his division. He was awarded two Purple Hearts and the Bronze Star.

In April of 1945, he had the option of a battlefield commission to Lieutenant or a 45-day furlough. He chose the furlough and was on his way back home to the states. Departing Germany, he made his way back through the lines, eventually departing France on April 21 headed for England. He departed Southampton England April 23 for the voyage home to New York.

During this cruise back home there was a slight problem with the ship he was on. It was a captured German vessel with electronic controls that jammed, and they were on a collision course with another ship. Orders were given to man life jackets and board lifeboats. This was startling to my dad who never knew how to swim. With all the combat he endured, he was left with the thought that he might drown on his way home. Fortunately, the problem was corrected, and he arrived safely in New York on May 5. His welcome home to Bryn Mawr happened to be on VE day, May 8. He had earned enough points while in combat to muster out of the military receiving his honorable discharge June 1945.

Now with his sights on the future, he landed a job with Bell Telephone of Pennsylvania due to his military experience in communications. He started on the Line Gang working as a lineman trainee. In addition to his career, he returned home to the girl he loved and promised to marry if she could wait until after the war. Although they had contemplated marriage prior to his departure, he had not wanted to burden her in the event he was seriously wounded during the war. So on October 5, 1946, Jim married Elizabeth Ann Ward at St. John Vianney Church in Gladwyne, Pennsylvania. Soon after, their first child was born, James Jr., August 14, 1947, with five more children to follow: Paul, Bob, Maria, Lisa, and Tom.

As children growing up, we all knew Dad was in the War and that many of our friends' parents had served the nation, too. Within the household, any discussion of the war was left mainly to funny incidents while in training, stealing food from the commissary to have on board ship when they sailed for England—things of that nature. As we boys grew older and began to study about WWII in school, some conversations occurred, but mostly to say that war is horrible, hell on earth. His hopes were that his service to the nation would protect all of us from ever having to face combat.

As we grew older, more discussions were held, and I began to take him to various reunions in his later years. My respect for these men, the sacrifices they made, and what they endured to protect our precious freedom grew every time we would meet other men of his generation and of the 83rd. These men never thought of themselves as heroes. Many times veterans would state that the heroes were still in Europe with a white cross on their graves.

It wasn't until I was in my late twenties that I ever heard my dad speak specifically about the war. He spoke to an older friend of mine, an Army veteran who fought in the Pacific. It's the only time I ever saw my dad break down and cry openly in sharing how a buddy of his was killed in very close proximity to him. Those men who have experienced combat have a unique and cohesive bond with one another that most of us will never fully understand—nor could we

* Background; French flag James McNabb brought home from the war in 1945.

without ever participating. I believe they chose not to speak about their gallant efforts to shelter us, the children, from the reality and horrors of war. Dad's generation simply looked at the war as a job that needed to be done.

With victory in hand, they moved on in life, for the most part, without ever looking back. They had careers, raised families and retired. My father pretty much lived out his life in that manner—God, family, and country were of the most importance to him. He had a very deep faith. Both he and my mom raised us in that manner.

One time, in discussing the war with my dad, I asked him about his deep faith, and he answered that faith deepens every time it is tested and his was tested on numerous occasions during the war. He went on to say, "How can you explain that you're running alongside another soldier and suddenly come under enemy fire. Then, when it all settles down, the guy next to you didn't make it, *although you were only four or five feet apart*. I had the good fortune to survive."

Divine intervention was his answer. God was looking out for him, and he never forgot that in all his ninety years of life. He lost my mother to cancer soon after he retired from Bell Telephone. He eventually fell in love with my brother's mother-in-law, and Selma and Dad were married in 1985. Dad was seventy-one at the time, and they enjoyed many happy years (nineteen) until his death in 2004.

As a family, our parents ensured that we had vacations, and all the holidays were celebrated along with birthdays, etc. Dad particularly enjoyed Christmas, and one pleasure that he would indulge in was contacting his WWII buddies by phone on Christmas Eve. Dad would be busy catering to all our needs, but as we grew older, we realized how important these calls were to him. He would call four or five men from Company K. But in particular, he remembered Coop—Captain Marion Cooper from Crawfordsville, Indiana. It was a small gesture on his part to call his buddies, but it always made his Christmas complete and was very meaningful catching up with them and their families.

The men of the Thunderbolt 83rd Infantry Division played a significant part in the United States being victorious but being part of the greatest generation. They did not seek out notoriety, they just elected to get on with life. The real stories are left untold for the most part. This was their right, for whatever reason, not to discuss. We owe them a tremendous debt of gratitude for their service and sacrifice with the documented history of what they accomplished, but even more so for the horrible memories they endured, taking many to their graves, all so we might have a better life as their children.

Thank you again, Dad, for all you have done.

Following my father's footsteps in Europe! Many thanks to: Jean Paul Pitou, Glyn Nightingale and family, Antoine Noslier, Gilles Billion, Willem Doms and family, Jelle Thys and family, and Eddy Monfort. It was a privilege and honor to walk in the steps of my hero, James F. McNabb.

Lendersdorf, Germany

ARMY BUDDIES

"Mac" McNabb and "Bud" Merrill from Training to Home

Submitted by Robert McNabb and Jack Merrill, Sons

Bud & I the Mutt & Jeff outfit.

Me, Hughie Houser & Bud. Hughie and I pitch tent together and always stay together while in combat.

Bud and I all set for a ride

Here in that Mutt and Jeff team again dear

ARMY BUDDIES

Lexington, Kentucky 1999 reunion.
Seated L-R; Wilder Mathena, Manny Epstein, Norm Malo.
Standing L-R; Bud Merrill, Paul Ours, Everett Rogers, George Baker, Jim McNabb.

Lexington, Kentucky 1999 reunion.
Seated L-R; Norm Malo, Wilder Mathena, Manny Epstein.
Standing L-R; Frank Horvath, Jim McNabb, Bud Merrill, Paul Ours, Everett Rogers, George Baker.

HAROLD L. "BUD" MERRILL, S SGT

83RD INFANTRY DIVISION, K/331ST, EUROPEAN THEATER

Submitted by John "Jack" Merrill, Son

HAROLD LAVERNE "BUD" MERRILL was born May 8, 1919. He was the seventh of eight children born to Willis and Jessie Merrill of Elkhorn, an early California pioneer family. He worked in the family dairy while going to school. While in high school, he met Isabella "Isabel" Mainland of Lodi and they married May 31, 1941.

In July 1942, my dad enlisted in the U.S. Army and trained at Fort Bridger and Fort Warrior, Wyoming; Camp Breckinridge, Kentucky in 1943; and Camp Atterbury, Indiana in 1944, before shipping out to England to prepare for the Normandy invasion. Prior to the invasion, his division lost much of their equipment in heavy rains and they did not go in until two weeks after D-Day. His tour of duty took him through France, Belgium, Luxembourg, and Germany. He received three Bronze Stars for bravery under fire and three Purple Hearts for wounds received along with other awards: the Army Good Conduct Medal, American Campaign Medal, European-African-Middle Eastern Campaign Medal with one Silver Star, World War II Victory Medal, Army of Occupation Medal with Germany Clasp, Presidential Unit Citation, Combat Infantryman Badge, Expert Marksman Badge with Carbine and Rifle Bars, and Honorable Service Lapel Button-WWII. He was discharged from the U.S. Army in October 1945.

My dad never talked much about the war until the last years of his life. He always said he never did much until I started researching into his medals. I knew he had a Purple Heart and Bronze Star, but when I sent in a search request for unissued or awarded medals, I found out he had many awarded which he had never received.

His first daughter, Joanne, was born in March of 1943 followed by Susan (1946) and myself, John "Jack" (1947). After my dad's return from

the war, he went to work for Isabel's father. The Mainlands owned a little retail nursery on Lodi Avenue which they started in 1918. He took over the nursery in 1952 after John Mainland's death and continued in the business until his retirement in 1999. With the help of his son-in-law, David Hildenbrand and myself, we oversaw the small enterprise grow into a large commercial wholesale nursery serving the west coast.

Bud enjoyed golfing, fishing, and going out to an early morning breakfast with his friends. He attended the 83rd Infantry Division Reunions where he became reacquainted with many of his old army friends. He was a member of the 83rd Infantry Association, Woodbridge Golf and Country Club, Lodi Sirs, Lodi Rotary Club, Elks Club and American Legion.

His wife, Isabel, died in 2002 after an extended illness. Bud passed away surrounded by his family on January 8, 2014.

THE UNITED STATES OF AMERICA

TO ALL WHO SHALL SEE THESE PRESENTS, GREETING:

THIS IS TO CERTIFY THAT
THE PRESIDENT OF THE UNITED STATES OF AMERICA
HAS AWARDED THE

PURPLE HEART

ESTABLISHED BY GENERAL GEORGE WASHINGTON
AT NEWBURGH, NEW YORK, AUGUST 7, 1782
TO

STAFF SERGEANT HAROLD L. MERRILL
ARMY OF THE UNITED STATES
FOR WOUNDS RECEIVED
IN ACTION
ON 14 AUGUST 1944 IN FRANCE
GIVEN UNDER MY HAND IN THE CITY OF WASHINGTON

THIS 17TH DAY OF OCTOBER 2012

DOLORES J. GATES MILLER

Our Mother and Artist, WWII Paintings, c. 1944

Special Tribute from her Children and Grandchildren

ERICH ANSCHUTZ

Deserted the German Army at Age Sixteen, April 1945

Submitted by Nils Hagemann, Grandson

MY NAME IS NILS HAGEMANN and I would like to share some stories as they have come to me about my grandpa's experiences in WWII, as well as those of his brothers and his father.

Erich Anschütz, my grandpa from my mother's side, was born in 1929 in Siebleben, which is part of Gotha, Thuringia in central Germany. In 1945, at the age of sixteen, he was drafted and went to basic training outside of town. He said they gave him a semi-automatic rifle, a helmet, and some ammunition. They trained a lot on the "Panzerfaust," an inexpensive, single-shot anti-tank weapon. They practiced firing at wooden silhouettes of tanks in fields from a range of about fifty meters. They went on marches and slept in the woods.

Shortly before the Americans arrived, his commander sent my grandpa to Gotha with a covered wagon, driven by a Polish prisoner of war, in order to pick up some equipment from a stockpile there. My grandpa was selected to go because he knew the town well, having lived there before being drafted. When they arrived in town, he decided to have a short visit with his parents. On his way to their home, he saw his father on the street and he told Erich to come home with him immediately. His father, Louis Anschütz, had fought in World War I and had been secretly listening to the BBC's German radio channel and knew that the Americans were close. His parents buried or burned his uniform and hid my grandpa for the final days of the war. This must have been in April 1945. People say that his parents helped several men who were deserting. Young men would knock at their door and asked them to hide their uniforms and give them a bit of food.

Then there was my grandpa's brother, whose name was Helmut Anschütz. He was older than my grandpa and had enlisted earlier. He served in the RAD (Reichsarbeitsdienst, i.e., Reich Labour Service). It was a military service that worked on construction projects. After his service there was over, he went into the army as a Non-Commissioned Officer. He served in Holland and France at the beginning of the war. Then he was transferred to Russia, where

he went missing in action in 1943, near the town of Kursk, the site of the largest tank battle in history.

There is a story about how he went missing. A comrade of his who managed to escape their situation sent a letter to his wife. He asked her to send a letter to Helmut's father (my great-grandfather) to explain what happened to his son. Although this comrade was killed a few weeks later, he, fortunately, had already sent the letter. His wife then sent the letter to my great-grandfather. In the letter, he said that they were being attacked by many Russians and had to retreat through a cornfield. The cornfields at Kursk were more than two meters tall, so you could not be seen in them. They heard Russians talking and shouting nearby. One of the German soldiers was wounded and Helmut did not want to leave him. He apparently stayed with his wounded comrade and either was killed there or maybe taken prisoner and killed later. His name is inscribed on a memorial in Kursk. I have not yet managed to go there, but I did get a picture of it from the German war graves commission. I also have a medal Helmut received in 1942 for military merit and bravery.

My grandpa had another brother, his name was Karl, and he was in a Luftwaffe ground unit during the war. My grandpa says that he was captured at the end of the war and stayed as a prisoner of war in France after the war where he was required to work on a farm. In the late 1940s he returned home with an infection and died in 1952. They all lived in the eastern part of Germany which was then under Soviet control. Medical supplies and care were very poor which is probably one of the reasons why he died.

My great-grandpa, Louis Anschütz, whom I mentioned before, fought in WWI. He joined the army in 1915 and served with the 6th Thuringian Infantry Regiment No. 95. He also fought at the Somme in 1916. In 1917, he was transferred to the 71st Infantry Regiment and fought at the Siegfried line, where he was wounded in April. A bullet entered his right hand and went straight through his arm and exited there. He was sent home and spent the rest of the war in a military hospital in Gotha, the town where he and his family lived. His wound prevented him from being drafted in WWII. He passed away in 1977. My mom said that he talked about the war quite often and that a Frenchman shot him. She also says that there was a very deep hollow area in his hand where the bullet entered, and he couldn't move his arm or hand normally.

L-R: Ben Nightingale, Bill Spriggs, and Nils Hagemann

VIRGIL D. MULFORD, CPT

Medic, 343rd Engineers, European Theater

Submitted by Cami Haddock, Granddaughter

My grandfather, Virgil Mulford, served in North Africa and fought North through Sicily and Italy to Germany. He started in the engineers, but because he had a degree and there was such a need for medics, at some point he became part of the medical group and helped treat many wounded men. He never told us too much about that part of the war, but we do have a few stories.

He was in Sicily as an engineer following the path of General Patton but was not under Patton's command. At one point, they were required to build a bridge over a river, but every night the Germans would bomb it, and they would have to rebuild it the next day. This went on until the U.S. Air Force shot down so many German bombers that the bombing stopped.

Grandpa was proud to own a Ka-Bar knife. I am not sure how he ended up with it because it is typically the combat/utility knife adopted by the U.S. Marine Corps and U.S. Navy (USN is on the handle).

He also found a German Steyr pistol, 9mm. Grandpa sent the pistol home piece-by-piece to his mother who had it reassembled by the time he got home. It was stolen from my parents' house in the 1990s.

His unit took a town in Italy from the Germans. In one of the basements was a shop where the enemy was assembling Mauser rifles. He and his buddy took a couple of the rifles and shot targets with them until the gun barrels were glowing red. We think this might have been where he picked up another pistol for which he traded his American camera.

One time, he took shelter in a town that people had evacuated but left their animals behind. Grandpa found some chickens and collected two dozen eggs. He built a fire and hard-boiled the eggs inside his helmet. He kept the eggs all to himself and ate them over the next few days because all they had were K-rations.

When Grandpa's unit was traveling through Spain, he played his guitar in a small town. A Spanish lady enjoyed Grandpa's guitar playing so much she made him a special cloth to polish his guitar. The cloth and guitar are still in the family.

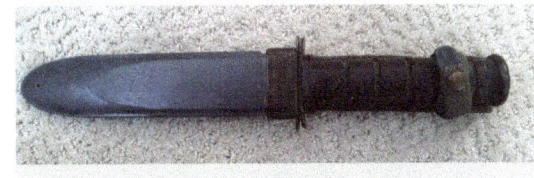

WILDER C. MATHENA, T SGT

83RD INFANTRY DIVISION, K/331ST, EUROPEAN THEATER

Submitted by Linda Tuller, Daughter

WHEN MY FATHER WENT into the U.S. Army, he was a 21-year-old man who had been raised on a farm in the hills of Southern Ohio in Pike County. He had barely traveled anywhere and had lived a very sheltered life.

These are *excerpts* from Dad's personal dates and memories which he shared with me in January of 2001 when he was seventy-nine years old:

October 30, 1942: Dad went by train to Camp Atterbury, Indiana for basic training assigned to the U.S. Army, 83rd Division, 3rd Battalion, 331st Regiment, "K" Company.

From June 1, 1943, to Mid-March, 1944: Dad was sent to training camps at Tennessee Maneuvers and Camp Breckenridge, Kentucky.

March 29, 1944: Dad and the other soldiers of the 83rd Division left Camp Breckenridge to fight a war, but they didn't know which one. Were they headed for Europe or Japan? What a horrible trip that must have been. Dad, who had barely been away from Pike County, was headed for a harbor where he was to take a ship to a foreign country. He and the other men didn't know if they were headed for Japan or Europe. I don't believe one place sounded any less frightening than the other.

April 6, 1944: Dad arrived in New York and boarded the ship, *USAT George Washington*. The *George Washington* had been captured from the Germans in World War I and hadn't been used until then. At this point, Dad knew he was headed to Europe because soldiers leaving for the war in Japan left from the Pacific Coast. He spent thirteen days at sea and suffered only a mild dizziness, while many others were chronically seasick.

April 18, 1944: The ship arrived in Liverpool, England. From there they were sent out into the countryside where they pitched tents and stayed the night. The next day they were sent to a "tent camp." Upon arriving there, Dad had a bad rash on his hands and was sent to the hospital where he stayed seventeen days. If a soldier was in the hospital more than seventeen days, he could not return to his own company but was sent to the "Seventh Replacement." That was a unit of men who could, and would, be sent anywhere in Europe where they were needed to fight.

A Captain by the name of Deger came to the hospital and made sure Dad got out in time to get back with his company.

May 1944 to June 15, 1944: Dad was sent to Wales for two weeks of "mountain maneuvers" and then returned to the "tent camp." Dad then boarded a British ship to cross the English Channel. By now the war was building to its full strength in Europe. Dad did not know it at the time, but his division was in reserve for the initial landing at Normandy Beach. I am so thankful Dad did not end up in that initial landing, D-Day. So many men were there on D-Day and half of them tragically died that day. Thankfully, the ship Dad was on had to stay afloat on the English Channel for three days due to rough water.

June 18, 1944: The waters finally calmed. The ship was close to Normandy Beach, and the soldiers left the ship by climbing down rope ladders and boarding small boats. Dad could not swim. When they got as close as they could, they had to wade to shore. The boats could not get closer due to all the debris and dead bodies of the soldiers from the initial landing. I asked Dad, what in the world he was thinking at this point. His only comment was that he was thinking about a lot of things. He said that he and all the others just kept going because that was what everyone else was doing!

Normandy Beach was being bombed by the Germans, aircraft were overhead dropping bombs, and the nighttime was lit up as bright as broad daylight. Dad said that there were huge balloons that were about 20-feet in diameter very high up in the air to keep enemy aircraft from coming too low. Though Dad and the other men didn't know it, the British were attempting to take Utah Beach at the same time they were attempting to take Normandy Beach. Dad said he believes Utah Beach would have been even harder to take because the soldiers had to climb steep cliffs with hooks and ropes not knowing what was waiting for them over the top edge.

June 26, 1944: The 83rd Division relieved the 101st Airborne Division in Carenton, France. Dad and they other men of K Company were online for twenty-three days with no relief.

Photo # NH 85263   USAT George Washington in port, during World War II

July 4, 1944, Dad's first involvement in an attack. So many men were wounded or KIA (Killed in Action) beside him and around him that they had to wait for replacements before they could continue to push forward. Sadly, Dad lost many of his friends that day. From there, the soldiers of K Company crossed the Brittany Peninsula using a tow path because the Germans had blown up all the bridges. Makeshift bridges were made by lashing pontoons together. Once they crossed the Peninsula they were surrounded by Germans. Out of 150 soldiers, excluding the men who were killed in action or wounded, only three escaped, and one was Dad! I don't think he wanted to admit how hard they ran to get out of there, but I'm sure glad they did! The Germans had blown up the tow path, so they went through a low swampy area. He thinks they crossed back over using pieces of the pontoons.

From there, they went to the small country of Luxembourg, defeating the Germans from town to town. After many relentless battles, they liberated that country from German command. Needless to say, the people of Luxembourg were openly grateful for their freedom.

Then they were on their way to Germany.

November 1944: Dad says at that point, they asked for non-commissioned officers to go back to Luxembourg and help set up defense for an ordnance company. Dad volunteered, because his uncle, Charles Ralph, was in the same company. Dad did get to see Charles and also got to eat a real Thanksgiving dinner in a hotel, eating off of real plates for the first time in months.

By then the weather was bitterly cold. The men suffered from frostbite and trench foot. They carried extra socks inside their clothing to dry them and slogged through snow and mud. They slept in holes in sub-zero temperatures. I believe for Dad the appalling cold was one of the things he remembers the most. He said he would wake up in a foxhole, crowded up against other soldiers, with his toes so frozen he would have to wiggle them a little at a time to try to get the circulation going again.

I asked Dad if they could really sleep with the bombing going on through the night, not knowing if your foxhole was going to take a direct hit. It seemed to me, that sheer terror would keep you wide awake! He said, "Yes, when you are to the point of exhaustion, you can sleep anywhere."

The next major battle Dad was in was getting through the Hurtgen Forest. This is where Dad met Captain Daniel Halladay, who was now his Company Commander. Dad says that Captain Halladay was a real nice fellow and a good Company Commander.

December 1944: Dad was also involved in the taking of the city of Gey, Germany, which was one of the major German strongholds. Gey sat on very low ground and was constantly being shelled by the Germans who were trying to stop them. It was during this period of the war that Captain Halladay recommended and filled out the paperwork for Dad's advancement in rank to a Platoon Sergeant.

December 16, 1944: The famous Battle of the Bulge began in the Ardennes Forest in Belgium. Germany had lost this area to our armed forces, but came back with tanks and reclaimed it until General Patton, and the 3rd Army took it back again.

December 25, 1944: Company K left Duren, Germany and took their position in the Battle of the Bulge and fought on the front lines of this fierce battle for sixteen days. Dad explained how respectful both sides were concerning the medical personnel and hospitals. Medics could clear the fields of the wounded and dead and not be fired upon. Nor would they bomb each other's medical facilities.

January 10, 1945: Dad was wounded in the Ardennes Forest. He was hit in the left forearm with a piece of shrapnel. Each soldier carried a first aid pack with eight sulfa tablets, and if they were wounded they were to immediately take the tablets. Dad said he took a few, but the water in his canteen was frozen, so he crushed the pills and ate them. A medic by the name of Samples tried to wrap a bandage around Dad's arm, but the shelling was so fierce he couldn't continue. Dad finally grabbed the bandage and wrapped it around his arm himself. He then ran, dodging artillery and small arms fire, and headed back to where he knew there was a first aid station. When he arrived there, they started him on more sulfa and ten shots of penicillin every four hours.

January 23, 1945: In a tent hospital in France, a doctor finally unwrapped his arm and looked at it for the first time. Dad said it was so infected and smelled terrible; it had what looked like white cottage cheese caked all over it. The next morning, they removed the top layer of infection with a tongue depressor and then made an incision in his arm and removed what they could of the shrapnel. When the doctor stitched it shut, the stitches started to tear out, so they made another good sized incision on the underside of his arm to relieve the pressure on the wound. Finally, they stitched that new incision together a few days later. The muscle was so mutilated in his forearm that there was a good-sized dip in his arm. There were also small pieces of shrapnel still in his arm; they said he would have to keep those as a souvenir!

GEORGE E. DOSCH, CPT

3rd Marine Division, 21st Marines, 2nd bn, Co. G, U.S. Marine Corps, Pacific Theater

Submitted by Jane Dosch, Daughter

THIS IS NOT A story about going to war. It's not about fighting a war. It's about coming home and living.

My father, George E. Dosch, was a hero. It says so on his citation for the Silver Star he received for heroism February 24, 1945, on the island of Iwo Jima as a Second Lieutenant in the U.S. Marine Corps. The words documented on official letterhead, "upon the recognition of your conspicuous gallantry and intrepidity in action against enemy Japanese forces," confirm his war hero status.

He never talked about the war except to tell funny stories about latrines breaking and other stories about his war buddies. I remember him talking to a guy on the phone who served with him in the Marines and later became a priest. Their shared experiences and private conversations were possibly the therapy they both needed. To see this man, my father, as I knew him as opposed to a heroic, military man, is like day and night. This story is how I remember him.

My mom spent the last ten months of the war serving as a nurse in New Orleans. When Mom and Dad were married in 1945, both wore their military uniforms for the ceremony. The Marine war hero and the Navy nurse made a striking picture. Dad's nickname in the service was Salty, and my mother called him Salty his whole life.

When I was ten or eleven we lived in Union, Missouri and on Saturday mornings, I would hang out with my Dad. We would go downtown, stop and buy a newspaper, and visit with the guys while having a donut and coffee at Schultz's bakery. They would talk back and forth while I would eat a crème-filled donut with coconut on top. Then we would walk around the square and stop in businesses to talk to people. He was so friendly, and everyone enjoyed him coming in to talk. I wanted to hang out with him and didn't want to do anything else on Saturdays.

We lived in Missouri but joked about him being a hillbilly since he was from Brooklyn. One Christmas my mother gave him a corncob pipe (he liked to smoke pipes and cigars—I still love the smell). One time, he posed with his corncob pipe and we took a photo of him to show his sense of humor.

My father grew up being told he needed an education. He was very smart and good in school, scoring the highest grades in high school. His plan was to take advantage of the G.I. Bill but life got in the way.

For several years Dad worked as a traveling salesman for a farm equipment manufacturer. As he drove during the week on sales calls, he would hang his arm out the window, and he always had a sunburned arm since he was so fair-skinned. He stayed in hotels during the week and would return home with the little soaps from the hotels—which I thought were the greatest thing ever. I remember

watching out the window on Friday nights, just waiting for him to come home. I would grab his suitcase and put everything away for him. He would always hide the little soaps in his suitcase for me to find. To this day, when I am staying at a hotel and see the little bar of soap in the bathroom, I think of him.

Dad and I would watch old movies together—the Fred Astaire black-and-white type movies. We had a routine; I would jump up in the middle of the movie to fix him a sandwich and

SARA DOSCH RECALLS SPECIAL times with her loving father:

I loved accompanying my father on business trips. One time after dinner, we headed back to our hotel room, and I begged to play a game before lights out. After one game I challenged him to another, the stipulation was that, if I won he would take me for ice cream. I won! We got redressed and out the door, and we went for my victory cone.

We had a two-door car with a front passenger seat that could be laid forward to allow back seat passengers into the back seat. We three kids were in the back, and I was standing up leaning on the back of the front seat. When he made a quick stop, the seat and I went forward and bumped his right arm. He yelled angrily at me to sit down. Later at home he called me in and apologized for losing his temper and told me he understood it was accidental and he should not have lost his temper and yelled at me. How many parents apologize and discuss with their children when they make a mistake?

He taught me by example to stand up straight, don't buckle, and never cry in public.

He was an honorable, honest, compassionate, and wonderful father.

get him a beer. He would say, "Be sure you put butter on the sandwich and not mayonnaise." I would always say back, "I KNOW, DAD!" He called me Button or Bunny, and during the commercials, he would swoop me up and dance around the living room—I thought I was in heaven. Those were precious times.

He would never talk seriously about the war, but he would joke and tell us a few things that were humorous. However, one time, it was no laughing matter. My brother and I had a BB gun and we wanted to shoot birds. My father quickly informed us that we were not shooting birds, if we wanted to shoot a gun, he would put up a target for us … and he did. Another time, I innocently questioned him when he mentioned that he once had a Japanese machine gun. I asked him why he didn't bring it home with him … he smiled and said, "They wouldn't let me bring it on the plane." When I continued my barrage about how he got it, he remarked, "Let's just say I took it away from someone."

When I was 18, my Dad passed away from cancer at the age of 47. He had a terrible struggle for three years before his death. At the beginning of his cancer, it developed on his arm. Then, he developed a tumor on his spine that paralyzed him from the waist down. We would have to drive to the Veteran's Association Hospital in St. Louis to see him. I hated to see him in so much pain; physical pain like he must have endured in the war. Near the end, he was able to come home to Springfield, Missouri where he spent his last days being cared for by my mother, aunt, my sister, and me. It was on my watch one evening when I went to his side, and he thought he was in the war. He grabbed my arm and said, "Get down, they are shooting, they are dangerous!" I was with him when he died. A true peacefulness came over him, and he quietly passed. It was such a huge loss for me.

People liked my father. He was very handsome. They were drawn to his quality, stature, and strength. He had a great sense of humor, and people liked being around him. He was a lifelong Republican (he didn't like Kennedy, but was very patriotic). The day of Kennedy's funeral—I walked into the living room, and he was watching the funeral on TV. His hands were clasped with tears coming down his face. I noticed he was watching the parade, the flag-draped casket. I never said a word and sat down next to him and watched.

My father is buried in the National Cemetery in Springfield, Missouri. As a fair-haired soldier during the war in the South Pacific, he struggled terribly from chronic sunburn. He is now forever protected from suffering by a shade tree lovingly planted beside his grave.

THE SECRETARY OF THE NAVY
WASHINGTON

The President of the United States takes pleasure in presenting the SILVER STAR MEDAL to

SECOND LIEUTENANT GEORGE E. DOSCH,
UNITED STATES MARINE CORPS,

for service as set forth in the following

CITATION:

"For conspicuous gallantry and intrepidity as a Machine Gun Platoon Leader of Company G, Second Battalion, Twenty-first Marines, Third Marine Division, in action against enemy Japanese forces on Iwo Jima, Volcano Islands, 24 February 1945. When his Company Commander became a casualty, Second Lieutenant Dosch immediately assumed control of the company which was then suffering heavy casualties. Carrying out a personal reconnaissance in the face of heavy hostile small-arms fire, he skillfully withdrew with minimum losses two of his platoons which had been located in positions extremely vulnerable to enemy fire. Quickly reorganizing his company, he directed the consolidation of the position and held it despite intense hostile fire. In the afternoon, he led his unit in an attack which resulted in the seizure and occupation of a salient dividing the Japanese forces, thereby contributing materially to the success of the operation. By his aggressive leadership, tactical ability and coolness under fire, Second Lieutenant Dosch upheld the highest traditions of the United States Naval Service."

For the President,

Secretary of the Navy.

ROBERT A. MITCHELL, LT COL

Captain, 83rd Infantry Division, F/331st, European Theater

Submitted by John Mitchell, Son

OUR DAD, ROBERT ALFRED (Bob), was born in Plainfield, Connecticut to his parents Alexander Michaud and Lumnia LaBonne, on October 8, 1918. He was the youngest of five children; Ursula was born in 1910, and Gabriel in 1912 in Jewett City; Dona was born in 1914, and Alexander 1917 in Plainfield. At the time of his birth, his father, Alexander, was 36 and his mother was 31. His mother passed away seventeen days after his birth from the flu. The children were brought up separately. Bob was raised by his Great Aunt Albena and moved to Bristol, Connecticut.

Prior to entering the military service, our dad worked for the E. Ingraham Clock Manufacturing Company in Bristol Connecticut. At the age of twenty-two, he was inducted into the military from Hartford, Connecticut on March 20, 1941, and was sent for Basic Training at Camp Shelby, Mississippi. He was assigned to the 169th Infantry of the 43rd Division.

Dad served one year and nine months as an enlisted soldier and was promoted to Corporal prior to his leaving the enlisted ranks on September 22, 1942. He was then assigned to the 23rd Company, 2nd Student Training Regiment, ISSC, Fort Benning, Georgia, enrolled from September 23, 1942, and graduating December 21, 1942, from the Officer Candidate Course at The Infantry School at Fort Benning, Georgia and was commissioned a 2nd Lieutenant.

Two months later he was assigned to Camp Atterbury, Indiana and was assigned with the 331st Infantry Regiment 83rd Division as a 2nd Lieutenant. His duty assignments starting, from January 1, 1943, as a 2nd Lieutenant, ranged from a Rifle Platoon Leader and Executive Officer. He was promoted to 1st Lieutenant December 9, 1943, and continued with assignments as Battalion Transportation Officer,

Mortar Platoon leader and weapons Platoon leader. August 1, 1944, he was promoted to Captain. He was a Company Commander from July 1, 1944, to December 31, 1944. From January 1, 1945, to April 25, 1945, he served in Belgium, Holland, and Germany.

On the morning of July 9, 1944, during the final drive on Sainteny, as a 1st Lieutenant he assumed command of his company when the Commanding Officer of his company became a casualty. Within an hour, his company had turned the direction of a fierce battle and broke the defenses of the village, which resulted in its capture. On July 13, 1944, his company led the advance from Bois Grimot to Chateau d'Auxais. His citation reads ". . . so thorough were his plans and preparations and leadership that his company advanced more than 2500 yards in six hours, captured ten prisoners and killed approximately twenty enemy soldiers." Although he was wounded by shrapnel to his hip, he was treated at an aid station and returned to duty. He was awarded the Bronze Star for meritorious service in action against the enemy in Normandy, France.

As depicted in a drawing sketch dated August 8, 1944, by American Artist, William Reusswig, he received the Silver Star for taking a fortified Hill near LeGue, France. Dad led his infantry unit through barbed wire, concrete, and steel tank obstacles. It was during this month he was wounded by concussion grenades to the head. He returned to active duty a week later after being hospitalized for a week.

On March 1, 1945, in Germany, in a tank-infantry attack against Loveling, he rode the lead tank in face of enemy small arms fire to direct the tanks into the town. The citation for the Bronze Star with Oak-Leaf Cluster was awarded for his tactical maneuver in directing his unit quickly and attaining and securing the military objective.

After the war, our dad served in Korea as a Civil Affairs Officer within headquarters of the 3rd Infantry Division, from October 26, 1953, to July, 25, 1954. After the "cessation of hostilities" in Korea, he assisted in the administration of humanitarian and economic aid. In May of 1954, he took over the responsibility for planning, supervising, and ensuring the successful handling of indigenous

personnel. He oversaw the insurance of an efficient and equitable division or issuance of plots of farm land, building supplies, equipment, and clothing. He was active with the orphanages, with estimates of over 100,000 homeless and parentless children left from the war's aftermath. By the end of 1954, there were over 400 registered orphanages in Korea. During 1954, the orphan population was still increasing with over a thousand children a month.

In 1958, Dad got a reassignment back to France, only this time during much better circumstances. He was promoted to the rank of Major, and his assignment was at the HQ USASCC Maison Forte, APO 58, Harbord Barracks, in Orleans, France. Mom, myself, my older sister, Sandra, and younger brother, Paul, all moved to Loiret, France to a caretakers house at the Chateau des Bordes. After some time, we got to the top of the vacant housing roster and moved to the dependent's military housing, Marechal Foche Housing Area in Olivet.

In July of 1961, Dad was transferred back to the States, assigned as Commanding Officer to U.S.A. Recruiting Main Station in Boston, Massachusetts. He was promoted to Lieutenant Colonel on December 20, 1961. His active career came to a close August 3, 1962, as the result of an automobile accident in Wareham, Massachusetts. Photos taken during his military service reflect his self-confidence, military pride, passion, and love for his military vocation. Simply put, he was a patriot who devoted his life to the service of his country and to his country's allies. A son of France who returned to France and will always be remembered for his dedication, love, and service pride.

Decorations: Silver Star, Bronze Star with two Bronze Oak Leaf clusters with letter "V" device, Purple Heart with one Bronze Oak Leaf cluster, Croix De Guerre with Silver Star, Army Commendation medal, Good Conduct medal, American Defense Service medal, American Campaign medal, European-African-Middle-Eastern Campaign medal with one Silver Star with three battle stars, World War II Victory medal, National Defense Service medal, Korean Service medal with one Bronze Service Star, Armed Forces Reserve medal, United Nations Service medal, Expert Badge with Carbine Bar, Combat Infantry Badge 2nd award.

Captain Robert A. Mitchell and 1st Sgt. George P. Terhanko are proudly remembered with the men of the 83rd Infantry Division, 2nd Battalion, 331st Regiment at the site of this memorial.

Normandy, France

83rd Infantry Division
2nd Battalion 331st Infantry Regiment

En hommage aux soldats et officiers du 2/331ème R.I. 83ème Division d'Infanterie, libérateurs de Sainteny. Ici, leurs mitrailleuses ont couvert et soutenu leurs frères d'armes du 1er et 3ème bataillons dans leurs tentatives courageuses mais désespérées de s'implanter sur la péninsule de La Varde. Par leur bravoure, leur courage et leurs actions, Auxais a été libéré.

Dedicated to the soldiers and officers of 2/331st IR 83rd Infantry Division Liberators of Sainteny. Here, their machine guns covered and supported their brothers in arms of the 1st and 3rd Battalions, in their brave but desperate attempt to gain a foothold on La Varde Peninsula. By their bravery, their courage and their actions, Auxais was liberated.

GEORGE P. TERHANKO, 1ST SGT

83RD INFANTRY DIVISION, F/331ST, EUROPEAN THEATER

Submitted by Rick Terhanko, Son

GEORGE TERHANKO WAS A tall man—you could tell that even when he was sitting in his chair, his hands resting on the head of his cane. He was a kindly gentleman who asked if you are OK—would you like something to drink or eat? He smiled when he talked about his granddaughters. But when he started to tell his war stories, you suddenly realized what a tough soldier he must have been.

He told us about how he and Shoemaker and a couple of other non-coms confiscated a stateroom on their troop ship. He liked to point out that he still had the keys to the room somewhere. One of his great stories he liked to tell was how he yelled an obscenity at someone who asked about the foxhole he was digging. Terhanko emerged from the hole to find General Eisenhower and his aide looking down at him. He thought for sure that he would be busted. Instead, Eisenhower commended him for his foxhole digging skills.

The more somber stories he told were about the bodies he had to step over when they landed at Omaha Beach and about how he was wounded four times and buried alive twice. "I was hell on wheels," he said. "We were all scared, but we had a job to do, and I figured we would do our job and not worry about what would happen to us."

He was wounded four times, three times in a three-week period; First Sergeant Terhanko never saw the inside of a hospital. The first time he was wounded was on June 29, 1944. He was carrying a bag of hand grenades when German mortars began firing at him. "I was lugging them in one of those double mortar bags. Then the Germans threw in some heavy mortar. Hot shrapnel tore into my hip. An inch closer and it would have cut my spinal cord." He told the runner who was with him to cut the shrapnel out of his hip, but the soldier protested, saying that he did not have a knife. Terhanko pulled out his own trench knife and handed it to his friend. After the impromptu surgery, Terhanko tried to continue his mission, but he was bleeding

S/Sgt. George P. Terhanko, aged 30, of 546 W. Princeton Ave., has every good reason to believe he has what it takes in the way of digging a foxhole because Supreme Commander Gen. Dwight D. Eisenhower praised his ability, a news dispatch from the invasion front in Normandy reported. Terhanko, son of Mr. and Mrs. George Terhanko Sr., has been serving overseas about two months with an infantry unit. When General Eisenhower visited the front lines, he saw the Youngstown man digging a slit trench. Turning to his staff officer, Eisenhower remarked: "Now there is a soldier who is properly concealed." Terhanko formerly was employed by the Great Atlantic & Pacific Co. here too much. The captain told him to go to the aid station, where they wanted to send him back to a field hospital. He refused to go. So they bandaged him up, loaded him on a jeep with his leg draped over the front, and sent him back to his company.

Terhanko recalls that when they finally made it through the hedgerows, they had to cross open terrain between Carentan and Periers.

Buried in a House – George Terhanko

As we moved along everything was quiet. Then all of a sudden the Germans started to fire at us. Six of us ran into a building that looked like a two story house to take cover. It also had a basement or shelter under it which was uncommon for a house in France. Hidden under the first floor were steps leading down to the shelter, which was about 10' by 12'. The Germans had seen us run into the house and started shelling it.

After a few near misses they scored a direct hit, bringing down the building on top of us.

Captain Mitchell tried to call in to report our position but the radio was knocked out. He finally got the radio operating and reported to the General Macon. The General was not pleased with our progress and sent help to get us out.

It took the outside help about two hours to dig us out while still being shelled. In all we were buried in the rubble for about 5 hours. We rejoined the rest of the company and continued.

Sergeant Terhanko was shelled again during the Brittany campaign.

Buried on Hill 48 – George Terhanko

We arrived late in the afternoon at the base of Hill 48 near the town of St. Briauc. We started to set up our night defensive positions. The area contained fox holes and a trench system that the retreating Germans left intact. We were to attack the hill in the morning from the west flank.

It was decided that this would be a good time to enjoy a hot meal and one was ordered from the rear. It arrived just as it was getting dark. A chow line was started and about half of the men were served before we started getting shelled by the Germans. They were using mortars and artillery.

I was straddling a trench directing the men to the chow line. As the rounds started coming in closer I heard one that sounded like it would be real close. I yelled for everyone to get down and dove into the trench I was standing over. The shell hit where my right foot had been, caving in the trench on top of me. I was completely covered with only my two feet sticking out of the ground.

The men dug out my head first or I would have suffocated. After they dug me out I went back to the chow truck and used their water to clean up with. The shelling was over. I was sore but lucky nothing was broken.

On another occasion, Terhanko was nearly run over by a tank.

Buried by a Tank - George Terhanko

We were crossing an open area when all of a sudden three German tanks appeared. They started for us. The area was covered with foxholes that the Germans had dug. I dove into one of them.

One of the tanks headed my way and drove over the foxhole I was in. When it got over top of me it stopped and twisted back and forth trying to cave the hole in on me. After trying this the tank moved on along with the other two.

We (the men in the other foxholes and myself) waited a few minutes and got out of the holes and started forward again. The tanks continued behind us and we were not bothered by them again.

At the end of the war, Sergeant Terhanko was somewhat reluctant to return home. He had plenty of points, but he said he had it made. Put in charge of a POW camp; Terhanko had a seamstress to repair and clean his clothes and a cook to prepare meals for him. It was quite a change from what he had experienced in the previous year.

The Silver Star was earned when artillery and tank fire had disorganized the company outside a small town in Luxembourg. 1st SGT George Terhanko took a group of men and acting on their own took over a section of the town.

The Bronze Star for a series of actions that he can't recall now.

The Purple Hearts were as follows;

1. On or around June 29, 1944, 1st SGT George Terhanko was carrying satchels of grenades to his men when the Germans spotted him and mortared him. He got hit with a piece of shrapnel that missed his tail bone by about an inch. He had one of his men dig it out with a knife.

2. On or about July 11, 1944, 1st SGT George Terhanko was walking back to the CP when he felt a sting in his shoulder that he thought was a bee sting. When he got to the CP one of the officers noticed a tracer bullet sticking out of his shirt.

3. On or about July 18, 1944, 1st SGT George Terhanko company was advancing when the bazooka man had the bottom of his ear shot off by a sniper. He dropped the bazooka and ran. 1st SGT George Terhanko went forward to retrieve the bazooka but was held back by sniper fire. As he was laying there, the company that they were to meet up with came marching by without drawing any fire. Terhanko stood up and was shot through his left knee by the sniper.

4. On or about December 9, 1944, 1st SGT George Terhanko was hit with a piece of shrapnel in his lower leg.

His decorations include the Silver Star, the Bronze Star, the Purple Heart with 3 Oak Leaf Clusters, the European-African-Middle Eastern Campaign medal with 5 Bronze Stars, the World War II Victory medal, the Army of Occupation medal, the Combat Infantryman Badge, the Presidential Unit Citation, the Meritorious Unit Citation, and the Good Conduct medal. In May of 2005 Mr. Terhanko was inducted into the Ohio Military Hall of Fame for Valor.

LAWRENCE L. CHITTENDEN, 1ST LT

83RD INFANTRY DIVISION, I/330TH, EUROPEAN THEATER

Reprinted with Permission by Beth Chittenden, Daughter

**An excerpt from *My Father's War* by Beth Chittenden
An Oral History of the Experiences of
Lawrence Lee Chittenden During World War II**

MOST OF OUR FIGHTING was in towns or villages. We'd pull up on the perimeter, unload out of the trucks and infantry would form, and we'd start towards town. This general was an armored general, and I thought he was a pip, a wonderful guy. He didn't sacrifice his infantry. He did all he could to save 'em. He'd bring them old tank destroyers up on a hill somewhere, and they'd start laying 90mm shells down the streets of the town and stone buildings. Those 90s would ricochet from one building to the other through town and scare 'em out. They'd take off, and when they took off out the backside, then the Air Corps was there, and they'd just slaughter 'em. It was really… it really chewed 'em up. It was terrible. After we'd done that for a few days, that's where we'd begin to get a lot of prisoners. We turned the prisoners over to the Free French.

I had this one truck driver, a black sergeant from a truck company. I had two trucks for my platoon, and one of these drivers, the first time we got out to go up to do a little fighting, why here he came. He had his carbine and was crawling right along with the squad that was in the lead. I said, "What are you doing here?" He said, "Sir, I'm here to fight this war just the same as you," he says. "If we're gonna whip 'em, then I'm gonna help." He wanted to fight. Well, I didn't stop him, and he did.

But he's the same one that we got such a kick out of when we'd get out of our trucks to go and fight, and then we'd come back to the trucks to move on, and at nights we'd stop with the trucks in an assembly area, and he'd take his entrenching shovel and go off into the weeds or the bush and go to the bathroom. And *every time* he'd come back leading one or two prisoners. (Laughing) It got to be a joke. We'd say—I can't remember his name, he was a sergeant— "There goes ol' Sergeant So-and-So to take a crap. I wonder how many he'll get this time." We laughed at that.

Among the French towns they passed through, Morlaix will perhaps be longest remembered, as it was here they learned something of the gratitude of the French people, who had been living four years under harsh German rule.

I think that's also where I had one of the most interesting experiences happen. It was hot. It was August, and we were walking now. We're moving, and we were along this railroad marching along. We went in there with woolen ODs (olive drab uniforms) and all those gas protection things, and you hadn't had a chance to bathe or anything. This French lady came out to me in kind of a Red Cross outfit, it was kind of a blue and white striped uniform, and kept wanting me to come, "Come, come."

Well, I couldn't speak any French, so I grabbed my runner and another enlisted man and went with her. And she took me to this little cafe, kind of like an old railroad diner, and I'll bet there were six tables in there just completely full of bottles of liquor. I have never, ever seen so many different kinds. "Have some," you know, "Help yourself." And they were, "Vive la France," "V for Victory," "Have it, drink it, come on, Vive la France." Well, it was hot, and in the summer there was no way you'd touch that stuff. But they just … they were so happy to see you. That's what made fighting worthwhile.

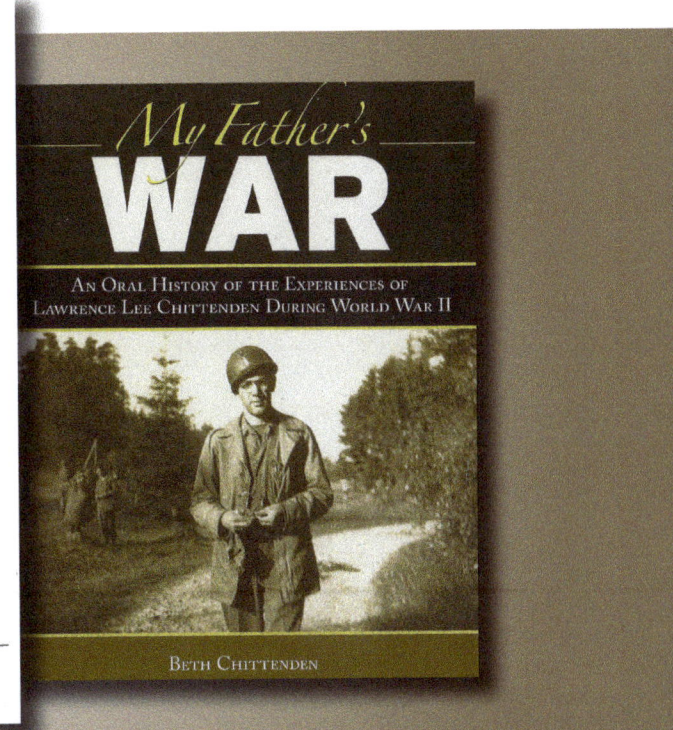

MYRON H. MILLER, S SGT

83rd Infantry Division, K/331st, European Theater

Stories Our Dad Told Us by The Miller Kids

Learning How (Not) to Ski – Camp Carson, Colorado
by Lynette Miller Ballard

MY DAD, MYRON MILLER, had all of us laughing so hard we cried when he told about being in training at Camp Carson and going with some other soldiers to the mountains to snow ski. They went up a mountain with borrowed skis and were going to have a great time skiing at top speed down the mountain. However, Daddy said, no matter how hard he tried, he could not keep his balance and kept falling off his skis into the cold, wet snow. Other soldiers were having a fine time; not he. Finally, he surrendered to practicality. He simply sat on the skis and propelled himself downhill, not as a racer, but as a hunkered-down farm boy. He tipped over several times, but at least that did not threaten to break any of his bones. After a long, tiring trip down the mountain, he joined his buddies and went back to Camp Carson, never to ski again.

Alles Kaput
by Del Miller

THE END OF WAR was only days away. The 83rd Division had crossed the Elbe River and they were now out on one of their last patrols. They were almost out of danger and they would soon be going home. It was a good day.

As they came to a bend in the road, three German soldiers suddenly stood up from the ditch, hands above their heads, "Alles kaput," one of them said, "It's all over." At their feet was a machine gun, its barrel pointing straight down the road from which they came.

The war was not over and had those Germans done their duty, my father and his men would have been mown down.

My father and his men took them as prisoners, politely.

Locked and Loaded
by Del Miller

I THINK OF MY father, a soft-spoken Ozark farmer, and it's hard to imagine him as the sort of guy who kicks down doors in hopes of finding heavily armed men who wanted to shoot him. But, in fact, he was exactly the sort of guy who kicked down doors and charged headlong into a darkness full of potential gunfire and rife with bad outcomes.

House-to-house fighting was scary business, so my father would trade in his M1 rifle for a Thompson submachine gun from which he could spew 45 caliber rounds into the darkness of someone's former dining room at six hundred rounds a minute. The problem with all this firepower was that the Thompson's ammunition magazine held only 20 rounds, so the math says that my dad had about two seconds of ammo to deal with a whole houseful of enemy soldiers.

So imagine yourself in my Dad's shoes: You have just barged, uninvited, into an enemy combat position, shot up some fraction of the bad guys in this dark and now smoke-filled room, and now you're out of ammo. The bad guys you didn't shoot are now pulling out an assortment of weapons and the time for discussion is clearly over. The process of pulling the spent magazine out of your gun and then fishing around in your bag for replacement ammo and then inserting the fresh clip into your gun, all while in the dark, in a room full of people with guns who are really angry with you, will almost certainly lead to some extremely tense moments.

It turns out that my Dad was not one to mess around with this kind of thing so he taped three magazines together, offset so each mag could in turn fit in the receiver. This way he could burn off an entire magazine and reload by simply pulling the magazine out of the gun and jamming it right back yet. That gave him a whole six seconds of ammunition to take on a building full of enemy soldiers.

So this was his gear when he burst into that farmhouse on a cold overcast day. Weapons were firing and artillery exploding throughout the town as Company K cleared the town. The enemy was holed up everywhere and his job was to drive them out. It was horrifying work, knowing that behind this door could be the bullet with **his name on it.** With his stomach in knots, he took one last, deep breath and **charged through** the doorway. And that's when he got hit …

… by a goat.

From out of the darkness flew a big angry billy goat that butted him against the hard stone wall like he was a rag doll. Hard. *Twice.* Then it ran away. There were no Germans in the house.

My dad said he sat there for a long moment and then he laughed out loud.

CLAUDE K. ROBERTS

Boatswain's Mate 1st Cl, USS Bridge, U.S. Navy, Pacific Theater

Submitted by Dayna Linton, Granddaughter

FIRST CLASS BOATSWAIN MATE Claude Knowlton Roberts was born on November 21, 1920, the twelfth of thirteen children to Orville Clark Roberts, Jr. and Persis Young Roberts in Redmesa, Colorado.

At the ripe old age of seventeen, Grandpa joined the Navy to see the world. There was a story he told about crossing the international date line. There is some ritual for those crossing the first time, and as we recall, it involved shaving the pollywog's heads.

Our brother's favorite story Grandpa told about his Navy days was when he was on his ship and was getting seasick, he would barf so much he would end up with the dry heaves. A shipmate told him, "If you feel something round and hairy in your throat when dry heaving, don't spit it out because that is your asshole."

Grandpa did talk a little about his time in the Navy, but really, as many others of his generation, not much.

Grandpa was contemplating whether to re-enlist or leave the Navy when Pearl Harbor was attacked, bringing the U.S. into the fight and inspiring Grandpa to re-enlist.

He was aboard one of the first ships to land at Pearl Harbor after the attack. It took his ship two weeks to reach the islands. Grandpa said sailors would volunteer to go down in scuba gear (the old-time gear) and then walk back toward the beach along the ocean floor. The bubbles from the oxygen would lift the bodies and, if a soldier turned around, they would see several bodies following them. Those sailors who volunteered would be given a very short amount of time to do this as it was very traumatic for them. We recall that they were only allowed to go down twice.

Grandpa was aboard the *USS Bridge* for the majority of the war. The *USS Bridge* was the lead ship of her class of stores ships and served in both WWI and WWII.

During WWII, the *USS Bridge* expanded her Pacific voyages to include the Fiji, Tonga, and New Caledonia Islands. Between the 10th of August and the 20th of October, 1942, she shuttled cargo between San Francisco and Alaska, and then returned to the South Pacific.

Between October 1942 and April 1943, she carried cargo to the Hawaii, Tonga, Loyalty Islands, and the Samoan Islands. From the 2nd of April until the 3rd of July, 1943, she ferried supplies between Nouméa, New Caledonia, and Auckland, New Zealand. In July, she steamed to San Francisco and thence to Alaska, where she operated until October. She returned to Pearl Harbor on the 3rd of November and operated between the Hawaiian and Ellice Islands until April 1944. Between the 19th of April 1944 and the 27th of April 1945, *Bridge* operated exclusively between Pearl Harbor and the Marshall Islands. During the 9th–22nd of May and the 11th of July–the 13th of August 1945, she landed supplies at Okinawa, returning to Pearl Harbor each time. *[Source: Wikipedia]*

In Claude's short "Life's Sketch," he writes: *During the War, two ships were sunk that I was supposed to be transferred to and one that I was transferred off of.*

He was a man of few words.

Grandpa would chuckle about how the sailors would sleep on the deck of the ship because it was too hot below. They would stretch canvas to protect themselves from the rain, but when the rain fell, Grandpa would poke the canvas with his finger, which would then make the rainwater seep through and hit the sailor below it.

The only other thing he mentions about the war in his "Life Sketch" is this:

> I loved many girls but when I heard about this young widow, that I had known most my life, and her small daughter, I started correspondence with her. When the war was over, after serving the Navy for almost eight years, I got a discharge and headed home. My father had died while I was out to sea. That was very sad as I loved my father very much. My mother now lived alone in Redmesa, so that is where I went. On February 14, 1946, I married Doris [the young widow—our grandma].

When we asked how come Grandpa was nearly bald, he told us he played the role of the King in *The King and I* and he had to shave his head over and over again for the part until his hair pretty much just stopped growing back.

Though Grandpa was the only grandpa we knew, as our biological grandpa died when our mother was only six-weeks-old, we think he was the best grandpa and great-grandpa ever! We were his only grandkids, and they spoiled us rotten!

Grandpa worked for the U.S. Post Office until his retirement and then he and Grandma moved to Pocatello, Idaho to be closer to our mother and their grandkids. The boys loved going out to the farm, feeding the animals and spending time with Grandpa and Grandma.

When walking next to the electric fence at the farm, Grandpa got our brothers Scott or Mitch to try to electrocute a grasshopper, knowing full well that the electricity passes right through the bug and shocks the person holding it. He would also grab the electric fence and try to touch one of us to shock us.

Grandpa would spend long hours driving up and down the field in his truck with us being towed behind on a sled. We got cold before he got tired of doing it.

He taught us to shoot with his bolt action .22 rifle. He taught us proper shooting and gun safety.

Our Grandpa loved to tease, and if you were barefoot, you could count on him grabbing your feet and pulling your toes. He also loved to rub his stubbly face on our skin just for fun, but our brother, Greg, didn't think it was fun when Grandpa did it to Greg's sunburned back.

When our parents divorced, and we had no father figure, Grandpa tried to step in. He told our brother, Greg, that if he had any questions about sex, he should ask him. Being embarrassed, Greg just smiled and told Grandpa that if *he* had any questions, he could ask him, too.

One time Grandma and Grandpa took the boys to see a movie called *"Avalanche."* There was a scene early in the movie where a guy gets out of a huge shower to answer the phone. While he is talking on the phone, the topless woman who was showering with him, came over to him. When Grandma saw the boobs, she *freaked out*! She was trying to keep hands over Greg, Scott and Mitch's eyes while telling Grandpa they needed to leave! Grandpa just sat there smiling and staring at the screen. The boys thought the guy behind them was going to crap his pants from laughing so hard.

Grandpa was there for every game, concert, recital—anything his grandchildren or great-grandchildren were involved in—until the day he died. We always knew Grandpa would be there to watch us and always early *really* early.

Grandpa also loved to read, even though he had only received an eighth-grade education, he could frequently be seen reading. He enjoyed reading at least two books, and usually four books, at a time. Grandpa loved Louis L'Amour, Zane Grey and books and movies about WWII.

On New Year's Day, 2008, Claude K. Roberts, at the age of 87, joined his twelve siblings, our grandma, and many other loved ones for a heavenly reunion.

He has been dearly missed.

ROBERT C. FERGUSSON

28th Infantry Division, 1st BN, European Theater

Submitted by Stephen Blaes on behalf of Richard Coyle, Friend

I WAS BORN IN Ponca City, Oklahoma on August 1, 1924, and entered the U. S. Army on June 1, 1943, just three days after graduating from high school. My unit trained for a year at anti-aircraft replacement camps, and then I was put in the U.S. Infantry when the Army had a greater need for soldiers on the ground instead of anti-aircraft personnel.

In September 1944 I arrived at a replacement depot in Verviers, Belgium, where I was assigned to the 1st Battalion of the 28th Infantry Division as a telephone lineman. The next day, two other soldiers and I went by Jeep into the Hurtgen Forest. Near the town of Vossnich, we came under German artillery fire. Laying telephone lines and repairing breaks in lines was a dangerous job and I came under fire many times.

On the night of December 16, my platoon was quartered in a hotel in the Luxembourg town of Diekirch, when the hotel was struck by an artillery shell. The Battle of the Bulge had begun. My crew went out to repair a broken line when we were alerted that German forces were just down the road headed our way. Returning to the town, we found the hotel had burned down and all our gear was lost. On Christmas Day, the cooks prepared us a turkey dinner. After two weeks of cold, hard fighting, it was the first hot meal we had had.

The next month, our unit moved into the Alsace area of France in relief of the 3rd Division. One time our crew was running a line to a mountain location when one of the guys, "Swede," tripped a personnel mine which exploded, sending a piece of shrapnel through my clothes, cutting my rifle strap and just missing me.

We moved back into Germany and lived in the woods. We were in position perhaps ten or twelve miles from the Rhine River preparing to make the crossing when, after a couple of weeks, we heard the Remagen Bridge had been captured intact by an American division, making it not necessary for us to cross. The end of the war was near, and the Germans surrendered in May 1945. Occupation duty was light, with each company forming track teams and competing in meets.

In August we embarked on ships out of LeHavre, and after an eight-day crossing, we arrived in New York Harbor. We passed the Statue of Liberty, and a small boat circled our ship, and we could hear the Andrew Sisters singing "The Pennsylvania Polka."

CHARLES T. DAVIS, SR.

83rd Infantry Division, 1/331st, European Theater

Reprinted with Permission by Dana Bryan Greene, Author

THESE TWO CHAPTERS, REPRINTED from the book, *See It Through: A Memoir of Charles T. Davis, Sr.*, tell a great story about Charles getting wounded in France and the process of communication during the war.

ACROSS FRANCE

After Patton took over we headed for the Brittany Peninsula to clean it out. The Germans were expecting us to come ashore at the mouth of the peninsula, and they had their guns pointed that way, but we were coming in the back way! Few Americans have heard the names of towns like Dinard, St. Lunaire, St. Brieue, and dozens of others, but those of us who fought our way through them remember very well. On August 3 and 4, we moved through Coutances and Avranches, France. Our tanks were shooting in every direction. Here we were faced with the enemy's main lines of defenses, consisting of a series of concrete pillboxes connected by several feet of reinforced steel tunnels and trenches. One company made a 400-yard assault through railroad spikes anti-tank obstacles, and double-apron barbed wire to knock out an enemy blockhouse. We then charged into Paramé. We were the first troops to penetrate this St. Malo suburb on August 8, 1944.

We were taking the town, street by street. One of our boys, Gardner Lee, got shot and was down in the street. We provided fire cover for some others to pull him out of harm's way. The Germans we were firing at took off running into a house. When we chased in behind them, they ran out the back door. I ran to the back door to see where they went, and just as I did a bullet hit the facing of the door. I told the boys that I had seen where he shot from. I said, "He's over behind that boarded fence in the back yard. I'll take a grenade, throw it over the fence and that'll take care of him." I took the grenade, pulled the pin and was fixin' to throw it, but when I stepped in the door the German soldier shot me. I held on to the grenade because I had pulled the pin and I knew if I dropped it, it would blow us up. The bullet knocked me to my knees, but I thought if I could get up I would be all right. I was trying to get up and the boys said, "Don't get up, he'll shoot you again!" One of them grabbed me by the pants leg and pulled me down. One of the men took the grenade out of my hand, crawled over to the door and without standing up, threw it over the fence as hard as he could. He didn't know where the Nazi soldier that shot me was positioned, and he didn't really care if it hit a German. He just wanted the grenade out of that house and the sooner the better.

Why that bullet didn't come through me is a mystery I'll never understand. A shell that size could go through a dozen men. When someone gets shot, you can't stop to help him. You've got to keep going. You depend on the medics coming along behind to take care of the wounded. The guys took me to the house where we had put the other wounded man. He was shot in the stomach. We lay there on the floor and talked for a while, until he went into shock. We were there by ourselves and he never came out of shock. He died, and there was nothing I could do. I was afraid that I would go into shock, but I didn't. Right after that the boys came back to get me and took me to a church. There were three people there. I guess one was a priest and the other two were nuns. It was around lunchtime. I couldn't tell what they were saying in French, and they didn't understand me. Later in the afternoon I was just lying there. I said to myself, "Ain't nobody fixin' to come and get me, and these people don't know what to do." But late that afternoon two of our boys came back with two German prisoners. They put me on a homemade stretcher and they made the two prisoners walk me back to the aid station, which was a mile or two away. The reason for all the walking is that a vehicle could not get in there because the roads were mined. Our boys tried to get a jeep in to get us, but the jeep hit a mine and we lost one of our soldiers. He was sitting on the back of the jeep when they hit, and it blew up. I truly believe had they been able to get into us, Gardner would have made it. Those medics could do wonders if they could get to a soldier fast enough. They patched me up at the aid station and carried me over to the field hospital where I stayed the night. They had a makeshift runway there so planes could land. They put all of us wounded on stretchers, laid us in the plane and flew us back to a hospital in England.

THE TELEGRAM

The U.S. Army has a long history of getting lots of things wrong. Sometimes those mistakes can break a person's heart. While I was lying in a bed in a hospital in England with a bullet one inch from my spine, the Army made a blunder that was almost unforgivable.

No mother wants her son to go to war, and it is even harder when she has only one son. My mother was no different, and she was convinced that if I went to war, I would not come back alive. I may have been wounded, but I was determined that I would prove her wrong. I would come back!

Somehow the War Department got a false report that I had died from my wound. The Army is quite efficient in some things, and one is immediate notification to families of soldiers who have been killed in action. So when the War Department in Washington received news of my death, they wasted no time in sending a telegram to the post office in Arlington, Georgia stating that I had been killed in combat. Hours later the Pentagon received the correct report that I was wounded, not killed, but the post office was already closed. We had no telephone, and they didn't know anybody else they could contact. As soon as the post office opened the next morning, the Army officials called Mr. Roy Powell, Arlington's postmaster, and instructed him not to deliver the telegram. Mr. Powell replied that it was too late because the mail carrier, who happened to be his daughter-in-law, Sara, had already gone out on her route and he didn't have any way to communicate with her.

To their credit, the Pentagon officers didn't give up. They learned that the telephone closest to our farm belonged to Judge W. R. Taylor, and they called immediately. Frances, the Taylor's daughter, answered and they hurriedly described the situation and asked her to intercept the mail carrier before she got to our place. Frances responded that the mail carrier had already delivered the mail to their house. What was worse was that the Taylors were gone in the car and Frances had no way to try to stop the carrier. Her only hope was to run out to the field back of the house and see if one of the farm hands could take a mule that was pulling one of the plows and ride it over to our place. She told the man she was talking to on the phone what she was going to do and took off running out to the field.

When the men saw Frances running towards them, they knew something was going on. They stopped plowing, and she told them about the telegram and that somebody needed to stop the mail carrier before she got to Mama. All around the farm country where we lived, everybody knew one another, and if one person had a problem, then everyone else had a problem. All of us, white and black alike, stuck together. Upon hearing the story, one of the men quickly unharnessed a mule, knowing that time was a-wasting. The mail carrier was driving a car, while he would be riding a barebacked mule. That old mule must surely have wondered what in the world was happening, 'cause he gave it all he had. The poor rider was holding on to the mule's mane and had his feet rammed into the animal's sides. He hung on for dear life, bouncing all over the mule's back all the way on the rough ride down that dirt road.

Bessie, my sister, and Bernard happened to be visiting Mama at the time. Bernard was in the backyard, playing in the dirt with some of his toys. Bessie was sitting on the front porch with Mama when Sara Powell drove up with the mail. It was unusual for Miss Sara to get out of the car on her deliveries. She normally would put the mail in the box and drive on, but this time she stopped the car and got out. The two women on the porch were getting more concerned with each step that Miss Sara took toward the house, expecting something real bad. Without a word, she handed Mama the mail, with the telegram right on top. Knowing that it was going to say what she feared, Mama tore it open and began to scream, "I knew it!" Bessie grabbed the telegram from Mama's hand and added her repeated screams, "Charles is dead!" Scared by all the ruckus he heard going on out front, little Bernard came running and crying to see what in the world was going on. Miss Sara was trying to comfort the women, but her efforts were in vain. The only thing she could do was to stay with them till somebody else came up. Daddy was out in the field working, and he had no idea what was going on at the house. Mama kept saying, "I told him not to go. I knew he wouldn't come back. I told everybody!" Bessie continued sobbing uncontrollably. Even Bernard's hugs couldn't stop her tears.

Mama went into a kind of shock. Her worse fear had come to pass, and she couldn't handle it. She was just sitting in her rocker with the telegram in her lap. Bessie couldn't be still and was pacing back and forth, wringing her hands and crying as hard as she could. Miss Sara turned her attention to Bernard, holding him and trying to assure him that his mama and grandmother were going to be all right. He had never seen anybody carry on like this before, especially these two women.

As the reality of things sank in and numbness began to overtake the ladies, they saw off in the distance a stirring cloud of dust moving toward them. Even before they could see him clearly, they heard a man yelling from the cloud of dust, and he got louder as he got closer. Directly, they saw the farmhand riding that bare-backed mule as hard as he could. In a little bit, they could make out the words he was shouting over and over: "It's a mistake! He's alive! Charles is alive." The panting messenger pulled the exhausted mule to a stop right at the porch and began to pour out an explanation of the mistake and all the efforts of the War Department in trying to stop the delivery of the telegram.

Now Mama had another problem. Her only son was half a world away and hurting and they couldn't do anything to help him. She didn't know the extent of his injuries, but if the Army thought he was dead, then his wounds must be bad!

Mama thanked the field hand for his kind deed and expressed to Miss Sara her appreciation for staying with them to comfort them. Then she told Miss Sara to continue on her route, assuring her that she and Bessie would be all right. After a while, when things calmed down, she told Bessie to take Bernard and go home, 'cause they all needed to try to get some rest after all that upheaval. When they left, Mama folded the telegram and put it in her apron pocket and went to bed. She and the Lord needed to have a conversation.

It was sundown before Daddy came in from his day's work in the field. He made sure all of the livestock had been fed before he made his way to the house. Before stepping into the kitchen, he made his usual stop on the back porch to wash his face and hands of a day's worth of plowing dirt. Mama had regained her composure and calmly described the events of the day and put the telegram on the table before him.

When Daddy said the blessing that night, he thanked the Lord that his son was alive and asked Him to heal his body, continue to protect him, and bring him home alive. My parents were the kind that believed it was a sin to worry. If you could fix a problem, you did, and if you couldn't, you trusted the Lord to take care of the situation.

It is my understanding that the War Department asked that the telegram be returned to them. After learning that I was alive, my family received sympathy telegrams from the governor and several other state officials. My family thought that was strange, but they were sure the governor and the others had good intentions.

KENNETH MOORE

83rd Infantry Division, K/331st, Medic, European Theater

Submitted by Annette Moore, Daughter

MARILYN EM (ANNETTE MOORE) has written a loving tribute to her father, Kenneth Moore, titled *Amazing Spirit: A Tribute to Dad* (AuthorHouse, Bloomington, Indiana, 2007). Her book covers a wide range of family history, and Chapter Two, "Coping with the Great Depression," includes several references to her dad's service in the Civilian Conservation Corps, and following that, the experience of being an Army medic on the front lines in Normandy. Much of what she learned was by attending the reunions of the 83rd Infantry Unit and talking to her dad's 331st "K" Company buddies.

- His buddies remembered him as "Doc," the medic who didn't stay in one place too long, and who didn't get much sleep, as he tirelessly helped to rescue and treat the wounded.

- His platoon sergeant, Norman Malo, verified that the medic had been captured and held as a POW by the Germans after he was wounded in the leg from shrapnel on July 19, 1944. Kenneth's story about being wounded was that "a great big Kraut" rescued him by slinging him over his shoulder and telling him, "Hospital soon." His captors "were merciful, fed him well, and nursed him back to health." Mr. Martin, another medic, whom Marilyn Em met at one of the reunions, remembered that both sides, Allies and Germans, despised what the horrors of war were doing to human beings.

- Sgt. Malo provided Kenneth's daughter with a photo of the farewell dinner held by the 331st before they returned home from Germany. In that photo, highlighted by a sunbeam, was her father's face. She felt that sunbeam showed what an angel her father had been to so many others during the war and in the years to come.

- At one of the reunions, Kenneth's daughter met General Patton's grandson Benjamin who was interviewing veterans for a documentary he was working on for public television in New York. Young Ben readily agreed to have a photo taken with Kenneth's granddaughter Libby.

- Kenneth Moore did his Army basic training at Camp Breckinridge in Kentucky.

- Kenneth met his wife at a USO dance before he was sent to France. She was a dedicated USO volunteer while he was in Europe. They eloped in 1946 while they were both living and working in Toledo, Ohio. They raised four lively youngsters and ran a significant "hobby farm" while he supported it all by working in a factory for about 38 years.

...and they all returned home with a smile

HUBERT D. 'HUGH' KLINE, 1ST LT

102ND AIR FORCE RESERVE, MAXWELL FIELD, ALABAMA, USA

SUBMITTED BY KAREN KLINE CHRISTOFFERSEN, DAUGHTER

DAD ENLISTED ON MARCH 27, 1942, at Baer Field, Ft. Wayne, Indiana, just across the border from the little town of his birth, Wren, Ohio, and his family's farm near Van Wert. He was a small man, just over 5 feet 7 inches, weighing about 150 pounds, but he never seemed short. He had a powerful presence; when he walked into a room, everyone was glad to see him.

Hugh, as he was known to his family and friends (also sometimes as "H.D."), had 20/15 vision in both eyes and was a pretty bright guy, probably a shoe-in for pilot training.

After his enlistment, he was assigned to Maxwell Air Field in Alabama, probably for basic training.

On February 5, 1943, along with 218 other cadet pilots, he received the rank of 2nd Lieutenant from Brigadier General L.A. Walton, Army Air Forces West Coast Training Center Headquarters.

Dad's training as an Aviation Cadet–Student Pilot took one year, one month and twenty-three days. The next records I located had him at the Army Air Forces Advanced Flying School, Roswell, New Mexico, and, upon graduation, he was awarded a certificate dated May 20, 1943, from the Roswell Army Flying School.

I recall a story Dad told that may have occurred sometime in December of 1943 (I only know this as there were a mandatory four days of "excused for medical reasons …" in his papers with that date.) He "accidentally" landed his aircraft on top of an elevated mesa, breaking his nose and squashing his pride, I am certain.

On his Enlisted Record, it mentions in his health physical when he was "discharged" as a 2nd Lieutenant (to become a 1st Lieutenant) as "Good" and his character as "Excellent." That did not surprise me as his character was excellent, but it made me smile—hugely.

Later, he was stationed at Maxwell Field, Alabama where he trained pilots, so he never crossed the seas to join his brother, Russell Kline, who flew bombers in WWII. He was honorably discharged in late 1945 but remained a part of the 102nd Air Force Reserve until his honorable discharge by the President of the United States on January 12, 1956, signed by Colonel James T. Quirk.

My father never experienced combat and the trauma of the battlefield on the ground or in the sky, but he was brave, and he was strong, and if called upon to serve in any way, I know without a doubt that he would have done anything to keep our country free and protect the innocent. I never thought of this before, but Hugh Kline was, and is, indeed a hero. He is one of the best men I have ever known. He died of a cerebral hemorrhage on June 25, 1980 at the young age of 65. It was a devastating loss to my family and me. But I thank Father in Heaven that I had him for 26 years.

RICHARD FAZZIO

Coxswain, U.S. Navy, D-Day, Omaha Beach, European Theater

Submitted by Joe Nadeau on Behalf of Eugene Peloquin, Friend

RICHARD FAZZIO KNEW HE had to go and join the Navy and leave his Lincoln Street home in Woonsocket, Rhode Island, even if his parents, Philomena and Charles, didn't like the idea.

But Fazzio's brother, Frank, then 21, had already gone off to fight in World War II with other young men from his neighborhood, and Richard Fazzio saw the Navy as the place for a guy like him—someone looking for great adventures.

The Navy didn't quite agree with that view. He made repeated trips down to the recruiter's office to begin his induction only to be sent home because of his youthful face. His father had even warned at one point that if they turned him down once more, he would stay home. Fazzio didn't come home after the next visit to the recruiter. After training for a year, he found himself in England preparing with the Allied Forces for the Invasion of Normandy in June of 1944.

Fazzio was assigned as the coxswain of a Landing Craft Vehicle Personnel (LCVP), a Higgins boat designed to land soldiers on the beach of an invasion zone. He was to pilot thirty soldiers ashore to Omaha Beach with the three other members of his crew—a Cumberland, Rhode Island friend Wally Lawton, Gabriel Balas, and Robert Breen.

The crewmen were assigned to boat No. 5 from the *USS Henrico*, a troop transport ship that would earn a heroic record in battles through the course of the war.

The Henrico's Higgins boats were deployed early in the morning of June 6, 1944, as part of the first attack wave and began circling in an assembly area with their cargoes of troops while the coxswains, like Fazzio, followed a well-rehearsed plan to carry them to the Nazi-held shores of the Normandy coast.

Fazzio, now 91, recalled recently how he was supposed to find a certain church tower in the town near Omaha Beach and use it as a landmark to bring his boatload of troops ashore. Luckily, the training prepared him perfectly to see what he was looking for. He

Eugene Peloquin (L) and Richard Fazzio (R)

spotted the church tower on fire after it had apparently been hit in the bombardment leading up to the beach attack. "You could see it was exactly the same layout, right down to the obstacles in the water," Fazzio recalled.

The scene the boat crews encountered as they neared their target zone was as horrendous as any in war could be. Fazzio remembers bullets from the enemy gun emplacements smacking on the water and against the steel-armored sides of his boat. The lifelong memories he earned that day included seeing all but one of the thirty soldiers his boat carried die as they made their run to the beach. The one young soldier who hesitated for a moment in the Higgins Boat could not go back with the crew and Fazzio had to wave him off to meet his fate with the other troops in his unit. Fazzio still doesn't know what happened to that one young soldier.

During his recent recollection of the battle while visiting a restored Higgins boat in Rhode Island, he credited Lawton with saving his life and those of his fellow crew members. A bullet tore into Fazzio's right armpit as he signaled the young soldier, and Lawton somehow got the ramp of the boat back up so Fazzio could back away from the beach. "Wally was the hero there because if he hadn't brought that ramp up when he did, we all would have been dead and no one would have come off that boat alive," Fazzio said. Fazzio and his three crewmembers made it back to the *Henrico* with him piloting half the course and Balas taking over when he collapsed.

Fazzio and the crew participated in other battles of the war in Europe and survived. He did not have to go on to fight in the Pacific, because of the dropping of the atomic bomb, but his family had felt the cost of that part of the war when his brother Frank was killed at the age of 23 in the fighting in Leyte Gulf on Dec. 2, 1944.

Fazzio remembers his brother's sacrifice and those of other Lincoln Street residents lost to the war when he visits a plaque in their memory still located not far from his former neighborhood today. It is hard for him to re-live what he experienced on D-Day but he does remember it now as the sole survivor of his crew.

He lost his wife, Frances, too, but has his children and his grandchildren to pass his memories on to another generation.

FRANK J. HORVATH, M SGT

Platoon Leader, 83rd Infantry Division, K/331st, European Theater

Submitted by Jelle Thys, Interviewer - 2015, Louisville, Kentucky

Frank: MY NAME IS Frank Horvath, and I was born on April 2, 1922.

Jelle: How did you get into the army?

Frank: I wanted to enlist in the U.S. Air Force, but I was rejected by the fact that I didn't pass my physical. So, within two months, I was drafted by the U.S. Government to be in the Army in October of 1942.

Jelle: When and where did you receive your basic training?

Frank: I received it from October 1942 into January of 1943. I was with the 83rd Infantry Division when they re-formed, and I was one of the original 83rd Infantry Division members. I joined the 83rd at Camp Atterbury, Indiana. My training was from October 22 and the first three months were what you could consider basic training, other than that it was advanced training.

Jelle: Which unit in the 83rd did you serve with and what was your role?

Frank: I served in Company K, 331st Infantry. I advanced from Private PFC to Corporal, to the point of Platoon Guide, which is directly under the Platoon Sergeant and Platoon Leader. My final role was a Platoon Leader in the 83rd Infantry Division with Company K.

Jelle: How do you look back on your time as a member of the 83rd?

Frank: Very favorably. I had the opportunities. The only thing is that I was denied admission to the Officer Training School because of an abundance of infantry officers at that time. When I was able to get in, I was already alerted for overseas deployment.

Jelle: Would you want to share any wartime stories or anecdotes?

Frank: We departed from New York in April of 1944 and arrived in Liverpool, England. Upon arriving in Liverpool, we went to Wales and received some mountain training for approximately one month and a half. Right before June 6th, D-Day, we were sent down to a receiving point in southern England, Plymouth. There we waited for departure for the coast of France. But it was terrible weather over the ocean and we just couldn't get off the ships on to the LST's. That took about a week and quite a few people were terribly nauseated, so things weren't looking too rosy at that time.

We came in to Isigny and advanced to Carentan, and then to Saint-Lô, Périers area. There we encountered the hedgerows of Normandy. That proved a difficult assignment because the Germans were there for four years and knew exactly what to do in the defensive position, making our task very difficult.

We advanced for maybe 100 or 200 yards and then we retreated for 100 yards, so we were just like not moving anywhere until July 26 when they began Operation Cobra. Airplanes bombarded the area in front of us. Then we went into General Patton's Third Army and went motorized, generally speaking. We went through Avranches and got to Saint-Malo where our Platoon Leader was killed. Our Platoon Sergeant advanced to another platoon, and I became Platoon Leader of the 3rd Platoon of Company K. I was assigned the position in Saint-Malo of clearing any Germans from the area of the beach to the first street adjoining the beach.

Our first obstacle was a fortification containing a cannon that was pointed out to the ocean, a very formidable fortification. We dropped hand grenades and white phosphorous bombs into their ventilator pipe, but nothing happened. I was able to speak with them and asked them to surrender. They were fearful that we would shoot them, and they didn't surrender. I don't know why. I used a bazooka man to fire two shells, but that didn't produce any results. Then I asked three men if they would join me as volunteers. I wanted to see whether we could get into the fortress entry anyway. Doing that, I went down on one of the two sets of steps of this fortification and looked inside to see what it contained. I found it was just a stone building with probably a metal door which was concealed. While I was observing all of this, a pistol fired and a bullet ricocheted and hit my leg. It came out of a little ventilator where the German was able to observe someone standing in the front area. They removed me and sent me to a French aid station, which was actually the French Red Cross. Upon arrival there, they treated my wound hastily, put me on a Jeep, and sent me to a field hospital. I stayed in the field hospital till that evening when they flew me to England.

That was the last time that I was with Company K, 331st Infantry.

Jelle: What happened then?

Frank: I flew to England, and I ended up in a station hospital in Ipswich, about 60 miles north of London. It was in the direct flight path of the V1 and V2 bombs, which we heard constantly coming over the hospital area. They determined that the bullet wound hit my thighbone but did not fracture it. The result of the ricochet was that the speed was reduced so much that it hit my leg right by the bone. They had a difficult time deciding how to operate to get it out. After about five weeks they finally decided to operate from the posterior section of the leg. They removed the fragment and gave it to me; I have that as a souvenir.

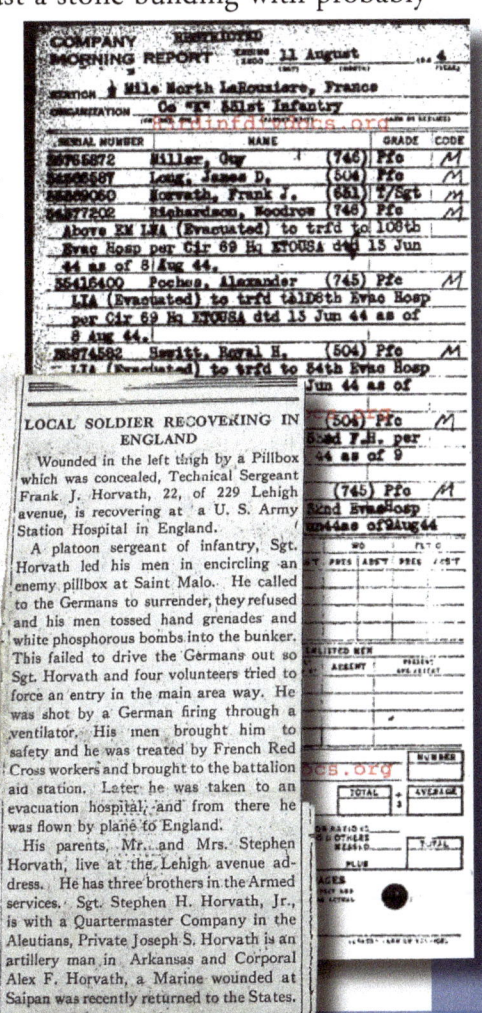

Then they determined I would have to lie on my stomach for ten days to two weeks and take nourishment that way. I had a recuperation period with crutches and canes until December 9, when I was released from the hospital. I was put on limited service and scheduled to be flown back to the United States. However, they found out I had my training as Platoon Leader and a knowledge of tactics, so they decided to send me to what they called the 5th Retraining Regiment in Compiègne, France.

It was a detachment of the 16th Reinforcement Depot. At that training center, I became Sergeant Major of that regiment. There they retrained survivors of the Battle of the Bulge. I was there from January until the beginning of June.

The 5th Retraining Regiment was headquartered in a chateau in Compiègne which was the place where the signing of the World War I declaration took place. Compiègne is close to the border of Belgium and the Battle of the Bulge was at the Belgian border. All the officers that were retrained in Compiègne in the 5th Training Regiment were a two-hour drive from their new assignment in the Battle of the Bulge.

Jelle: So this was for the remainder of the war.

Frank: Yes. And the war ended in May 1945. In June, I was asked by my adjutant if I'd be interested in going to the Biarritz American University in Biarritz, France. I told him I would.

I went there as a First Sergeant and was in the university orchestra of Biarritz. I played with the band at the base and at some private engagements. I left Biarritz University in November 1945 by ship from Marseille and came back to the United States around December 4, 1945.

Upon being discharged, I served in the Army Reserves as a Master Sergeant for six years. After that, I went to the Pennsylvania National Guard and served for three years as a Master Sergeant.

Jelle: You were in France at VE-day. So how did you feel when the war was over?

Frank: Great!

Sept. 3, 1944

Dear Frank,

The duffle bags are up and you know what that means. They bring up a point in question. What to do with your stuff. Particularly your banjo. First I was going to send it home for you then I decided to just hold it until we heard from you on the subject. I had Joe Gagne box it up. So you tell us what to do with it. Also your duffle bag is still with it. We'll hang on to that too.

Quite a time we had after you left. Four days later I was C.O. Been that way ever since. C'est le guerre. Right now we're cooking with gas. Can't lose with you've got those duffle bags you know.

We sure miss you. Hope you are getting along okay.

As Ever
T. Anderson

Dublin Ohio
Jan. 28, 1969

Hello Horvath,

I received your address in the 83rd Thunderbolt I got a day or so ago. It sure was good to hear someones name from good old co. K. I believe you will remember me Mathena, I was with Ernest Renzetti 2nd plt. tho I dont believe he was with us when you left us,, the 8th of Aug. wasnt it in St. Malo? It was me and another kid William E Lamm that helped you back to the french hospital wasnt it? How serious were you wounded? It was your leg wasnt it? Did you get back to the states or were you reassigned? On the way back up Lamm was killed by a sniper. I stayed with the Co. untill Jan. 10, then I got wounded in the battle of the Buldge in Belgium, in the left arm not too serious. I guess we were lucky getting back home huh? I got back with the 83rd The 17th of May the war ended there was only two left of the plt. that I knew.

Why dont you write and tell me what you have been doing since I saw you? For myself I got home Nov. 45 worked on my fathers farm for two yrs. in southern part of Ohio then I mouved 100 mi. north close to Columbus Ohio farmed for my uncle 10 yrs. in 58 I started working for the city of Columbus Zoo and I am still here. We have two wonderful daughters, Linda is married and expecting in Mar. I will be grandpa ha. The other one is Kimberly and she is 15.

I have been to 6 or 7 of the 83rd reunions. This year it is in Detroit Mich. and Im going to do my best to make it,, sure hope I can see you there. I was just telling a fellow I work with a few days ago about you taking your banjo across with you.

Well I must close hoping to hear from you soon.

As ever a pal,
Wilbur Mathena

(over)

WILLIAM ALLEN, SGT

83RD INFANTRY DIVISION, D/331ST, EUROPEAN THEATER

COMPILED BY KEN MILLER ON BEHALF OF THE ALLEN FAMILY

SERGEANT WILLIAM ALLEN OF Alta, Illinois entered military service in December 1943 and served in the European Theater until his tragic death on April 19, 1945 near Tochheim, Germany. He had made it all of the way through, within weeks of the war being over, to be killed when his jeep struck a land mine. His letters home were collected by his family into a volume called *Dear Folks, Love Bill*. He had been a teacher and drama coach before the war and his letters are beautifully written and keenly descriptive. We have chosen a few excerpts to share:

Dec 12 '43 Camp Wheeler, Georgia

... Here I learned the first two rules for being a good soldier: (1) He is the best soldier who spends the most time doing the least work and (2) Never do with one man what can be done with fifty (I have since discovered that these do not always apply at Camp Wheeler, thank goodness). However, I would have awarded the accolade for that day to the bartender, who spent the entire afternoon on the stool in the latrine. There's one thing that I don't understand about the army. They issue you a good comb and then cut off all of your hair.

Dec 25 '43 Camp Wheeler, Georgia

... All of which leads me to a discussion of every infantryman's pet of pets, his constant headache, his ever ready enemy in time of leisure, the cause for many sore muscles, the cause of many extra hours of K. P. and latrine duty, the greatest weapon yet devised by the genius of man —the U. S. Army Rifle. (Type—a military secret.)

We listen to many hours of lecture on the assembly, care, cleaning, and use of it. All day long we hear the constant howl of the non-coms. "Soldier, hold that butt in! No, not yours—the rifle's!" Every waking spare minute is spent in cleaning it. We take hours to clean all the oil out, and then we immediately put more on to keep it from getting rusty. We go out in the dark and have to take it apart and put it together again with only our finger tips to guide us. We are told that it will some day save our lives. It had better—to repay us for all the misery that it causes!

July 9 '44 England

... I cornered a little English paper boy the other evening at one edge of the camp and subjected him to about an hour of questioning. He was fifteen-years-old and worked as a "clark" in a local grocery. For those who suffer from rationing in America, he informed me that at his store the citizen got, for their ration coupons, one egg per week, two slices of bacon, two ounces of sweets, two ounces of butter or fats, a family of four is allowed one and one-half pints of milk per day. I asked him about gasoline rationing and he looked puzzled for a moment before he replied, "You mean petrol? Why no one here drives a car unless it is engaged in essential war work." One of the men in our platoon tells about giving one of the lads one of our oranges the other day, and the chap ate it peeling and all.

August 6, '44 France

... I'm convinced that Americans never need worry about the appreciation of the French people for what is being done for them. I've been flower bedecked and kissed by enough teary-eyed civilians to repay me for all that I've gone through to bring me this far. I might be just sentimental enough to believe that what I'm helping to do now is by far the most useful thing that I ever hope to accomplish.

It's a thrill that no money can buy to pass down an endless line of cheering liberated people who are waving French and American flags, throw flowers at you, throw their arms around you and kiss you, shove an endless supply of cognac and wine (which must have been buried deep these past few years) at you, shake your hands off and shout "Vive l'Amerique!" (long live America!) which makes you feel so good that even the blisters on your feet and the memory of recent experiences almost vanish.

August 22 '44 France

... We've come to the conclusion that in at least one instance, fiction is fact. French girls are beautiful. Such figures! Such complexions! Such smiles! Right now there is a swarm of about a dozen little children around us. Already they have practically all our noon rations.

Sept 12, '44 France

... I didn't plan to say anything about it, but I've been told unofficially that I've been recommended for a Bronze Star Medal. It probably won't get through the necessary channels to the actual awarding, and I really don't care. However, it may give you a certain amount of satisfaction to know that my leaders recognized the fact that when there was a certain job to do Little Billy was on hand and able to master the situation. Also it's for helping to save lives and not for destroying them, and that's so much to the better.

Sept 27, '44 France

... A good G. I. can sleep anywhere and in any position. I honestly believe that I could lie down in the middle of Main St. in Peoria and sleep during the busiest part of the day. So we, soaking wet and in the midst of a strong winter gale, proceeded to pile on top of each other in an open truck—headed toward we knew not what—and go to sleep.

October 16, '44 France

... I received a V Mail from Lee last week and took the air mail envelope and stationery in your last letter and hurried off an answer. As to that crack about the Infantry Badge, which no Marine could possibly earn, and the three box tops from "K" rations, you can write and tell him that it took just one. That was all I had as I had been living on raw potatoes and carrots and green apples the previous week. And beside that, in order to earn it, I had to personally eliminate an entire company of Germans one morning before I breakfasted on the one "K" ration. You'd have read about this deed in the papers, but it seems that all the reporters and photographers are sunning themselves on some island with the Marines where they know they'll be safe. Also, I informed him that the front line fighting men of Company "D" consider battalion headquarters, and organization his address tells me he is a part of, as belonging to the rear lines.

October '44 Luxembourg

... The Luxembourgers were not quite so enthusiastic when we arrived as were the French. Some attributed their coolness to the German heritage of the country. I'd like to think that the lack of demonstrativeness is due to a difference in the temperament of the people.

There's no doubt in my mind that liberation was welcome. The story Anni told me this afternoon is typical. When the Germans arrived, they completely possessed all resources of the country; when they left, they took everything which they could get their hands on. This family lost a new radio, an automobile (all automobiles in France were apparently confiscated for the retreat. Hundreds of them are still bullet-ridden along the roads—thanks to our airforce), all liquor supplies, and some cows.

I asked if money was given for what was taken. She told me, "No," but that the soldiers gave them a piece of paper listing the articles. That was the Germans' way of making the transaction legal. An official document stating, "We have stolen the following articles from this family: "Yes, everything's on the up-and-up, and Der Fuhrer's law has been obeyed to the letter."

October 24, '44 Luxembourg

... In my opinion, General Bradley is the military brains in this theatre. We were with his army in Normandy, where I believe the hardest fighting until now took place. I believe that the big push through France was overplayed in the press. You probably read in the papers where our division took the 20,000 prisoners in one operation. That was much easier than taking just a few in other places.

December 17, '44 Germany

... Someday when I reread this letter I may like to recall that I wrote it on the edge of a freezing, water filled bomb crater in the middle of a sugar beet patch where I dug my way out of one unpleasant day when it was then "No-man's land," and our crew was escaping the fire of enemy machine guns three hundred yards away. Now for three days, I've lived in this hole and am fixing it up like a home. The enemy—well, they've been taken care of, too. It was cold the first night, but now we have our blankets and sleep as comfortable as bugs in a rug; or should I say "foxes in a hole."

December 26, '44 Germany

... I'm seeing my first German civilians today as the people of this town walk by this building and silently stare at us. You probably know that there's a $65 fine for our speaking to them. I couldn't help contrasting the move which we have just made to the victory marches we made through France last summer. The flowers, wine, fruit, hospitality and kisses are noticeably lacking.

December 30, '44 Belgium

... I've never appreciated hospitality quite so much as some we've been getting from the Belgium people. Of course, if you're reading the newspapers, you'll understand why we're so welcome. A German news broadcast I heard recently mentioned that Belgium towns were being "liberated" but what I've seen hasn't led me to believe that they are seeking the German "liberation." ... Anyway they do little things, like the man who found us an empty house when we pulled into a village late one night and built a fire and carried water for us to wash with.

Jan 19, '45 Belgium

... This has been the closest physical contact that I've had with the enemy and more like the fighting that you read about in the history books. Someday I'll tell you all about the three Panther tanks which I could have reached out and touched and the house we fought our way into one morning at 3 A.M. only to be surrounded and cut off. German soldiers kept coming right up into the house the rest of the night. Some of them actually got in before they knew we were here. They did not get out.

March 6, '45 Germany

... We finally caught up with the civilians and a section of Germany which hadn't been completely destroyed and are enjoying a rest in the fine modern homes. The colonel ordered that our men should have the best billets available and it was up to me to help order the surprised occupants to vacate. I almost felt sorry for the innocent, sweet old ladies and men until we found a "Volksturm" arsenal in one of the back rooms and saw pictures of German soldiers every place. So out they go, not quite able to conceive that they are a conquered people and the U.S. military government is running their country.

April 9, '45 Germany

... If there has ever been any doubt in my mind as to the guilt of the German people, it has been removed as I have traveled the cluttered roads of late and witnessed the results of twentieth century slavery. There are hundreds of Poles, Russians, French, etc. In polite language they are probably referred to as "displaced nationals," but I'm, sure that our Southern slavery was just as kind to humanity. They're truly wretched specimens who have led a blank existence these past few years. Now that they're turned loose, heaven only knows what will become of them. I've seen at least one die of starvation. They can only live by looting and stealing. ... There are old women with enormous packs on their backs, old men pushing loaded bicycles; but young or old-they all look alike. It is difficult to tell whether they are sixteen or sixty by looking at them. For the most part, they just stare at us. Once in a while they smile and that smile is just as significant as all the cheers we received coming through France.

April 14, '45 Germany

... The roads have been lined recently with pitiful specimens in striped suits and today I discovered what they are: Concentration camp prisoners. Most of them are Jews, and everything we've heard about them, must be true, for there certainly isn't much of the human being left to some of them. The first ones I saw came stumbling across a field yelling "Americano" a couple of days ago. They were barefooted and fell several times before they reached us and, weeping, climbed aboard a tank and attempted to kiss the startled doughboys thereon. They looked 99% starved and were munching raw sugar beets which they had dug up in the fields. ... The English prisoners, which we have freed recently, tell wild stories about their treatment in the hands of the German army. They say that all of them would probably have starved had it not been for the Red Cross parcels which were gotten through to them.

April 16, '45 Germany

... I've really seen some beautiful and historic country lately. None of us can understand why the Germans weren't satisfied with what they had without causing misery all over the world. For the most part, we're happy about the progress we're making. But I have long since been convinced that the war here will be over only when there is an allied soldier on every foot of Germany. They apparently want us to destroy some more of their country, and believe-you-me we have the means at our disposal now for doing it. It does seem tragic, though, that a few stubborn soldiers should cause the destruction of an entire town and so many of the innocent civilians who can't help themselves.

RALPH E. WITHERS, CPL

671st Bomb Squad, U.S. Army Air Corps, European Theater

Submitted by Norma Jean Withers Harris, Daughter

THE ONLY THING MY father told me about the war was that he was on a train during the middle of the night as the train passed through Dixon, Missouri, his hometown. His folks didn't have any idea that he was so close at that point, and he had no way of letting them know. He remembers being very homesick as he gazed through the dark windows as the engine rattled down the tracks.

From his Honorable Discharge papers, I know that he entered the service on December 15, 1942, and was discharged on October 24, 1945, both times were at Jefferson Barracks, Missouri. He was awarded six Bronze Stars and a Good Conduct medal for the following campaigns; Ardennes, Rhineland, Central Europe, European Air Offensive, and Normandy.

DALTON L. CLARK, M SGT

Army Combat Engineers, U.S. Army, Pacific Theater

Submitted by Bill Harris, Son

DALTON LINDSEY CLARK WAS a career soldier, retiring after twenty years of service in the U.S. Army. His years of duty spanned World War II and the Korean War. He spent his WWII years in the Pacific Theater as a member of the Army Combat Engineers, building and maintaining landing strips and aircraft facilities on several Pacific islands. He retired in 1970, MSGT E-8.

He was born in Texas, and his military career led to his family making their home in Dixon when he transferred to Fort Leonard Wood from Camp Wolters, Texas in 1957.

JAMES W. STOKES, PVT

63rd Infantry Division, Co C, U.S. Army, Pacific Theater

Submitted by Kay Stokes Wilkinson, Daughter

THE U.S. ARMY GAVE my father the middle initial "W" as he did not have a middle name. Dad would never watch a war movie. He said if you lived it, you never wanted to see it again. He told me that one time, they sent his unit out and only he, and one other guy came back. His job was to go into caves and places to see if the enemy was there. If he came back, the rest could go in. My sisters and I are certainly glad that he made it back home!

GEORGE F. STUDOR, 1ST LT

83RD INFANTRY DIVISION, AT/329TH, EUROPEAN THEATER

Submitted by George Studor, Son

Excerpts from
One Soldier's Story - A Rembembrance by his Wife
as told by Dorothy B. Studor

THE FOLLOWING IS A composite of memories, facts, and stories derived from various letters, pamphlets, and books, among them the *History of the 329th Buckshot Infantry Regiment*, *83rd Thunderbolt Rag-Tag Circus*, and *The Thunderbolt Across Europe*.

George F. Studor received his U.S. Army 2nd Lieutenant Officer's Commission during graduation ceremonies on the Syracuse University campus, June 8, 1942. During his four years of ROTC classes, he was a member of the Pershing Rifles and Scabbard & Blade honorary societies. I remember feeling disappointed that he had to wear his army uniform instead of the traditional robe at graduation. The very next day, he reported to Fort Ontario, New York for assignment.

Now the serious business of Army training would begin at the Infantry School, Fort Benning, Georgia, and he joined the 28th Infantry Division already in training. The men were trained for mountain climbing in Tennessee, beach landing in Florida, and other specialties. We were married December 1, 1942, in Syracuse while he had a week's pass from Camp Polk, Louisiana. I returned to my graduate studies in Detroit at The Merrill-Palmer School, part of Wayne University, while he continued maneuvers with the 28th. The following June, I joined him at Camp Pickett, Virginia for their final preparation for the overseas duty. During his last medical exam, the doctor told him he couldn't "ship out" with his unit, as he had to have a double hernia operation at Walter Reed Hospital in Washington, D.C. He was really upset (I wasn't) to be leaving his "boys."

After a fairly long hospital stay and medical leave, George's next assignment was to Camp Croft, South Carolina for reassignment. New Year's Day, 1944, found us on our way to Camp Breckinridge, Kentucky to join the already trained 83rd Infantry Division. He was a replacement officer assigned to lead the three Squads (about 15 men in each) of the 2nd Platoon, Anti-Tank Company, 329th Infantry Regiment. Suddenly, and unannounced, on March 24, 1944, the division left by train for Camp Shanks, New York. The 83rd embarked on April 6th on the English converted liner *HMS Samaria*, carrying over 5,000 troops. This ship was one of many constituting the largest convoy ever to cross the Atlantic. After twelve long days, the northern coast of Ireland appeared, and the ship docked at Liverpool, England. More training was in store for the men in the cold, wet mountains of Wales. At this time, the 83rd was transferred from the Third Army (under General George Patton) to the First Army (under General Omar Bradley) and settled at a temporary base near Chester, England.

Thunderbolt Across Europe relates that the 83rd left England, June 19, 1944 at the "sausage area" outside Plymouth and Falmouth. What was to have been a short crossing turned into a miserable four days. A strong sea storm appeared out of nowhere and made landing impossible. Their ships tossed and turned on the rough and choppy English Channel, along with thousands of other "Liberty" ships waiting to unload men and equipment. Nearly all aboard became seasick until the 23rd of June, "D-Day +17," when the sea became calm enough to land their Landing Ship Tanks (LST's). None of the men had any real knowledge of what lay ahead for them in battle. Omaha Beach was littered; gunfire was constantly heard amid the sounds of a "Jerry" always overhead firing down on one ship or another. On June 28, they left the assembly area and marched through the recently taken town of Carentan to relieve the 502nd Parachute Regiment of the 101st Airborne Division in the vicinity of Auvers.

The 4th of July was a day the Thunderbolts would never forget. They launched their first attack between Carentan, Sainteny, and Périers. Normandy was a land of hedgerows and swamps. Every farmer's field was hedged or walled-in and heavily mined by the German occupation troops. The Allies could only gain one or two hedged-in fields a day and only after hard and close-in fighting. One mined field taken was only followed by another hedged-in one. Many were killed here in the tough countryside. From July 4 to 13, casualties mounted, as the enemy had every field zeroed in with accurate artillery and mortar fire. Finally, on July 25, the great break-through came, and the Battle of Normandy was ended.

For the next three months, the 83rd Division traveled north and east moving further into the European countryside until they arrived near Sy, Belgium. George told me he found a fairly large stone home here and decided this would be a good place for his platoon to bivouac. The woman who came to the door, Madame de Hepc'ee, after four years of occupation by the German invaders, was very happy to see the liberating American soldiers. It had been a real reign of terror and she was glad to welcome them. He told her he needed a place for his men to stay out of the cold and that they would protect her and her young family of four boys and a girl. Her husband, an official of a large industry in Liège, Belgium, had sent his family

Dotty + George Ft. Ontario
July 1-12 1942

to the country to be safe from the bombings. In fact, their home had been nearly destroyed. They had been under German control and living off the land. Despite the fact they were not poor, there was very little food or clothing to buy. He assured her the men would leave them alone and that they could live upstairs and the men downstairs. They would give the family any leftover rations as well as the embers from their cooking fires, for which they were very grateful.

Madame de Hepc'ee, Mona, was a well-educated, tall, and stately woman, and she and George became friends. The young boys and the soldiers became friends. That friendship developed over the years by mail and we kept in contact with pictures, gifts, etc. Madame de Hepc'ee was an English teacher and had some children's books published, which she sent to us. She was also a weaver and made two wool jumpers for our little girls. When we wrote to her about our planned trip to Europe on "D-Day + 40 years," she insisted we stay a few extra days and visit them in Liège, which we did. By then, she was a widow, but we visited each of her boy's families all in the countryside near Liège. There were many stories the boys remembered about the American soldiers staying in their country home.

On December 23, the 329th moved near Aachen to be part of the Ninth Army on reserve, and on Christmas Day they enjoyed a turkey dinner. Later that day, their pleasant, but short stay around Aachen ended as they were moved sixty-five miles, crossing into Belgium to the First Army's sector by the next morning. They knew the move had something to do with containing the German push into Allied lines, known as the Ardennes Battle or the "Battle of the Bulge." By now, winter had surely set-in with cold, snow, fog and icy roads. There was heavy fighting, the toughest since Normandy, with many casualties and numerous frozen feet in the sub-zero temperatures. There was incessant fire from enemy tanks, but finally, the 329th liberated the towns of Petite Langelier and Langelier. Not much sleep could occur in wet, snowy foxholes, which incidentally were hard to dig in the frozen ground.

From the Rhineland, the 329th moved quickly, dashing 280 miles in thirteen days to cross the Elbe River. The 83rd was dubbed the "Rag-Tag Circus" by correspondents. General Robert C. Macon had issued orders to supplement the division's transport with anything that moved. They threw away the books and improvised, hurriedly repainting left-behind German tanks, trucks, cars, jeeps, motorbikes, buses and two fire engines. Out in front, with infantrymen hanging all over it, was one of the fire trucks. On its rear bumper was a large flapping banner which read *Next Stop, Berlin*. General Bradley said, "Advance on order to the east and exploit any opportunity for seizing a bridgehead over the Elbe and be prepared to continue the advance on Berlin, or to the Northeast."

As the units advanced, and captured town after town, Germans were surrendering to the Allied Forces, as they would do anything to avoid capture by the Russians coming from the East. Many times, a Mayor of one town would be *influenced* to phone ahead to the next town to advise. The Mayor there said that, "If he wanted the town to remain standing, he better surrender now. Put white sheets in the windows, or else." He would *pour it on*, telling his neighbor that the Americans had hundreds of tanks and thousands of troops. The ruse usually worked.

George received a second Bronze Star (below) in the capture of Barbie on April 12. On April 13, spearhead units of the 83rd crossed the Elbe River at Barbie. Colonel "Buckshot" Crabhill even helped push the assault boats across. "Don't waste this opportunity," he yelled at a boatload, "You're on your way to Berlin. Don't wait to organize! Don't wait for someone to tell you what to do! Go over there in any shape you can!" Within a day, the engineers had finished a pontoon bridge across the Elbe and even put up a sign calling it the "Truman Bridge–Gateway to Berlin over the Elbe." This was done in honor of the new U.S. President, who succeeded after Franklin Roosevelt's death on April 12.

I remember George showing me part of a white flag, the only one he ever used, which was attached to his lead jeep when his job was to take a column of soldiers and trucks about 25 miles behind the Russian area to liberate a German prisoner of war camp. He met columns of Russian soldiers heading west and was amazed to see many Russian women drivers. The camp was not a pleasant site, as it was also a slave-labor camp. Many have said they would remember the beauty of the country as well as the horror hidden beneath.

Meantime, our daughter Ginny, who was born October 29 the year before, had become ill and was hospitalized at ten months old, weighing only eleven pounds. The Red Cross alerted the Army to have George flown home, but by the time the message was received, he was already homeward bound. He left Marsailles, France on September 11 aboard the *SS Admiral Copps* troopship, and landed September 20 at Hampton Roads, Virginia. It was with very mixed emotions that I met him two days later in New York City after eighteen months of separation. I was so happy to see him but also sad that I had to tell him of his seriously ill baby hospitalized in Syracuse. Ginny recovered and we had six more children.

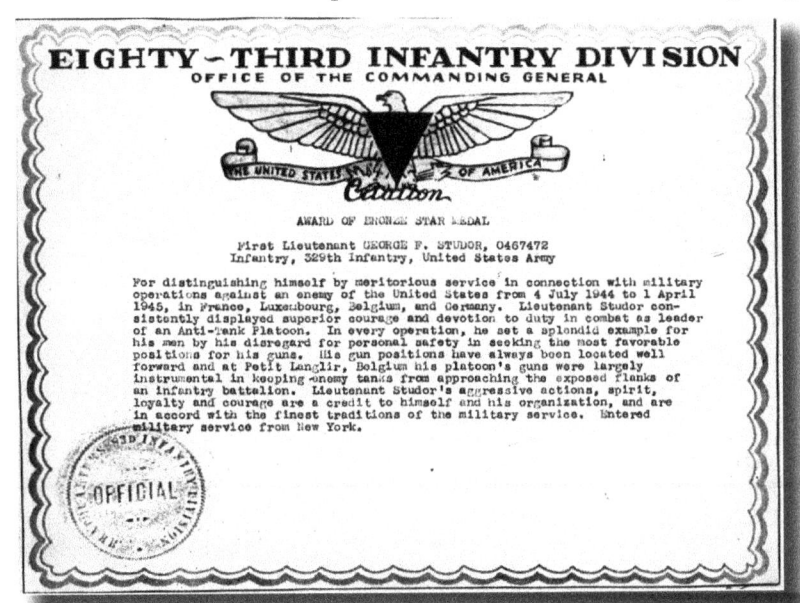

JOHN G. 'MAC' MCNAMARA, MAJ

Capt, 83rd Infantry Division, 908th FA Bn, European Theater

Submitted by Nancy McNamara Hamilton, Daughter

JOHN GILMORE MCNAMARA (MAC) was born on January 6, 1921, in Bellaire, Ohio, the son of Anna and John McNamara, of German and Irish heritage. He took a year of prep school at Braden's in New York after graduating from Bellaire High School, having earned a spot in the United States Military Academy in the class that began July 1, 1939. In 1941, Pearl Harbor was bombed, the war was declared, and the crucial need for officers precipitated an early graduation in January 1943. Mac graduated into the Field Artillery.

On December 9, 1943, Mac became the first ground member of his class to make captain. He went to England as the commanding officer of the 908th Field Artillery Battalion with the 83rd Infantry Division. He earned five battle stars on his European-African-Middle Eastern Campaign ribbon. His Bronze Star came from an incident in Germany on April 18, 1945. "In the vicinity of Steckby Forest the 1st Battalion, 331st Infantry was fiercely counter-attacked by two German infantry battalions and several tanks overrunning the main line of resistance of one of the lead companies. Captain McNamara, the Artillery Liaison Officer, moved to a position from which he could direct fire on the enemy. Although under artillery, high velocity and small arms fire he continued to direct devastating artillery fire on the enemy crushing the counter-attack. His courage and heroic devotion to duty merit the highest praise and uphold the finest traditions of the military service."

Before D-Day while in England, Mac met a redheaded nurse, 1st Lieutenant Anne McClure from New Jersey, who would soon be nursing patients in an evacuation hospital closest to the Battle of the Bulge, the 16th General. They courted throughout the war, finding time between the chaos to see each other, and eventually marry in Paris, August 7, 1945. Anne went home to her family in New Jersey at the war's end, but Mac had to stay for another year with the Army of Occupation. When he returned, his first assignment was at Fort Sill, Oklahoma. In 1951, the family moved to Bowling Green, Ohio, where Mac was assigned to the R.O.T.C. at the University there.

After the war, this U.S.M.A. class was hit by the promotion freeze, and Mac was one of those affected. Thus, six years of captains whom he ranked were pushed ahead of him to major, reserve captains being promoted in an unequal manner. He was made a major in 1951. Mac had always wanted to be a mechanical engineer, so he resigned from the military in 1954 after eleven years of service, and got his degree in that field from Toledo University, near the family home in Bowling Green, Ohio. His first job after that was in Seattle, Washington where he worked for Boeing. Next was a ten-year stint as superintendent of engineering for Olin Mathieson in Hannibal, Ohio. For ten years after that, he was safety director for all the plants of Consolidated Aluminum Company, in St. Louis. In 1978, he was project engineer for the same company, living in Shadyside, Ohio.

He became ill suddenly, and unexpectedly died within a short time on January 18, 1981, at the young age of 60 years. He is buried in Mount Calvary Cemetery, Bellaire, Ohio. He is survived by his daughter Ann (Nancy) Hamilton of Houston, Texas, husband Ted, granddaughter Katie Koy and her husband Lance; his son John McNamara of Washington Pennsylvania, wife Adele; and daughter-in-law Mary McNamara, grandchildren Molly, John and Joseph McNamara. His wife Anne died 1995; his younger son Michael, died in 2004.

ANNE R. MCCLURE MCNAMARA, 1ST LT

NURSE, 16TH GENERAL HOSPITAL, EUROPEAN THEATER

Submitted by Nancy McNamara Hamilton, Daughter

Journal:
WWII Memories of Anne Rita McClure, 1st Lt.
History of WWII Events
(Reprinted as written with permission)

Feb. 1, 1943 - Reported to Fort Dupont, Delaware. Helen Rydeski entered the A.N.C. (Army Nurse Corp) with me.

Feb. 2, 1943 - Only 12 nurses there. We were treated like queens. Met Jane Young, Ruth Cray, Margaret O'Malley & Esther Kinney. Kinney was chief nurse and a nice lady. Some of the male officers: Dr. Delta Penna, Col. Compton, Major Vogel - all are doctors.

Aug. 3, 1943 - Helen & I transferred to Fort Devens, Mass. New Stanton Hospital. We are assigned to 16 General Hospital.

Aug. 23, 1943 - moved to quarters 22. Helen is my roommate. She's on night duty and in a bad mood. Met Darcie, Mitch, Shep, Audy - we and 15 others went on duty at Lovell Hosp. I loved it there. We had lots of dates. I worked the Officers Ward. Got to know Mitch, Audy and Shep quite well - nice kids. Went to the Officers Club to a dance - 100 men to 1 lady.

Dec, 1943 - First Xmas away from home. I called and everyone cried on both ends. We got all our uniforms. Mine fits very well.

Boston, Dec. 29, 1943 - Left Devens for the boat. It was an adventure and I wasn't afraid-thought I would be.

Jan. 1, 1944. Pulled out next day & allowed on deck to wave bye bye to Boston. After the 1st night we were not allowed on deck so didn't see the moon for 4 nights. We met some officers and played cards until 2 a.m. Mitch met Pete Andre. Elaine tied up with Sammy somebody. We even got sandwiches from the cooks. One morning we saw Ireland. All I could see was two big rocks but people kept telling me to look.

Jan. 8, 1944 - Next day we landed in Liverpool England. We like the way English talk. Gave kids oranges and candy. England looks dirty & wet. They would yell, "Hey Ginger" to me.

Jan., 1944 - We went to Oulton Park - a camp place and crummy. There were 38 in a hut with 3 pot stoves. Elaine kept us awake being comical and I froze. The latrines were outside with no doors - water on the floor & wet toilet paper. I caught a slight cold on the boat and it became worse in this dump. We had a fireplace in this place. Mitch and I goldbricked every chance while the others went out to drill. A real cute Sgt. is our drill instructor. We stayed here 5 days. I still have bad cold.

Jan., 1944 - Overton - now at 304th Station Hosp. There are 25 girls to a ward. All my friends except Shep are with me - It's paradise compared to Oulton. Everyone nice to us. Lots of bicycles here so Mitch and I borrowed two bikes from a couple of Sgts. Went for a chest X-ray. Put in Hosp. 304th, think I have pneumonia. Slept well 1st time since we got off the boat. There's a lot of sick people here with me, from the 16th. Helen & others went to a dance. Had fun. 3rd hospital day - We had inspection & then to patients mess.

Jan., 1944 - Heard today our convoy (we traveled from US in huge convoy) did have some enemy action & we didn't know it. We were issued a ribbon for being in action.

Jan., 1944 - One week in hosp. Had my chest stropped, feel 100% better now. Jean & Loubre ordered bikes for Helen & I. She can't ride. I'll teach her.

Jan. 25, 1944 - Out of hospital. Nurses were wonderful. Back with my group. We have to mop floors & clean latrines.

Jan. 28, 1944 - went to work on V.D. ward with Maluso? We had nothing to do. Even the 304th nurses have little to do. This type of nursing is strictly giving meds.

Jan. 29, 1944 - Hung around with Marie Maluso and Lee Batrato (both NJ).

Jan. 30, 1944 - went to air force dance - met a NJ Lt. Frank Blain. They have beautiful club. Most of the guys are youngsters.

Jan. 31, 1944 - USO show - very good. I get goose bumps when Star Spangled Banner is played. Had letters from brother Bill today.

Feb. 1, 1944 - Saw movie "Amelia Earhart, Flight for Freedom".

Feb. 2, 1944 - Bikes came today. Been doing lots of riding.

Feb. 4, 1944 - Darcy angry with us - we forgot to get her for supper. I'll get her to go bike riding with me. To leave the 304th grounds, we have to be in Class A uniform. Try wearing a skirt and riding a bike.

Feb. 5, 1944 - Mitch, Audy, Shep, Darcy and I went to Wrexham. The Sgt from the 304th took us. After tea we went to Winstay Arms for a drink. We got a bus back to Overton. I got fish and chips. Back to camp.

Feb. 6, 1944 - Helen and I went to a farm and got 1 doz eggs; shared them with the girls.

Feb. 7, 1944 - Went to Overton with Darcy, Mitch and Helen. Went to Canteen. Met two E.M. - Engineers. They were so glad to talk to American girls. We had trouble getting back on the bikes. - It was all downhill. I have given Rodrigues a 59 & Perm. Hope her hair doesn't fall out. Everybody is depressed today - we need to get out of here.

Feb. 9, 1944 - Mopped the ward and halls. Feel more cheerful. Had to wear gas masks for one hour. Rodrigues perm looks OK. Loubre set it. Anne Negro sat in kitchen sink and had a bath.

Feb. 10, 1944 - got letter from Esther Kinney.

Feb. 11, 1944- went to Overton to Mrs. Reeves - she fixed tea and cookies. Got letter from Dr. Art Ruccia?, an intern from St. Michaels. Mitch got bread, eggs (10) & fixed them - a real treat.

16th General Hospital Nurses arriving Liverpool, England, Jan. 1944

Went to an air force dance. Disgusted with the necking on the bus going home. Pilots. Shy American girls aren't as loving as English girls.

Feb. 13, 1944 - went to Overton on bikes. Helen, Mitch & myself. The Reeves served tea. I just love Cecil. Whole family is nice.

Feb. 14, 1944 - Valentines day and not one Valentine. Went on a hike today. Mitch played hookey. She hid behind a screen.

Feb. 15, 1944 - one year in army. Helen gave me a perm.

Feb. 16, 1944 - Planes are flying very low. We all jumped out the back window.

Feb. 18, 1944 - played softball. We won. Helen fractured a finger. She's in a stinkin' mood.

Feb. 20, 1944 - Left 304th. Moved to our own Hosp. 16th Gen. 7 in a hut. Latrines are outside & freezing. Mitch, Helen, Darcy, Audy, Shep, me and Martin share the hut. Martin is very quiet. The stove is a pain - its always out or going out.

Feb. 22, 1944 - Went to Wrexham with Elaine. She got a perm. She's a character.

Feb, 27, 1944 - Off to Manchester for the weekend. Made reservations thru Red Cross - they stuck us in a YWCA - a dump. We left and went to Midlands hotel. Went to 8a.m. mass. Church beautiful. Had lunch at R.C. & played ping pong. We caught 7:30 train & met English kids - gave us dupe on places to go.

Feb. 28, 1944 - Training started today - drill, classes

Mar. 1, 1944 - Got into argument today. Helen, Mitch & Audy won't take blackout curtain down during day. Bicycled to Overton. Met Guernsey & Cobb. Went to Ellesmere on bikes. Had tea.

Mar. 4, 1944 - Audy, Mitch, Elaine and I went to pub down road. What a dump - walked in and out. Got doz. eggs from Reeves. They are always hunting around for something - we feel let down. We have an officers club - It's OK.

Mar. 5, 1944 - Having nice time at 16th Hosp. Helen, Mitch, Shep & I rode to Bangor. 16 made trip. We visited a maternity Hosp.

Mar. 6, 1944 - Kids next door came back from London - Millie, Connie. They saw Queen Eliz. Major Cosner is back - She's O.K.

Mar. 7, 1944 - Off to London. O'Reilly sent back to U.S. She's pregnant – on account of London trip. Arrived at Red Cross 10 Charles St. at 4 p.m. We had room with all 6 of us in it. Note from Dr. Ruccia he'd pick me up at 6 for dinner. I was glad to see him. He's much thinner & nicer. We went to an Italian place - manager made a big fuss over us. Then we went to Savoy Hotel for drinks. He left me at 11 to catch a train. I met Avery at the Red Cross so Elaine & I stayed with Avery. Helen, Mitch, Audy, Shep never got in until 1 a.m. Darcy had met Oscar.

Mar. 8, 1944 - Went to see changing of guard at Buckingham Palace. We hired a guide - saw Hyde Park, Madam Toussauds, St. James Palace. Wed night - All of us went out with Paul a Lt. we met at ticket agency - also Scottie. We went to Savoy - had a great time. Other girls went to Parliament. I met Ruccia at noon. We went sight seeing. Had supper at Murabel? Hotel. Saw show "Lisbon Story" then went dancing.

Mar. 10, 1944 - Went with Mitch to see her girl friend. Out with Ruccia & more sightseeing. Mitch with Pete. Andre came with us to Landsdon for dinner.

Mar. 11, 1944 - Ruccia had breakfast with us & had to leave for camp. In p.m. Helen Mitch & I went to cathedral again. Climbed 614 steps to tower. One section of church is bombed - a mess.

Sat night – Helen, Mitch and I went to a play with some guys.

Mar. 12, 1944 - Mitch & I went to zoo. Audy & Shep went with Audy's brother & friend for several days. We went out at night with G.I.s we met at Cathedral - all of us had guys get dates so we could all go - all or none is our motto. There were 10 of us.

Mar. 13, 1944 - last day - Went to Reading with Helen, Ruccin met with a jeep & to his camp for lunch. Then we went to see Margaret Boylans cousin Mrs. Hunt. Back to the station & goodbye Dr. Ruccia. I could like him if I tried.

Mar. 14, 1944 - the Payoff, Mitch & I met 2 paratroopers - went to officers mess for supper. Left them & met 2 air force guys & Curtis, Oakes & Brad. They took us to a party at Curtis apt. Wild party. 2 more guys came in (Mac and Wink) they took us to an Embassy party. One guy got so drunk he was a fool. Wink took me home. We walked around Berkely Square at 4 a.m. But I got back O.K.

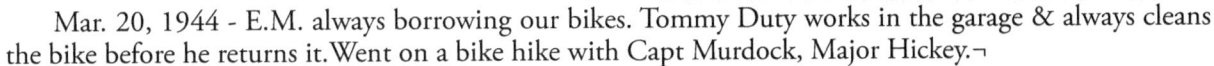

Mar. 15, 1944 - Back to camp. We heard London got bombed that night. Have a dog (sheep) named George - Mitch doesn't like him.

Mar. 16, 1944 - Col. Kubin spoke to us. Nice guy.

Mar. 20, 1944 - E.M. always borrowing our bikes. Tommy Duty works in the garage & always cleans the bike before he returns it. Went on a bike hike with Capt Murdock, Major Hickey.

Mar. 29, 1944 - Maluso & I went to clean our ward. Our ward Dr. is Capt. Morse. The ward is beginning to look good - No patients yet.

Mar. 30, 1944 - Retreat was awful. Capt. Moscato was upset with us.

Apr. 1, 1944 - Lots of pkgs today.

Apr. 3, 1944 - Tomorrow we have a dry run in the ward. I'll work with Maluso, Loubre & Dr. Morse. Fr. Barry is our chaplain - He's nice. We got to dance at Oulton Park - usually in a truck - very safe. Went as far as Whitchurch for tea.

Apr. 18, 1944 - Hospital opened. First patient Sgt Hendeson. Fr. Barrie, Capt. William, Major Sincarda all leaving for new posts. Canders, Aspero and Wheeler left the post in slacks - they caught hell.

Apr. 21, 1944 - Overton is packed with American troops. We met Chuck & Mac. Took them back with us - they wanted to borrow bikes. Mac is very nice. He's from Ohio. Elaine, me & Grace Larrabie wen to Llangotten. Larrabee left us. We met Mac & Churck & got lost. 9 Field Artillery men came to our hut. We all had dates - Shep got Mac but he likes me.

Apr. 24, 1944 - First day for my ward patients.

Apr. 30, 1944 - Have been dating Mac - nice guy. They are bivouacked out of town. Darcy has been dating Chuck. We have lots of patients.

May 3, 1944 - Mac & outfit moved 14 miles away. He comes every night, gave me his O.D. sweater.

May 7, 1944 - Nurses marched in Chester.

May 8, 1944 - Got 22 patients. Mac & Chuck came & took shower in our officers quarters. Wed - Maluso in Hosp. I've been working alone - very hard. We're opening other wards now.

May 13, 1944 - Mac & Chuck took Darcy & me to Trotting Mare Pub - 10 p.m. the lady yells "Time". Mac & Church come every night - Mac says I'm the one for him.

May 16, 1944 - Capt. Kelleher left to join a surgical team - He's a nice guy.

May 20, 1944 - We were told we are leaving our Hosp. I'll have to give George to a maid. Mac & Chuck are on maneuvers somewhere. Got a letter from Mac today. He's naming his jeep "Belle of Irvington". He hopes to come Sunday.

May 26, 1944 - Boys back from maneuvers - also Bill Smith. We all went to "Trotting Mare Inn". Mac, Chuck, Bill Smith, me, Darcy & Mitch go out a lot.

June 6, 1944 - Invasion started. Mac & I went to club

June 14, 1944 - Mac is leaving - wants to marry me.

June 17, 1944 - Battle casualties from France - I have 21 patients.

June 23, 1944 - Farewell party at club - I didn't go.

June 24, 1944 - Darcy got 2 letters from Chuck.

June 26, 1944 - 2 letters from Mac, Dr. Lt. Keleber back - He was on L.C.T. with 908th - Mac's outfit. So he's in France now.

July 9, 1944 - Ordered to pack immediately at 5 p.m. Be ready by 8 p.m. We pulled out of Renley Wales Halls at 8 p.m. Rode all night on train.

July 10, 1944 - Arrived England, Bridport

July 10, 1944 - 7:45 a.m. Billeted in big house, 7 in one Rm. All of Hut 5. We are near beach.

July 19, 1944 - Letters from Mac & Ruccia.

July 20, 1944 - still waiting to cross channel

July 23, 1944 - Went to Lady Pennsys house all day. 5 nurses, 9 E.M. Super time.

July 24, 1944 – Helen, Darcy gave me bracelet & spoon – nice, birthday tomorrow - July 25

Aug. 6, 1944 - Went to Weyhmouth & had tea. Cable from J Walsh, Ellen is born.

Aug. 10, 1944 - Col says we are hotter than hot

Aug. 11, 1944 - Left Bridport for South Hampton - living in huts - 5 hr train ride.

Aug. 13, 1944 - Crossing Channel. Left England 2:30 p.m. Slept on deck.

Aug. 14, 1944 - Saw France 7:30 a.m.

Aug. 15, 1944 - Still on boat LCJ.

Aug. 16, 1944 - Utah Beach. Arrived on beach 1:30 p.m. Went to transit area. Very cold. Left at 9:30 p.m. in trucks - all dark. Went to 25th Gen hosp 2 a.m. Slept in tents on ground.

Aug. 17, 1944 - Went to bivouac area. K rations - ugh.

Aug. 20, 1944 - Church filled, open field

Aug. 21, 1944 - Not allowed to go anywhere

Aug. 23, 1944 - living in field has its drawbacks. Bees are thick. Shep got a bite. Nice letter from Mac. We went to St. Lo-a, bombed out town.

Aug. 24, 1944 - Mitch, Johnny, two Larrabees (sisters) & me took off for Cherbourg. Saw quite a bit of France. G.I.s in jeeps gave us rides. Never got to Cherbourg.

Aug. 26. 1944 - Off to Cherbourg again. Got there 3 p.m. Went to R.C. to eat. To get back we got a ride in a weapons carrier. Gillard was furious at us - but she didn't squeal. Mitch's birthday. We celebrated.

Sep. 1, 1944 - Still here. We freeze at night.

Sep. 9, 1944 - 9 girls went to Granville. I can't go, I'm on shock team.

Sep. 19, 1944 - Softball game. We lost to Canadian girls.

Sep. 20, 1944 - I'm sick, have mono a Pt. in 25th Gen.

Sep. 27, 1944 - out of hospital

Sep. 30, 1944 - left cow pasture, going to Paris by train.

Oct. 1, 1944 - On train

Oct. 2, 1944 - Nights are bad- Arrived Paris 11 a.m. - We lined up in station in fatigues and helmets. People stared. The 16th is billeted in a chateau on a lake.

Oct. 3, 1944 - Went on detached duty at 365th station hospital in Paris – Helen, Darcy, Mitch, Audy & me. It's the American Hosp. at Neuilly. We have private rooms & tubs - we take care of American officers.

Oct. 5, 1944 - Into Paris and sightseeing. On duty, little to do. Off at 3:30 - Spend lots of time in Paris. We eat in officers mess in hosp.

Oct. 7, 1944 - Worked on WAC ward - to Paris after work.

Oct. 8, 1944 - Back to 16th. Laubu, Wheeler transferred – Helen, Darcy and I went to Engham.

Oct. 9, 1944 - Leaving for Liege Belgium

Oct. 11, 1944 - Arrived at Liege at 7 a.m. Living in a hotel. We eat with 15th Gen. Dr. Bob D'Agostini is with 15th.

Oct. 12, 1944 - Helen birthday. Nazi female collaborators were dragged into street & head shaved

Oct. 21, 1944 - Working at 15th Shock Ward

Nov. 6, 1944 - Cosner left today

Nov. 17, 1944 - 16th Gen opened a tent hospital. I have officers ward.

Nov. 18, 1944 - Ruccia came from Holland. Both areas strafed today by Germans. 2 boys killed.

Dec. 25, 1944 - We'll never forget this day. Buzz bombs and dog fights - all day. Saw several Jerry planes shot down. My patients gave me lovely gifts. We are on alert - told to get ready to leave. But we stayed.

Dec. 26, 1944 - 28th Gen Hosp hit by bomb. Couple of German P.O.W.s and one E.M. killed.

Dec. 30, 1944 - German planes strafing - killed POW, wounded 17

Jan. 1, 1945 - Air activity terrific. V-2 landed next to chateau - no one hurt.

Jan. 11, 1945 - Buzz bomb struck house across from hosp. Flattened med. supply. Uppy, Wright, Guernsey & 2 E.M. - dazed.

Feb. 6, 1945 - Assigned D-5. My old pal Thompson, my ward boy.

Feb. 8, 1945 - Mac came, stayed 2 days. I was off all day

Feb. 14, 1945 - Valentines dance, went with Mac - good time.

Feb. 15, 1945 - Mac came, I sent him to Audy's ward to sleep.

Feb. 18-20, 1945 - Mac here ever day and night.

Feb. 22, 1945 - Mac came last night. He is in Germany in the fight and takes off to see me. He's tired & dirty poor guy. Won't see him for awhile.

Feb. 25, 1945 - on night duty. We are getting Roer River casualties. Nice boys. I love nursing them.

Mar. 1, 1945 - Did see Mac a lot. He's a nice guy. Don Bymes (Intern St. Mikes) came twice.

Mar. 22, 1945- Norma came to see me - a friend from St. Michaels. Helen & Shep made 1st Lt.

Apr. 3, 1945 - got 3 days in Paris. We saw Betty, my sister, with the WACs.

Apr. 7, 1945 - Maggie our Chief nurse is leaving. I'm so glad. We got a Capt Patterson, seems O.K.

Apr. 21, 1945 - Went to Aachen. We saw Jawhawk Cemetery. 17,000 dead Americans. It is so sad.

Apr. 23, 1945 - Ruccia visited. He's a friend to all.

May 1, 1945 - Went to Cologne with some 82nd air borne, lots of sightseeing. They also did some looting.

May 7, 1945 - V-E Day - Everyone went to club.

May 9, 1945 - Official VE Day

May 24, 1945 - cruise on the Rhine.

June 10, 1945 - Letter from Mac - He got a bronze star for gallantry in action.

June 18, 1945 - Left Jupille - took 26 hrs to Chalms France. Live 18 in a room

June 21, 1945 - Night duty D4

July 1, 1945 - Betty visited. She's on her way to Berlin. She looks good.

Aug. 7, 1945 - End of War. Met Mac in Paris, got married - Happy day.

Aug. 24, 1945 - I got 1st Lt.

Sep. 7, 1945 - Brussels, 4 days with Mac

Sep. 12, 1945 - Helen & I to Switzerland 7 days. Johnny Johnson married there, Sept 20th 1945.

Sep. 21, 1945 - Back to duty. Told we are going to the U.S.

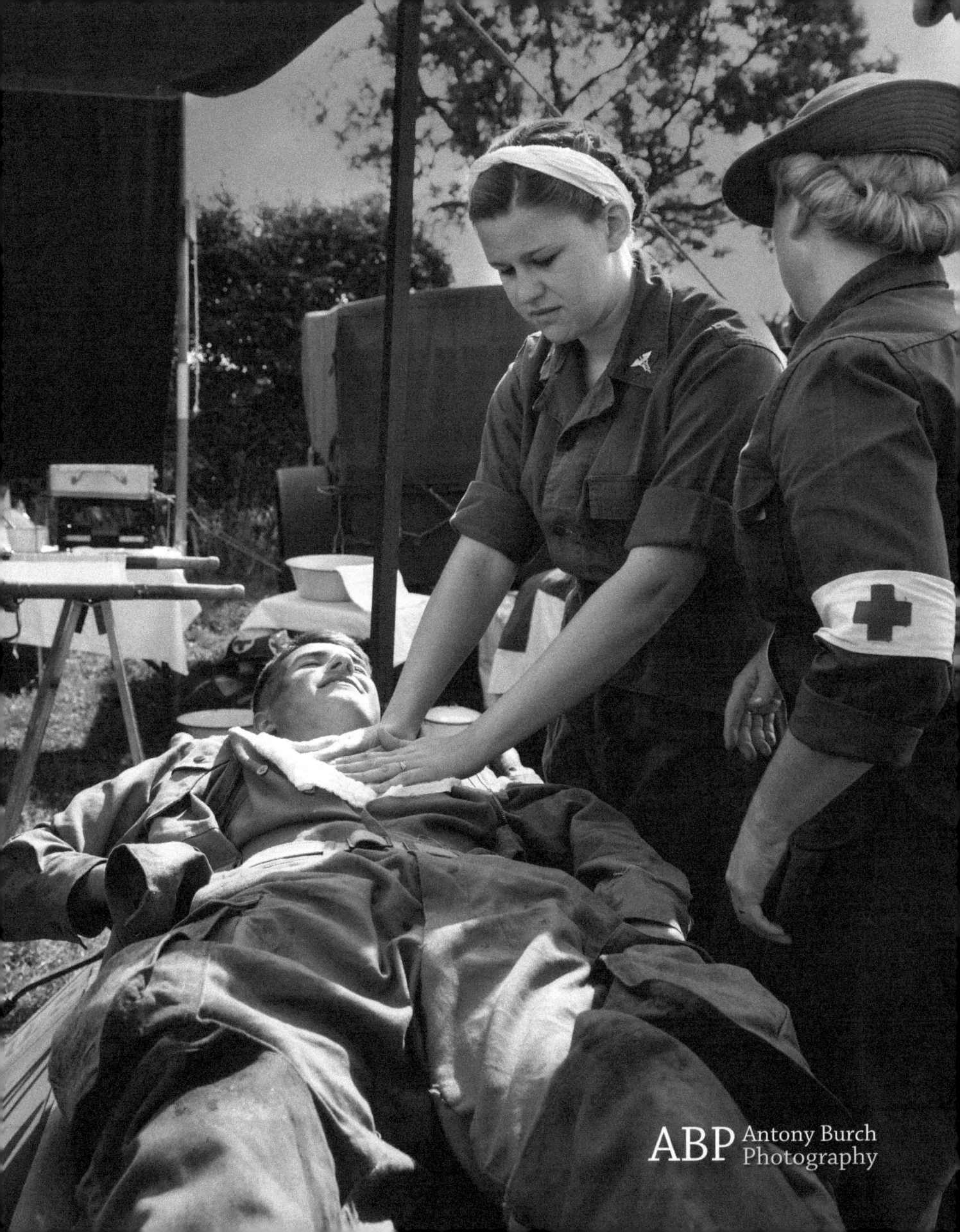

MYRON H. MILLER, S SGT

83rd Infantry Division, K/331st, European Theater

Stories Our Dad Told Us by The Miller Kids

The Cop
by Del Miller

THE WAR WAS OVER and my soldier father finds that he is now a military policeman. He had no experience as the sheriff in a land in which he didn't speak the language; land in which he had recently been the enemy.

So here he was, called out in a domestic violence complaint. It was the third time he'd been to the house and the husband was drunk and angry, and the wife was scared and injured. So my father instructed his translator to tell the man that if he ever had to come out again, he would shoot him.

There were no more calls.

Like Cows
by Del Miller

MY FATHER DID NOT go to war gladly. He was "Requested to enlist" is how he described his being drafted.

But he didn't think it was so funny at the time. Forced to kill other men while trying not to be killed himself. Living outside, "like cows" he would say with an edge to his voice, barely concealing a decades-old bitterness.

He said, "We all figured we were just pawns in a fight between powerful men." There was a long pause, then he'd cleared his throat and continued, "Then we got to the concentration camps." Another pause. "Then we kind of figured it was a good thing we were there …"

T. S. THOMASON, PFC

83rd Infantry Division, A/330th, European Theater

Submitted by The Millers for Tom Thomason, Son

PFC T.S. Thomason
83rd I.D. 330th/Co. A
Tom S. Thomason, Jr.
SWA 15th July 44
Remilly Sur Lozon

JESS F. 'JAY' DUDLEY, SGT

93rd Fighter Control Sq, Army Air Corps, European Theater

Submitted by Jayne Dudley White, Daughter

MY DAD SERVED THREE years in the Army Air Corps. Stateside, he was stationed at Fort Sill, Oklahoma; Santa Monica, California; and McDill Air Base, Florida. He then was sent overseas (England, Germany, Belgium and France) to work on B-26 planes. He spent Christmas 1944 stranded behind enemy lines during the Battle of the Bulge. This, the last major offensive campaign of WWII. It caught the Allied forces off guard and casualties were the highest for any battle during the war. To say that these young men were traumatized, would be an understatement. My Dad was awarded the Bronze Star for heroism during this battle.

When the war ended on September 2, 1945, my dad, along with all other G.I.s was told to "Go home, use the G.I. Bill to get an education, and go back to your lives." It was that easy … or not. He was sent home on the *Queen Mary*; the pre-war ship had a passenger capacity of 2,139. In an effort to return the young men, the ship's troop-carrying capacity was increased to 16,000 men. The ship was so packed that there was standing room only, with soldiers sleeping in shifts.

My dad returned to his hometown, Westville, Oklahoma, where he met Winifred, "Wee WAC," the nickname was given her because of her tiny stature, and they were married a few weeks later. Their marriage lasted 71 years until his death in August 2016. After the wedding, they immediately moved to Tahlequah, Oklahoma, where he began classes at Northeastern College in January 1946. They lived in some old army barracks that had been converted into apartments, Veterans Village. After my dad had graduated, they moved to the tiny community of Bunch, in Northeastern Oklahoma, where he became principal of Cave Springs School (grades 1 through 12).

I came along in 1949, three and a half years after the war's end. My earliest memories of my dad involve my

older brother and I playing "war" with our parents' helmets. Later, we used and abused their uniforms, boots, etc. To us, war was just a game. We had no idea of the horrors our dad had experienced so recently. One of our favorite "games" we played was to swing as high as we could, then as we jumped out of the swing we would yell, "Bombs away for Tokyo!" As children who had never known the horrors of war, our generation had no idea that tens of thousands of innocent people in Tokyo died from bombs.

I now understand why my dad would sometimes appear depressed and even sad, especially on cold, rainy days. I assume he remembered those frigid days in the Battle of the Bulge. He only told us stories of how they survived the long, cold nights by digging trenches where they slept "three deep," changing positions every hour. So, every two hours, he got to sleep in the middle. The unfortunate ones were on top and bottom. We were never told of the terror he faced. Instead, we heard about some of the other G.I.s he worked with, the places he saw and about his planes—both B26's. One was titled "The Seks Masheen" (named after the pilot, Major Sheen) and the other "The Silver Dick" (I have no idea where this one came from).

As time went by, we heard less about the war. He was busy making a living as an educator and taking care of our family. He worked twelve months a year as a school principal *and* running our 380-acre farm in Adair County, Oklahoma. He was the only principal I ever experienced. I guess I would say he was the best principal I ever had.

After retiring, my parents moved to Tulsa to be near my three siblings and their families. In retirement, they were busier than ever with helping care for their eleven grandchildren and volunteering. A highlight of their later years involved getting to travel to Washington, D.C. as part of the Oklahoma's Honor Flight Program. They loved seeing the WWII Memorial. They were so impressed that they became part of a group of organizers of this program and worked to help with every trip after that.

I am extremely proud of my parents, and almost daily I tell someone that *both* of my parents are WWII veterans. My dad actually fought the war on foreign soil, but my Mom served on the homefront. We could not have won that war without both groups.

Jess "Jay" Floyd Dudley
January 29, 1929 – August 6, 2016

'JAY' AND 'WEE WAC'
Together for 71 years

WINIFRED 'WEE WAC' DUDLEY

WOMEN'S ARMY CORPS (WAC), USA

SUBMITTED BY JAYNE DUDLEY WHITE, DAUGHTER

THE AMERICAN HOME FRONT was critical to the outcome of the war. When war broke out in Europe, my Mom's entire family left their farm and their spacious home in Westville, Oklahoma to move to Tulsa so they could all work at the Douglas Aircraft Company. They rented a small house near Douglas, and all four of them began work on building planes as their part of the war effort. The building was built without windows, so that it could operate under blackout conditions, twenty-four hours a day. While she enjoyed her work at Douglas, her "career" soon ended when the company made the decision that multiple members of a family could not work there. My mom told her Uncle James that she was now unemployed and that she needed a way to help with the war effort. Uncle James, a progressive Tulsa civic leader, responded, "Well, Freddie, they are taking women." She asked him what he meant, and he said, "They are accepting women in the military. The next day, my Mom signed up with the Women's Army Corp and within days, she was shipped out to Fort Oglethorpe, Georgia where she was nicknamed "Wee WAC" because of her small stature (4'11" - and never weighing more than 90 pounds). She also served at Love Field in Dallas; Grenier, New Hampshire; Romulus, Michigan; Goose Bay, Labrador;

Patterson Field, Ohio; Wright Field, in Dayton, Ohio; and San Antonio, Texas. She received orders to go to a base in India, but ten minutes before her flight was to leave the War officially ended. Mom's Military Occupational Specialty (MOS) was "Electrical Technician" but she also worked in Air Transport Command and as a Chaplain's Assistant. She laughed about this last assignment because she was raised Baptist but served as an assistant to a Catholic Chaplain.

While my dad actually fought the war and my mom also served, their wars could not have differed more. Mom enjoyed *every* minute of her time in the military. She went from small town farm to traveling the United States and "living with" tens of thousands of young men on military bases. When the war ended, her life once again changed drastically.

She met my dad at the end of the war, and they were married weeks later. Their first home was in Tahlequah, Oklahoma, where my dad began college on the G.I. Bill. She enjoyed their early years as part of being on a busy campus. Upon graduation, my dad took a job in tiny Bunch, Oklahoma where they would live for the next twenty years. One challenge my mom faced was the sudden isolation because they lived in the country and she did not drive. So, her life was pretty much being a wife and a mother of two little ones.

She tells me that one day after the recent move, she was standing at the kitchen sink and heard my brother and me laughing while playing on a big tree in the yard. As she was thinking how lonely she was, she watched us play, and it reminded her that children seem to find ways to enjoy life wherever they are and to thrive if given "half-a-chance." She realized that we were happy, Dad was happy, and she loved her family. She had a good husband, and she loved being a mother. At that moment, she made a commitment to God that she *would* be happy wherever He put her and find ways to help others. The next day, she got her uniforms out and began wearing them every time she could find a reason. She began working in their church and helping others in the community. Her dedication to serving others continues to this day. In fact, she still volunteers at the Tulsa Veterans Medical Center, works with the Oklahoma Honor Flight program, volunteers at her church, speaks in schools all over Tulsa on WWII, and helps anyone else who needs her.

When we were growing up, we knew our mom was in the military because we had two helmets to play with, but she never mentioned her military career. As adults, we noticed with pride how she took on the persona of a veteran. I think it would be safe to say that she has been pictured in Tulsa's newspapers more than any other veteran in Oklahoma. She and my dad served as parade marshals and were on the reviewing stand for Tulsa's Veterans Day Parade several times. At her retirement home, she is referred to as "The General." If it had been possible in the 1940's, no doubt my mom would have been a general.

BOTTISHAM AIRFIELD MUSEUM

Bottisham, Cambridge, England

Dedicated to the Brave Men and Women who Served at Bottisham During WWII

THE MISSION OF THE Bottisham Airfield Museum is to collect, restore, conserve and display items relevant to the history of Bottisham Airfield, including material relating to the Home Front in the local communities and local personalities. To promote and encourage interest in the Museum, especially among the local communities, young and old, and in relation to items or memorabilia that individuals might wish to donate to the Museum. To educate visitors to the Museum regarding the role of the airfield, the units that served there and the role the village played in the war effort.

1940 – The RAF Move In

Originally prepared in 1940 as a satellite of the Royal Air Force (RAF) Waterbeach, Bottisham was built as a grass airfield and was initially used by the Cambridge-based Tiger Moths of No.22 Elementary Flying Training School as a relief landing ground. During a two-year period beginning in July 1941, the airfield was then occupied by a succession of Royal Air Force Army Co-operation squadrons: Nos. 241, 652, 168, 654, 2 and 4 Squadrons, equipped with a variety of aircraft including Lysanders, Tomahawks, Tiger Moths, Austers and Allison-engine Mustangs. In October 1941, Bottisham's grass runways were reinforced with Army Track surfaces, but as these proved insubstantial, they were replaced by steel mesh Summerfeld Track the following summer.

1943 – The Americans Arrive

However, during the summer of 1943, the Air Ministry Works Directorate began work on enlarging and improving the facilities at Bottisham in preparation for the arrival of new tenants: the 361st Fighter Group, United States Eighth Air Force, comprising the 374th, 375th and 376th Fighter Squadrons, plus seven support units. Having arrived in the UK aboard the HMS Queen Elizabeth, the Group, Commanded by L/Col. Thomas J.J. Christian, Jr., was established in December 1943 as the last 8th Air Force fighter group to be equipped with the P-47 Thunderbolt and was tasked with providing escort to the Eighth's daylight bombing offensive as well as conducting ground attack missions. On 3 January 1944, RAF Bottisham was officially handed over to the Americans and the base was renamed Army Air Force Station F-374. On the 21st, the Group flew its first combat mission and, a few days later, the main runway was widened using Pierced Steel Planking (PSP) to allow for formation take-offs.

During the first four months of 1944, the 361st gave a good account of itself against the Luftwaffe, despite the range limitations of the P-47 but, in May of that year, converted to the long-range P-51 Mustang. Successes continued during the summer, but not without losses which included one of the squadron commanders and the Group CO, who were both killed in action over France. In September, L/Col. Joseph J. Kruzel took command of the Group and the 376th Squadron took a heavy toll of enemy aircraft on the 27th. However, by the end of the month, the Group had moved to Little Walden in Essex and Bottisham fell silent. In total, the 361st had flown 214 missions, claiming 148 enemy aircraft destroyed in the air and 86 on the ground, for the loss of 39 pilots.

1945 – The Belgians See It Out

Not until June 1945, did Bottisham see any more flying activity. On 1 June 1945, the airfield came into use as a relief landing ground for aircraft of the RAF (Belgian) Initial Training School, then based at RAF Snailwell. On 1 October, the airfield became a full satellite of Snailwell, and by 23 November the activities of the RAF (Belgian) ITS were divided between the two airfields. Training proceeded steadily into the following year, but by 9 March, 1946, the Belgians had departed for their home country. The airfield finally closed on 1 May, 1946, and was sold for agricultural use on 1 October, 1958.

2016 - The Bottisham Airfield Museum and Restoration Project

The Bottisham Airfield Museum was opened in 2009 to commemorate the sometimes forgotten role of the airfield at Bottisham in World War II and is the only UK museum dedicated to the Royal Air Force, United States 8th Army Air Force, and Belgian Air Forces. The purchase of the site was completed in September 2014. Buildings are being renovated and restored back to their original appearance while modernizing features to store and display items safely.

BOTTISHAM
AIRFIELD MUSEUM

This information is reprinted with permission from www.bottishamairfieldmuseum.org.uk in order to educate others about the need to support this educational museum and WWII renovation project near Cambridge, England.

CHARLES E. 'CHUCK' RUDLER, PFC

83RD INFANTRY DIVISION, L/331ST, EUROPEAN THEATER

Submitted by Mark Durfee, Grandson

MY GRANDFATHER, CHARLES E. RUDLER, was first documented as Missing in Action (MIA) on the After Action Report of December 12, 1944 during the 83rd Infantry Divisions attack on Gey, Germany. Company L was moving to the north side of the town during fierce house-to-house battles. Seven men were MIA on the same report. I do not know the fate of the others, but my grandfather tells us that he was taken as a Prisoner of War (POW) that day.

Veterans Day means a lot to my grandfather, because "many people don't have any idea the price that is paid for our freedom." He shares the story about how he was treated in a German POW camp with hundreds of other prisoners on Christmas Eve of 1944. He was chosen by the guards as one of 225 prisoners to be loaded into a boxcar in eighteen below temperature to go work at a labor camp. For three days and three nights, all he had to eat was a third of a loaf of bread. They were given one five-gallon bucket for a toilet. That bucket wasn't dumped during the duration of the three-day ordeal, and Chuck explained that there wasn't a dry place for anyone to sit down.

He spent five and a half months as a prisoner, nearly starving to death while wearing the same dirty clothes without any opportunity to wash. He slept on mud floors with a little bit of straw in a barn-like structure without heat. He ended up trading his precious cameo ring given to him by his girlfriend (now wife) for two loaves of bread.

On May 3, 1945, he was marched out of the POW camp and sent to the American lines where they carefully and slowly fed the malnourished prisoners. They were deloused and finally were able to take showers and receive clean new clothes. They were soon loaded onto trucks and sent home. "You don't appreciate what freedom is until it's taken away," he says. He explains that he was glad that he served and was part of the group that helped stop the Nazis from inflicting pain and suffering on more people.

Sources provided by Mark Durfee; Erie Times-News, by Valerie Myers, and Linesville Rotary Club.

GREAT MEN AND COMMUNITY LEADERS

Special Tribute to Two WWII Veterans

Submitted by Myra Miller, Friend

CHARLES E. HAROLD

Communications, Alaska/Aleutian Islands, Army Air Corps, Pacific Theater

LUTHER A. RIDDLE, ACR

USS U.S. Grant, U.S. Navy, Pacific Theater

EVERETT 'SMITTY' SMITH

Hq, 187th Regiment, 11th A/B Division, Pacific Theater

Submitted by GP Cox, Son

Blog:
Pacific Paratrooper
"Jungle Juice" – Letter X
https://pacificparatrooper.wordpress.com
(Reprinted as written with permission)

IN DOBODURA, NEW GUINEA, the 457th began to notice severe shortages in their sugar supply. As it turned out, there was a major boot-legging operation in progress. With the absence of alcohol, the men felt necessity would be the mother of invention, but they were caught with their stills in production. The makeshift liquor companies were immediately put out of business.

My father had other ideas. The following letter was one I never tired of reading; it always gives me a chuckle or two. My father's ingenuity was unfailing. He used to tell me, "If you think hard enough, there's a solution to every problem." After years of having tended bar, this was going to be right up Smitty's alley.

Letter X   *"Jungle Juice"*   *Monday 7/17/44*

Dear Mom, The title of this letter, at first glance, will no doubt puzzle you, but I suspect at the end you will know more than you do now. Before going any farther with this, allow me to explain the whys and wherefores of its origin and purpose.

The Army has been telling us, for some time now, that any day (they mean year), they are going to issue us hot, dry soldiers some beer. They haven't told us the percentages yet, but never fear, it will be 3.2. In the meantime, we're here in New Guinea patiently awaiting the day. We know, because our eyes and nostrils do not lie, that there is good whiskey slyly floating about. Try as we may to lay hold of some, as yet, none have succeeded.

There is an old saying, told to me by a much older and wiser veteran of this man's army that goes: "Take something away from a soldier and he will, in time, make or find a better substitute." Hence and forever after – Jungle Juice.

To begin the making of this liquor substitute, one must first overcome a few minor details in order to secure the necessary equipment and ingredients. First: You may try to cultivate the friendship of the mess sergeant. This is easily accomplished if one is well endowed with currency. Second: You may try getting on guard duty and taking a chance of getting the job of protecting the mess hall. (The odds against this working out is ten to one against you.) This is the hard way of acquiring the friendship of the mess sergeant and we will continue. With your new buddy's help, you now have in your proud and cherished possession a quantity of raisins, dried prunes or apricots and some sugar. (Very rarely will one come up with any yeast, so we will forget it.)

Now, we need something to put all this stuff into. To make matters worse, it cannot be metal and it must be waterproof. A nail barrel will do the trick, if we soak it in water, thereby allowing the wood to swell. You could go to the supply sergeant and get a saw, hammer, nails and boards, but in taking this route, you risk your supplier discovering your idea and you will have to pay him off with the promise that, when finished, he will receive a share. Not only is this undesirable, but now you will have to sit out in the hot sun and build a cask. My first suggestion of a nail barrel will not only save you labor, but also add an extra drink of this wonderful alcoholic beverage.

Now, we are ready to begin. Into the empty cask, put your fruit and sugar, making certain to add water. With your hands, (clean ones are advisable) stir everything around while crushing some of the fruit with your fists. This is what's called the "rapid juice extraction process." When finished, cover the cask with a clean piece of linen long enough to drape over the side. Here, you can also use a G.I. handkerchief or undershirt. (This is just a sanitary precaution and it in no way affects the product.)

Now, dig yourself a hole (under your bunk preferably) large enough to receive the cask and conceal it. This is a necessary precaution as the manufacture of Jungle Juice is frowned upon by the Army and especially you C.O. or Inspection Officer. The finding of such might cause embarrassment. This way it will only be found if someone should trip you C.O. and he inadvertently falls face down on the spot.

All you have to do at this point is use some self-control and patiently wait out the next two or three weeks as the fruit, sugar and water do their stuff. We all know from experience that you will only sit out two weeks, so let's get on with the last step. Surely you have kept busy locating empty bottles and cleaning them, so dig up the cask.

To accomplish the final phase, it is wise to get your mattress cover and put it over a clean, steel helmet. You will find that the Army had supplied you with a damn good filter. The whole parts stay on top and the liquid freely pours through, without blemish to the helmet. Pour the juice into the bottles and seal with candle wax, making them air tight. Here is the most difficult step because by this time, not only your curiosity, but your craving for a taste is so high — you're almost completely out of control. But, you must put your contraband away for one more week.

As the expected day approaches, I want to warn you to be on the lookout for newly acquired friends who start calling on you, regardless of the fact that they never came near you before. Yes, you are suddenly becoming the most popular guy in camp. When the hour approaches, marked as the time of reckoning, I would advise you to make up your mind that you are not going to finish it all in one sitting. Actually, this precaution is really unnecessary, as the Jungle Juice will decide that for you.

I won't describe the taste. For some it is bitter and others say sweet. No two batches are alike and in fact the Juice has no opposition. Even its most adamant foes agree that for variety, the Juice has no equal.

This recipe is given free of charge.

I hope to hear your hiccupping in your next letter soon. Your brewmeister son & never to be dry again,

Everett

General Swing decided, after the stills were destroyed, to bring ice cream machines and set up sports competitions. Teams were made up for volleyball, softball and tackle football. This proved not only to lift their spirits, but the activities kept them in top physical shape.

It always amazed me that such a letter as "Jungle Juice" made it through the censors without Smitty ever getting into trouble. His little operation was never discovered.

MYRON H. MILLER, S SGT

83rd Infantry Division, K/331st, European Theater

Stories Our Dad Told Us by The Miller Kids

The Candy Bar Incident
by Del Miller

HE WAS SO HUNGRY. After a day and night in the swamps of western Louisiana, chasing the enemy through briar patches and endless woods; they were all starving.

In their packs were D-Rations, a chunk of oatmeal and chocolate powder with the consistency of cured concrete and a flavor slightly tastier than a boiled potato. The D-Ration was conceived to be an emergency ration, and the army didn't want soldiers eating their emergency meal except under dire circumstances. Hence the D-ration–filling, energy rich, and as appetizing as a 2 x 4.

But the situation had been getting pretty dire, and a D-Ration was beginning to sound like haute cuisine. Indeed, they would have been gnawing on their chocolate-like bars had they not received very specific orders not to touch their D-Rations until commanded to do so. So it was not a surprise when they were back at camp to be lined up and ordered to show their uneaten rations. But to his horror, his ration was missing. *Gone.* Someone had taken his candy bar.

There was no chance to plead innocence. No opportunity to point fingers, and absolutely no chance for appeal when he was busted to buck private and booted unceremoniously to another unit already packing for war. My father felt humiliated and treated so unfairly. Someone else had broken the rules, but he would pay the price.

So off to war he went.

But he told me, that later on after the war, he found out that his original outfit had later arrived in the theater and had walked into a terrible massacre.

So maybe his trouble with the chocolate bar was not such a bad thing.

HENRY I. TANNENBAUM, PVT

83rd Infantry Division, F/331st, European Theater

Written by Del Miller as told by Sam Tannenbaum, Son

THE STORIES IN THIS book are mostly ones that our veterans told after they came back to us from the war. Here, we celebrate what they did and who they were, and these stories bring back our memories of them. We can see their faces and hear their voices from long ago and we are family once again.

But there are those who have no stories to tell. Some were but babies when the telegram came, and their mothers cried. Some were too young to remember their father's face and too young to understand that he would never come home. Their mothers' grieved, and then they moved on, leaving behind the pain, and with it, the stories of this man in uniform.

And, as the children grew, they began to wonder who this man was, their father. But their mothers, for oh, so many reasons, had little to say. Perhaps there were no portraits on the mantle, no medals in a frame. A few old photographs might be the only clues to whom this man really was. Her relatives didn't speak of him; the new family friends never knew him. Instead of a father, all this child had was a name and a hollow feeling where their father's love should be.

Private Henry Tannenbaum went to war, leaving behind a wife and a little boy named Sam. He never came back, for he died face down in the snow in a Belgian field. The news broke his wife's heart and her mind, and she was never well again. Sam had never known his father, and now he had lost his mother, too.

So, Sam grew up strong and independent, knowing nearly nothing of his father. As he grew older, he began to feel that tug on the heart that we feel when we need to connect to family. He began to search for his father to understand who this man was. But all he had was his father's name and a thousand questions: How tall was he? What did he read? Was his voice soft or was it gruff? Did he like sports? Did he sing?

Then Sam helped found the American World War II Orphans Network (AWON) and, with the support of so many people like himself, he began to find the answers. Sam discovered that his father was the youngest of three children. He was Captain of the Chess Club and was a member of the Latin, Greek and Hebrew Clubs. He was an idealist and an intellectual. He graduated from Brooklyn College in 1936, where he was President of the Classical Club.

After college, Henry Tannenbaum worked at the Office of Price Administration in Washington D.C., and he taught Sunday School at a Temple. In the Army, he conducted religious services for the troops in England, and he fought in France in August 1944. He was in Luxembourg in October 1944, where he received a medal from General Robert Macon.

He was wounded during the Luxembourg Campaign. He returned to the front on December 6, 1944, and on January 11, 1945, Private Henry Irving Tannenbaum was killed in action near Ottré, Belgium. It was here that Henry's fellow soldier, Tony Vaccaro, took a heart-rending photo of Private Tannenbaum lying dead in the snow.

One can only imagine the emotions that Sam must have felt when he finally saw this image. He had sought for years to know his father and now here was a photograph of his last moment, frozen in time. It was closure of sorts, I imagine, the moment when Henry Tannenbaum finally came home. But it was heartbreaking all the same.

Fifty-eight years later, Sam visited the Belgian field where his father died, and here he saw this monument to his father.

The story of Sam Tannenbaum's courageous search for his father began in tragedy but ended in honor. As a child, Sam only knew his father as a name, but now Henry Tannenbaum is a man for all time.

For all the World War II war orphans who never knew their fathers, Sam's journey is wonderfully inspiring.

We are so proud to know this soldier's story.

GERVIS H. KESTEN, SGT

485th Bomb Group, 15th Air Force, 829th Sqdn, European Theater

Submitted by Greg Kesten, Son

Excerpts from *We Didn't Know any Different* by Gerv H. Kesten used with permission from his son, Greg Kesten.

INDUCTED INTO THE SERVICE in Iowa, Gerv Kesten received aircraft mechanics and gunnery training and was assigned to a B-24 crew. His first overseas flight was from Bangor, Maine to the Azores Islands.

. . . It was overcast and so we climbed up to the altitude over top of the clouds and so we're flying and it's nice weather but you can't see the ground, you can't see the ocean, you can't see anything. Hank, our navigator, was really good, but after a while, I thought I'd go up and see what Hank was doing. I looked up and he's not in the nose. I looked back in the back and him and the gunners were back there playing cards.

"Hank! My gosh!" I said. "You'd better check the headings and be sure. We can't even see the Azore Islands probably."

"Well, I'll be up there in just a few minutes. When we get over the Azores, if there is a hole, we'll be over them."

He went up to the nose and he called back over the intercom.

"In ten minutes, look down and you should see the Azore Islands."

We looked down a few minutes later and there was a hole. It looked like about two inches. Right in the middle of the hole, we could see the Azore Islands. We had to let down through all of the clouds and land. We were just doggone lucky we had a navigator who was that good. Hank was always good.

When we were down in the Azore Islands, we were flying B-24's, like I say, there were B-17's, too. They would land at the same place and we got to arguing back and forth about which was the best airplane. The B-24 was always faster than the B-17. The B-17 probably could go higher, because it had a different type of wing, but we could outrun them. We got to arguing about that. I think we were going from the Azores to North Africa and I'm standing up between the pilot and the co-pilot.

"Oh no!" I said. "Look at this." This B-17 climbed above us, he had one prop feathered, and he was coasting.

"See! A 17 can pass a 24 with only three engines," he called down to us.

That's what you go through when you're in the service. Things like that happen to you. You never know what these clowns are going to do.

Gerv and his crew were then stationed in Venosa, Italy.

. . . We got about twenty-six missions and we didn't have much trouble. As we were flying our missions over there, they always sent an instructor pilot along for the first few missions and they also sent an instructor engineer. We were flying on our own and it was probably our fifth or sixth mission and we had our co-pilot back and we lost an engine. It's nothing serious, we've lost a lot of engines.

The pilot called me on the intercom and said, "Okay, now we've lost another engine. We can't make it back home. We are going to go to Switzerland and bail out and we won't have to fight the war. We'll be free for the rest of the war."

I came back on the mike and I said, "There hasn't been a guy in here of ten guys that's ever hit the silk. It could kill us all when we have to bail out. There is nothing wrong with this airplane that we can't take it home. Let's take this sucker home, where we should be going."

From then on, I was boss. Whatever I said, went. We took the airplane home and there were no problems.

One time, we lost two engines and we had to lighten the ship as much as we could. We dropped the bombs and threw our guns overboard. We threw everything we could think of overboard—even parachutes, we threw overboard, which is pretty stupid. But that's war.

I transferred all the fuel from the wing tanks into the main tank so we could get all the fuel we could possibly get because we knew we would need a lot of the fuel. When you are flying on just two engines, on a four-engine airplane, you've gotta use a lot of power and that uses a lot of fuel. We're getting pretty close back to the base and I didn't want to worry the guys, but I hadn't seen any gas in the sight gauges for probably twenty or thirty minutes. In this airplane, we had two glass pipes that were in the fuselage right up in the pilot's compartment and when you filled up the airplane, those pipes filled up with gas and when you were getting low on gas, you couldn't see any in there.

We were coming in on final approach and I'm standing between the pilot and co-pilot and the guy down on the field comes on and says, "Go around. We've got an airplane cracked up on the end of the runway."

The pilot turned to me and said, "We've got to go around."

"Set down over the top of him," I said.

The pilot went and set down over the top of him. We taxied over to the hard stand. The hard stand is where you park the airplane. We went to push all four throttles forward to kill the engines and all four engines died. We're getting out and here comes the CO, the guy that told us to go around and, man, was he mad!

"I told you to go around," he barked.

Air Crew
Italy

"Just a minute, sir, just a minute," the crew chief said. "They went to kill the engines and all four engines ran out of gas. That airplane was completely out."

"Thanks for bringing the airplane back," he replied. That's as much as we got out of that one.

. . . If you didn't keep cracking the bomb bay doors as you went up, they would get moisture on them and freeze up. Then they wouldn't open. I don't know whether I should tell this or not, but I told the bombardier to keep cracking the bomb bay doors and close them back up, just barely open them and then close them back up, and that would keep them from freezing. Sometimes he would do it, but if he didn't do it, I had an emergency control underneath my deck that I could open them up. I was underneath my deck doing something, probably checking the generators or some darn thing, and I wondered why our bomb bay doors were always freezing up. Up in the front end, going up on a mission, was the nose gunner up in the nose and the navigator and bombardier, the pilot, the copilot and me. Back behind the bomb bays was another little door. In back was the tail gunner and the radio operator was up with us. The ball turret gunner was back in the back end, too. Martin, upper turret man, sometimes would stay back there instead of up where he should be.

I'm wondering why the heck our bomb bay doors were always freezing up. We'd have to drop bombs through them. I happened to look back one time and the door opened and they were going potty on my bomb bay doors! I opened them up just a little bit and it flew back in their face and that was the last time I had to worry about them going to the bathroom on the doors.

Anyway, when the bomb bay doors would freeze, we couldn't get them open and we'd go over our target and we'd just drop the bombs right through the bomb bay doors. The bomb bay doors were on tracks. They had little pulleys that ran on tracks. When you dropped the bombs through them, it broke all these pulleys off and you couldn't close them back up. They just hung straight down. Well, you couldn't land with those down because they would drag on the runway. It was my job to get a cable, which I had a little cable hoist under the flight deck, and I would lay on my stomach and try to snare those bomb bay doors, which I always did, and then pull them up. Then I'd have to walk out between the bomb racks and get a piece of wire and wire them up and then catch the next one. That was quite a job, laying on your stomach. I couldn't do it now, looking down, and you're flying around 20,000 feet or better and you look down and all you can see is ground. This happened a lot of times. That was one thing that was bad about B-24's.

. . . I have to tell you a little about Capanzzi, the man who was the ball turret operator. He was so afraid to be down in the ball turret because he thought, "If something happens, how can I get out?"

"You gotta get down in there," I said.

"I'm just scared to death," he said. "Is there any way that I can do something that will look like I'm in there?"

"Yeah," I told him. "Let the ball turret down and leave the hatch open. You lay on your stomach on a flack suit so if any flack comes up, it won't blow you up. You reach down in and grab the controls and you keep moving the guns back and forth and people will think you are in the ball turret."

He never got in the ball turret after that. He just laid on his stomach with a flack suit on and a flack helmet—oh, about five flack suits laying underneath him. He was afraid he was going to get hit. That's the way he manned his ball turret, laying on his stomach in the fuselage.

. . . We finally finished our missions. We flew twenty-six, or something like that. We got double missions for flying one mission because it was so far. We had flack hit us and knock out control cables, which I had to repair as well as we could in the air, so we could land. But we never did get anything like a serious hit. We had a few holes in the wings and a few holes in the fuselage, but when we were flying through flack. If you have ever been on an old gravel road, and your tires of your car pick up the little stones and throw them up on the fender and it rattles, that's the way flack sounds on an airplane when you are just out of reach of it.

New bomb groups were coming over in new B-17's and B-24's. By the time they arrived, the war was over. So we were always very lucky. We flew a new B-24 from the States over to Italy and we got back down to Joya, Italy again and they said, "Here's a 24 that just came over. It's got a few hours on it. As quick as we can get it fixed up, you can take it home."

"What do you mean, fixed up?" I asked.

"Well, one generator doesn't work very well."

"I don't need all four generators," I said. "I can run this on three generators."

"You can't even start the engines with a generator out."

"I certainly can," I told him. "The batteries are all charged up, so it's all right. One engine will start and when that engine starts, I'll use that generator."

"Well, you have to start number three engine first and use that generator."

"That's what the book says," I told him, "but you can start any engine you want on here and then you just turn the generator on and it will charge the battery."

I got him to sign off the book and we brought the airplane home. We never did have any problems with the generator. We had three generators instead of four but I wasn't going to stay another week or two, waiting for him to fix the generator, which he probably wouldn't have done anyway.

I had always heard about icebergs. We were over the North Atlantic, coming back home in that new B-24 when I looked down and here are about four big icebergs floating down the Atlantic Ocean. On one of them was a bunch of birds. Boy, that was something, for me to see an iceberg. It was just bubbling all around it where it was trying to melt. That was really something!

We came back and I'm not sure where we landed. I think it was in Florida. Then everybody was sent home on a thirty-day furlough.

JAMES J. WHETTON, CDR

USS Montpelier (CL-57), U.S. Navy, Pacifc Theater

Submitted by Karen K. Christoffersen, Friend

During World War II, Commander James J. Whetton served on the light cruiser, *USS Montpelier*, as the General Quarters Deck Officer or two years. Jim served in the Luzon Gulf, Philippines Islands, and was witness to one of the largest sea battles in the entire war, during which the U.S. destroyed the Japanese fleet. During the battle, a Kamikaze pilot made a desperate run to crash into the cruiser, and Commander Whetton's gunnery division shot off one of the Japanese Zero's wings, avoiding a disaster. If the Kamikaze had been successful, a minimum of 500 seamen would have died. That was one of Jim's best crews, dedicated and eager to learn.

He had 20 to 25 seamen under his charge, assigned to four 40 mm guns and one 5-inch anti-aircraft gun, along with three turrets with 16-inch guns. Commander Whetton reported directly to four-star Admiral Ralph S. Riggs, who had command of the entire fleet in the very successful Luzon Gulf invasion.

Another story of note was one foggy winter when the *USS Montpelier*, a flagship, was headed for its home port in Boston. They had to travel through the bay of New York which was down to almost zero visibility. Commander Whetton could only see with radar, and the bay was full of ships. His best judgment told him to drop anchor and stay put, rather than risk impacting another ship. But his immediate superior, Captain William A. Gorry, refused. Not understanding the danger, Gorry relied on the commander to keep the ship safe, so Whetton ignored his order and dropped anchor. Captain Gorry chastised and punished Jim (confined him to his room for a week), but when Admiral Riggs heard of the circumstances, he was furious. Jim said you could hear the Admiral over the speaker system all over the ship. The Admiral told the Captain that Commander Whetton had just saved his a**.

After the war, Commander Whetton went on to serve as an active reserve, second in command of a battalion in Ogden, Utah. First in command was Commander Patrick Healy who chose Whetton as his Chief of Staff, where Jim served for four years.

After his release from active duty in the Navy, Jim went back to California where he was among the primary members of Howard Hughes' personal staff beginning in 1954. Mr. Hughes hired Jim as his Chief of Staff, and he had the opportunity to work very closely with him for many years. He co-authored the book; *We Knew Howard Hughes: A Collection of Memoirs* by James Whetton, James Leo Wadsworth and Wilbur Thain, published in 2012.

Through all the years of Jim's service, his beautiful, faithful, supportive wife, Marian Vader Whetton, cared for five children and kept the home fires burning.

To you who answered the call of your country and served in its Armed Forces to bring about the total defeat of the enemy, I extend the heartfelt thanks of a grateful Nation. As one of the Nation's finest, you undertook the most severe task one can be called upon to perform. Because you demonstrated the fortitude, resourcefulness and calm judgment necessary to carry out that task, we now look to you for leadership and example in further exalting our country in peace.

Harry Truman

THE WHITE HOUSE

SPECIAL TRIBUTE
Men Serving their Country after WWII
The Miller Family Honors Your Service

HAROLD D. PETERSON

On Behalf of The Peterson Family

ROBERT L. SOOTER

On Behalf of The Sooter Family

WALTER DICKENS
On Behalf of The Dickens Family

IRVIN "BUD" JENKINS
On Behalf of The Miller Family

FRANK E. BALLARD
On Behalf of The Miller Family

PAUL WOHNHAS
On Behalf of The Wohnhas Family

BOYD H. MILLER
On Behalf of The Miller Family

THE GATES BROTHERS — Brothers of Dolores J. Gates Miller

Myron C. Gates

Rector K. Gates

Conrad L. Gates

In the Footsteps
The Journey
by Marshall Miller

THE NUMBERS ARE STAGGERING. Of the 2.3 billion estimated world population in 1939, 70 to 85 million died. The United States put more than 16 million men and women in uniform. Nearly 700,000 of them were wounded, and more than 400,000 died. Numbers—statistics that boggle the imagination. How can they be put in perspective? How can you measure the sacrifices and dedication of the men and women who served?

That's impossible, but following Dad's footsteps through the European Theater provided an invaluable understanding of what he accomplished. S/Sgt. Myron H. Miller, a Dixon, Missouri native, and our father, was a rifleman in the 83rd Infantry Division. We started our journey only with a vague knowledge of his experiences in Europe, thanks to bits and pieces of stories and anecdotes he told over the years. Omaha Beach, the Taute River, a German town named Gey, —all were locations on a map. The goal was to fill in the blanks.

It all started when Myra, the youngest of the four travelers, watched a documentary about the war and wondered about Dad's role in that conflict. Enter the amazing world of the Internet. Before long, Myra had become friends with several European experts on the 83rd Division who suggested that she could follow her dad's footsteps. Myra was hooked. Now she just had to convince the rest of us to go along with this crazy idea.

Within days, all were on board except for the oldest sibling, Lynette Ballard, who was unable to join the rest of us because of prior commitments. She stayed virtually connected to us through Facebook and texts. Myra, Ken, Del and Marshall Miller declared all in, renting a 22-foot motorhome to tool around Europe. The biggest question: Would we survive each other?

Traveling to Europe and actually visiting the places where Dad fought seven decades ago was not anything we had ever imagined possible. When Myra first proposed this journey, we had images of visiting historical points of interest and museums and hearing educated guesses about the where's and when's of Dad's experiences. The thought was, we would be tourists with tour guides. We were not sure what to expect from them.

Boy, did we get it wrong! The reality was mind boggling. Our "tour guides", became new friends who have a deep passion for keeping alive the story of the 83rd Division and a reverence for the American soldier that stunned us. Their goal was not to just show us things but to honor our father's memory and the memories of all the men and women who liberated Europe. It proved to be a humbling and magnificent experience.

Omaha Beach

AT FIRST SIGHT, IT was just another sandy beach like so many throughout the world. But on June 6, 1944, the Normandy coast was the center of the universe. The D-Day invasion was an all-in attempt to restore world order. You catch a glimpse of Omaha Beach through the trees and your throat catches. All you can think of are the sacrifices made here 72 years before. You try to imagine the armada of ships filling the horizon, the thousands of troops coming ashore, the sounds of bullets and artillery shells—the death. It is overwhelming.

Our guide, Jean Paul Pitou met us there. As we walked down the pathway above the beach, we got our first view of the American Cemetery. We walked among the graves and saw the gravesites of many 83rd Infantry Division soldiers. Ken told us about a hometown Dixon boy, James "Ralph" Hickey, who never made it to shore at Omaha Beach on June 6. A memorial wall commemorated more than 1,500 missing soldiers, including Ralph Hickey.

Dad wasn't among the first invaders. The 83rd Infantry came ashore on June 18, nearly two weeks later. He was a replacement soldier and didn't arrive at Omaha Beach until July 17, six weeks after D-Day.

To find out more, we followed Jean Paul to a monument describing Mulberries, temporary floating piers invented by the British that were used to offload men and supplies after the initial invasion. Pointing to a spot where the Mulberry pier had been located, Jean Paul told us that Dad came ashore at Omaha Beach at this very spot. Bingo! Our first footstep!

The Hedgerows

DRIVING A SHORT DISTANCE from Omaha Beach to Sainteny, we arrived near the hamlet of Auxais where we were greeted with open arms by our hosts, Glyn and Elaine and their sons Ben and Sam. Dinner and great conversation followed until our bleary eyes couldn't take it any longer. They told us the next day was going to be busy. That was an understatement.

In the morning, we headed to the hedgerows and fields around Sainteny and Auxais for a history lesson. We were taken to the spot where the Battle for Sainteny started nearly three weeks before Dad joined his unit. We stood where the battle lines were drawn 72 years before

and made history come alive. In that field a German Panzer tank fired on advancing American troops; in that spot a machine gun nest was located; behind those hedgerows, American troops were huddled while trying to root out the Nazis.

They took us to the Chateau de Auxais, an estate which was destroyed during the Battle of the Hedgerows and today is home of Paul Cotelle. Paul gave us a brief tour and we learned the 331st Regiment (Dad's) used this area as its headquarters.

We were led down an old road, overgrown with weeds—the path Dad would have walked on his way to joining his unit. Another footstep. We then came to a field among the hedgerows, the location for K Company on July 21, 1944, the day Dad walked into camp. Footstep No. 3.

Auxais is a beautiful little village today but 72 years ago it was the center of the clash between the 83rd Infantry Division and a German unit blocking the breakout. The only way the 83rd could force its way through was a long causeway that crossed the Taute River and arrowed straight across the little valley which was flooded by the Germans. The causeway today is an asphalt road that took us from Auxais to Marchesieux, again in Dad's footsteps. To avoid horrendous casualties the Allied command developed Operation Cobra, a massive bombing campaign on the German positions from St-Lo to Periers. This opened the causeway route, and American forces were able to take Marchesieux.

We drove to a beautiful area overlooking a brilliant green valley. In July of 1944, the 2nd Battalion, 331st Regiment, placed a machine gun nest overlooking the Taute River Valley. Glyn said he had found more than 3,000 spent cartridges in the ground around this location, which offers a breathtaking view of the valley which spread out below us.

Peaceful—until the British arrived.

We where expecting British re-enactors in the Sainteny area, but didn't realize Glyn had arranged for them to meet us at this location. In full gear, riding in vintage jeeps, they brought the 83rd Infantry to life—right before our eyes. It was great fun and Skelly, a.k.a. Jon Skelson, invited Del and me to take a jeep ride. Off we drove into the French countryside, down an old sunken road which was the scene of some pretty fierce fighting in 1944. The day was exhausting. And the next day promised to be more of the same.

Saint-Malo and the Map

SAINT-MALO, FRANCE WAS our next stop. This seaport town was the scene of a major WWII battle. Strategically important as a potential landing site for men and supplies in the liberation of Europe, the 83rd Infantry was charged with taking the town from the Germans. Savage house-to-house fighting and fierce resistance by the Germans made this task extremely difficult.

We met our next tour guide here. Antoine Noslier is the 83rd expert in Brittany and quickly surprised us with a remarkable coincidence. Several years ago, Antoine explained, he purchased an old map on eBay that depicted the route of the 83rd Infantry through Europe from June 18, 1944, through May 1, 1945—Omaha Beach to Zerbst, Germany. It was obviously printed after the war, somewhere in Germany, and apparently was available to the soldiers of the 83rd. But this particular map was special. It was reverently displayed and featured, right across it the signature, "S/Sgt Myron H. Miller, Dixon, Missouri." His was among eleven signatures sprinkled across this very special map.

The map was a wonderful prologue for the tour of Saint-Malo, which started with a road that Antoine told us the 331st, 3rd Battalion, Company K, followed on its way into the city. More footsteps. Antoine pointed to a canal which cut through the flat coastal area and explained how the Germans had flooded the low-lying areas to inhibit the American troops from driving to Saint-Malo. The canal was much bigger in 1944, and the Americans had to cross the canal on boats or whatever they could find that would float. One story has soldiers crossing on a barn door improvised raft and Antoine pointed out locations where German tanks were positioned to stop the American advance.

We made our way into Paramé, a suburb of Saint-Malo, and were led down a street that was the scene of a famous photograph taken; it shows several soldiers peeking around a corner and moving across the street. This was the route Company L took during the advance. Company K was one street over when the photo was taken. We walked a block and once again were confronted by Dad's footsteps.

Another story in this book tells about Dad's buddy, Raymond Barnes, who was wounded at Saint-Malo. We hoped to find the spot where this happened so that we could share it with the Barnes family. We couldn't know the exact spot, but with Antoine's help, we did get within a block or two and knew that Dad and Raymond were together here for the last time in the war.

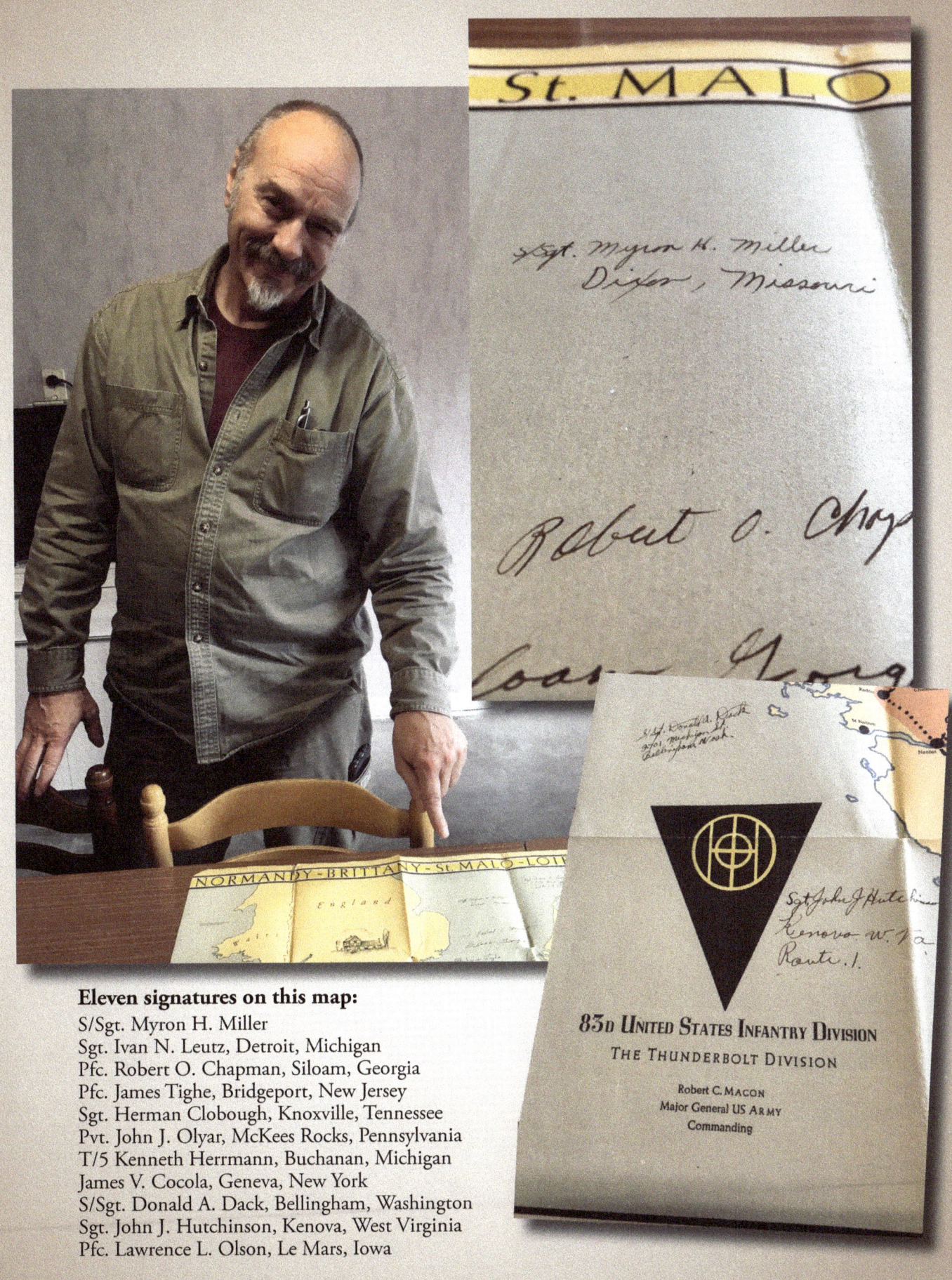

Eleven signatures on this map:
S/Sgt. Myron H. Miller
Sgt. Ivan N. Leutz, Detroit, Michigan
Pfc. Robert O. Chapman, Siloam, Georgia
Pfc. James Tighe, Bridgeport, New Jersey
Sgt. Herman Clobough, Knoxville, Tennessee
Pvt. John J. Olyar, McKees Rocks, Pennsylvania
T/5 Kenneth Herrmann, Buchanan, Michigan
James V. Cocola, Geneva, New York
S/Sgt. Donald A. Dack, Bellingham, Washington
Sgt. John J. Hutchinson, Kenova, West Virginia
Pfc. Lawrence L. Olson, Le Mars, Iowa

Honoring the Heroes

DAY THREE, WE WERE still a little jet-lagged but the adrenaline was pumping. The day was filled with ceremonies to honor the 72nd anniversary of D-Day.

The first was a brief ceremony at the Sainteny Cemetery honoring the citizens of the village and surrounding areas who lost their lives during the war. This ceremony was in French, so we depended on the universal language of tears and emotions. At the conclusion, we were introduced to Tom and Linda Thomason from Nashville, Tennessee. They too were following in the footsteps of Tom's father—an instant connection.

We moved on to a monument honoring 4th Infantry Division Major Richard J. O'Malley, who was killed in the liberation of Sainteny. Among other honorees were Jack Port, a veteran of the Battle for Sainteny and another member of the 4th Division, and several British veterans resplendent in their dress uniforms from 70 years ago. "The Star-Spangled Banner," "La Marseillaise", and "God Save the Queen" emphasized this solemn occasion. This was a big deal! We met two current members of the 4th Infantry Division who had been invited to witness the ceremony, and we discovered they had trained at Fort Leonard Wood, Missouri. One soldier's parents had lived a few minutes from Dixon, our hometown in central Missouri.

The entire assembly moved to a monument in the town square of Sainteny honoring the 83rd Infantry Division, Dad's unit. Jean Paul shared Dad's story—drafted and sent to France, where he joined the 83rd on July 21, 1944. Wounded in the Hurtgen Forest on December 16, 1944. His return to the 83rd in April of 1945. Discharged and home to marry our mother, Dolores and raise five children.

Jean Paul told the story of Tom Thomason's father, who also served in the 83rd Division. The ceremony ended with the town's children waving French and American flags and singing the French National Anthem, "La Marseillaise." We were surrounded by townspeople thanking us for coming to Sainteny and expressing how appreciative they were for the heroic actions our father and the 83rd Division did to liberate the town.

This incredible day continued with a champagne reception followed by a surprise three-course meal at Relais de Forges Bar. But our emotional day was not yet complete.

Returning to Auxais, we noticed a flurry of activity. A tent was being set up, and refreshments laid out. Once again, the little ceremony we were expecting was much grander than anticipated! Glyn had erected two monuments to honor members of the 83rd Infantry. The first was dedicated to Corporal J. J. Ricks of the 941st Field Artillery. The honor guard was made up of French military re-enactors. The mayor of Auxais read the dedication in French, my brother Del, translated in English. This touching event was yet another testimonial to what the American effort means to the French people.

In the second ceremony honoring the 83rd, Tom Thomason, Myra and I were honored to lay the wreath. The national anthems of the United States, Great Britain, and France were played again, followed by a moment of tearful silence. Myra looked out over the valley and saw movement. Walking up the wildflower-covered hill, like a scene from a movie, was a squad of American soldiers. Our British re-enactors had returned to surprise us.

We had expected to leave around 6:00 p.m. and drive to Germany, where a meeting with tour guide Willem was set for 10:00 A.M. But it was party time, and our timely exit wasn't going to happen. More than 90 people celebrated with us, including a group of Frenchmen dressed in vintage American uniforms, the British re-enactors and Brigitte, a former prisoner (as a small child) in a Japanese concentration camp.

The next surprise came with the roar of a 2½ ton GMC vintage cargo truck, compliments of the re-enactors. Myra, Del, Tom, Linda and I all piled in with several soldiers and took off. We headed to the Chateau de Auxais. We walked down a sunken road between the hedgerows and stopped at an old machine gun nest. Glyn's metal detector immediately started beeping, disclosing shell casings from 72 years ago. Finally, we climbed into the truck and headed back. The soulful sounds of a harmonica began to play, momentarily stunning us. Our Father had played the harmonica, and the sound hit us like a punch in the gut.

With great reluctance, we said our goodbyes and began our long drive to Germany. Our experience here will never be forgotten.

Gey and Kufferath

IN DECEMBER OF 1944, the 83rd Infantry traveled from the hedgerows of France to the forests of Northern Germany. The Hurtgenwald is a section of rugged terrain just outside of Aachen, Germany. The 83rd was tasked with advancing the Allied front into Germany.

The advance led through the little village of Gey (pronounced Guy) on the eastern edge of the Hurtgenwald. That's where we met Willem Doms, our expert on the 83rd activity in this area. Willem was accompanied by his fiancé, Vera, as well as Eric Thys and his wife, Nelly, who had driven from Belgium to join us. We would later meet their son, Jelle, another expert of the 83rd. After driving to the little village of Schevenhutte, Willem asked if we were ready for a little hike to the town of Gey, 3½ miles away.

As we hiked, Willem shared that in December of 1944 the 331st Regiment, 3rd Battalion, had moved straight down this road on its advance toward the German lines. It was warm and sunny for our trek. Not so in 1944. It was December, cold, wet and muddy. The 1944 road was little more than a couple of ruts running parallel through dense brush and trees. Complicating this march was the artillery being fired by the Germans at the American lines. Dad was walking into a bombardment that reduced the trees to stumps.

Halfway to Gey, Willem moved ahead to look over the terrain, and pointed to an area at the intersection of two roads. This V-shaped patch of ground about 50 yards on each side, was the location of K Company from December 7 to 11, 1944. As we walked through the trees, we noticed depressions in the ground—the foxholes K Company dug so many years before. A footstep. According to Willem, those four days in 1944 were anything but comfortable. The German shelling was almost constant, making it hard for the men to leave their foxholes. It was freezing, and on the 10th, it snowed. Finally, they got the order to move on to Gey.

We approached the town, just as our father had, and walked down the street into Gey. Here we met Willie Schumacher, a lifelong Gey resident who, as a 10-year old, was sent to central Germany as a refugee. He returned to Gey after the war and witnessed the devastation. Pointing, he told us the school was over there; the kids played over there, and over there is where a playmate was killed by a mine left over from the war.

Gey is much bigger today than in 1944, but many of the old buildings remain. After the war ended, many buildings were repaired using the very stones that had been blasted out of them. Many stones were marked where gunfire gouged out little craters in the walls.

Our next stop on this walking tour was Kufferath, a smaller village a couple of miles east of Gey. This stop was very important for our family. Years ago Dad had told us he was wounded while in a V-or L-shaped foxhole; while his companion had been killed by the mortar. Mom always thought it happened in Gey, but Willem determined that on December 16, 1944, Dad's Company had been sent to secure Kufferath.

We also discovered that American soldiers did not dig V-or L-shaped foxholes. The Germans dug zig-zag foxholes, which resembled the V or L shapes. Just outside of town, we were led up a hill where a grove of trees surrounded a line of zig-zagged foxholes. Company K had apparently advanced up this hill and used the abandoned German foxholes in which to hunker down. This might have been the spot were Dad was wounded. He never identified the soldier with him in that foxhole. Willem determined that the only soldier reported killed on that day from K Company was a Sgt. Joseph Ehmet. Though we'll never know for sure, he could have been the one in our father's foxhole.

After leaving Kufferath, we drove to Willem's house. Willem, Vera, and son David later told us about a war-time firefight that eventually made its way to the inside of their house. My brother, Ken, a gifted artist, sat at their kitchen table and sketched their home as it might have looked on that day in 1944, complete with Sherman tanks. This same story is depicted in the book Shavetail by William L Devitt, who was the lieutenant in charge of E Company's 3rd platoon of the 330th Regiment.

The next morning, we met Robert Hellwig, who recalled at age five hiding in the cellar with his mother as his village was shelled. He also explained how his dad was mortally wounded after the war when the tractor he was riding hit a left-over mine. Robert guided us through a local World War II museum displaying volumes of relics and artifacts.

We later traveled through the villages of Grosshau, Kleinhau and Vossenack before settling on Robert's patio where we enjoyed the opportunity to sample some fine German beer. A perfect ending to another emotional but satisfying day.

Remagan and Luxembourg

AFTER GEY WE TOOK a free day to explore, beginning with Remagan, a town on the Rhine River which was crucial in the Allied effort to bring a close to the war. The 83rd Infantry was not involved in taking the town and the famous bridge, but we wanted to see this historic location where American forces first crossed the Rhine on their way to Berlin.

In early 1945, the Allies were blocked by the Rhine. Up and down the river, the Germans had attempted to destroy every bridge. But on March 7th, scouts from the 89th Reconnaissance Squadron discovered the Ludendorff Bridge at Remagan still standing. Within hours, after suffering heavy casualties, the Allies took the bridge and were across the Rhine. Over the next two weeks, the Germans tried to destroy the bridge by artillery and planes, finally succeeding on March 17th when the weakened structure collapsed. But by that time, the Allies had secured the eastern bank of the Rhine.

Today, the town of Remagan sits quietly on the banks of the river. The Ludendorff bridge is long gone, while the massive bridge towers on each side of the river provide the only reminders of this crucial battle.

We left Germany and traveled to the town of Echternach, Luxembourg. This small city, located across the Moselle River from Germany, is the oldest city in Luxembourg. From the old abbey founded in 698 AD to the town square, we walked the maze of streets and marveled at the architecture, the quaint shops, and the old world feel of this beautiful city.

In tracing Dad's path, we realized the 83rd Division passed through here on the way to the Hurtgen Forest in November 1944. We followed the road along the Moselle for about 20 miles south to the village of Wormeldange. Dad had mentioned Wormeldange and Echternach but didn't pass on any details.

We stopped at a small gas station to get our bearings and determine our route to Luxembourg City. On one side was the river and the other a hill with a vineyard. It wasn't until our return home that Del discovered that hill was captured by Company K. This footstep we found all on our own.

We were lucky to find a campground with one available site north of Luxembourg City on the Sure River. Nestled between two pine-covered ridges, the beautiful River Sure flowed twenty feet from our motorhome.

In the morning, we visited the oldest castle in Luxembourg, Esch-sur-Sure. The first written evidence of this property dates back to October 773—a report that "Nebelungus" donated his properties and serfs to the abbey at Echternach. We climbed to the top of the ruins and looked out over the village. We saw the river that almost encircles the town, noticed the crumbling walls of the castle all around us, and observed the castle towers which appeared like sentinels guarding the village.

Leaving Luxembourg, we wished we had more time to explore and visit the ancient castles of the country known as Little Switzerland.

Battle of the Bulge

On December 16, 1944, the German Army made one last major effort to turn the tides of war and to at least salvage a negotiated surrender. That offensive is remembered as the Battle of the Bulge. The purpose was two-fold: to stop Allied transportation across the channel by capturing the port of Antwerp and to split the Allied armies in half so the Germans could encircle and destroy four different Armies. That result would have given Hitler the leverage to negotiate a peace treaty in Germany's favor.

The Germans completely fooled the Allied command with the surprise attack. The German units had driven deep into Luxembourg and Belgium before the Allies were able to stop the offensive. A couple of factors played into the Allied victory. One, the Germans could not maintain their supply lines and literally ran out of gas; and two, the Allies slowed the advance with several heroic stands. An example occurred around the crossroads of Bastogne, where the 101st Airborne Division, the 969th Artillery Battalion and elements of the 10th Armored Division staged

a legendary defense. When the German commander demanded that Brigadier General Anthony McAuliffe surrender he replied with the now famous quote, "Nuts." Cut off and alone; the American defenders held out against immense odds until the siege was broken.

We met Eddie Montfort, our 83rd Infantry expert in the Ardennes when we arrived at Bastogne. Joining us for the day were Eric and Jelle Thys, 83rd Infantry experts from Putte, Belgium. Dad's unit had passed through Bastogne briefly on its way to the Hurtgen Forest in November of 1944. The area at that time was securely in American hands, and there was no inkling the Germans were planning a surprise attack. It was while the first day of the Battle of the Bulge was fought that Dad was wounded. Subsequently, the 83rd was pulled out of Germany and repositioned north of Bastogne.

Eddie took us to the Battle of the Bulge Memorial outside of Bastogne. The magnificent structure, built in the shape of a star, features engravings of the then-48 states as well as the names and insignia of all the American units that participated in the Battle of the Bulge.

Traveling north out of Bastogne, we came to Malempre, Eddie's hometown. In December of 1944, the 83rd Division advanced on the German elements occupying the little village and ultimately liberated it. Now it was time for our next history lesson.

We climbed into Eddie's World War II vintage Dodge truck and toured the countryside. We drove through Foy, made famous in Band of Brothers, traveled down gravel roads and eventually arrived at Ottré. We stopped next to a field where Eddie noted the location where a famous photograph, "White Death" by Tony Vaccaro, was taken. The picture shows the body of Henry Tannenbaum half covered in snow after his squad was ambushed. Further on we saw a sign marking the location of the first V2 rocket launched by the Germans. Its destination—Paris.

Returning to Eddie's home, we learned about the liberation of Malempre. He told us how the 83rd held a position on the ridge behind his current home. He showed us where the Germans held the village. We heard first-hand from Eddie's father how, as a 10-year-old boy, he huddled in a cellar as shells thundered above him. He remembered that after the 83rd had driven the Germans out, the Americans built kitchens to feed the villagers. He remembered the burned out tanks, the devastation, and the joy of freedom.

Epilogue

AS THE JOURNEY DREW to a close, we drove to Putte, Belgium, to visit the Thys family—Eric, Nelly, and Jelle. We were invited to dinner and a tour of World War II sights around the city. They also showed us their collection of war memorabilia.

Jelle, now 22, had been interested in the history of World War II since he was eight years old. He has made considerable effort to meet with American veterans to study the personal side of the war. Jelle maintains a website for the 83rd Infantry Division Association Inc. at www.83rdassociation.com and has traveled to the United States to attend the 83rd Infantry convention at West Point. He has visited veterans in North Carolina, New Orleans, and Kansas, and he has adopted the graves of American soldiers interred in Belgium. He provides a remarkable example of how the people of Belgium, and all of Europe, appreciate the sacrifices of the American soldiers who liberated the continent from the Nazis.

Putte, Belgium, had set up a monument for Frank Klepper, a member of an anti-aircraft battalion who died while protecting the Port of Antwerp from the Luftwaffe. We visited the monument and the site of the anti-aircraft batteries and tried to imagine what it was like for the soldiers stationed here.

The final leg of our journey took us through Belgium and the French countryside en route to Paris and our flight home. We passed Waterloo and caught a glimpse of the battlefield where Napoleon was defeated in 1815. We saw road signs offering directions to the great battle sites of World War I and others to the battlefields of World War II. We remembered all the history lessons we experienced on our journey, lessons that helped us understand what everyone had been telling us for the previous ten days—NEVER FORGET.

June 1 to 10, 2016, was the experience of a lifetime. We met amazing people from France, Belgium, Germany, and Great Britain. We saw cities and countryside we had only read about in books or seen on television. But most of all, we followed in Dad's footsteps. No words can express our appreciation to all the friends who made this possible.

We thank you from the bottom of our hearts.

An Artist's View
by Ken Miller

AS NOTED IN THE Introduction, this book was from the beginning a *Let's-justdoit* kind of project that seems somewhat serendipitous. That is easy for me to say since the hard work of making this whole thing happen required much work on the part of Myra and Marshall, in particular. As the "official" artist for the project, I was allowed to take it one day at a time.

So Day One it seemed at least useful to make some paintings as gifts to all the great friends we had already made and were waiting for us. Since our efforts focused on our dad, Myron Miller, I decided some watercolors of the local Dixon, Missouri area that was familiar to him would be appropriate. Shown here are two paintings, for Glyn and Jean Paul. Our dad (with us!) raised Angus cattle, and his office as an agricultural lender was a few hundred yards from the Roubidoux Bridge.

One of the first places we visited was Auxais, France. The ruined church was within a mile of the place our dad joined Company K on July 21, 1944. The church, which was built in the tenth century, stands testament to the violent fighting which occurred. I added the Tiger tank, which we had seen in Brittany. Jean Paul later informed me that there were no Tiger tanks in Normandy at the time, so the picture couldn't be right. Lynette thinks the picture says something about peace and war, so I left it in. Later, Myra went back to Europe and presented a "corrected" Church of Auxais to their Mayor at a special ceremony! As an artist, you must get your details correct when it comes to the military.

Willem introduced us to Robert Hellwig who graciously shared his Hurtgenwald museum to us and took us to the military cemetery at Vossenack. Myra suggested I draw the contemporary/medieval statue at the cemetery entrance as a gift for Robert.

Our visit with Willem at his and Vera's house in Strauss offered a special opportunity. That very house was the scene of a small and terrifying battle. German troops had stopped a couple of American Sherman tanks by the house and occupied them and had fired on a platoon of unsuspecting Americans as they passed by, resulting in a battle that involved the entire grounds, including the interior of the house, as well. The Americans were ultimately victorious. The sketch was done over breakfast inside the house.

Eric and Jelle invited us to their house in Putte, Belgium where we were astonished by the professional quality museum this young man has created to honor the 83rd. Nelly prepared a beautiful dinner for us featuring a fantastic pasta dish with just-in-season white asparagus. While digesting that feast, I put this sketch in Jelle's guest book. The sketch is based on a photo in the 331st Regiment book *See it Through*, guys sawing wood to stay warm in the cold Hurtgen Forest.

One of the great surprises for me was fulfilling Glyn's request for a sketch of the soldiers, Captain Robert A. Mitchell, George P. Terhanko, and André G. Beaumont. Myra presented the picture to Glyn at the convention of the 83rd Infantry Division Association in Washington D.C. in July, 2016. It just happened that present at the convention was living veteran, André Beaumont, and the sons of Captain Robert A. Mitchell and George P. Terhanko. Here are the three holding my drawing (in that order). What a happy occasion!

Finally, here is a picture of one of David Pratt's reenactors from the UK whom we met at the great demonstration in Auxais. His friendly tip o' the helmet seems to sum it all up for me.

Examples of Ken's commissioned art can can be found on Facebook at Ken Miller Art Studio or on the Military Art tab, soldiersstoriesbook.com.

Index

Allen, William	252
Anschutz, Erich	208
Armontrout, Russell L.	89
Army Buddies - Mac and Bud	202
Ballard, Frank E.	300
Barnett, Jennings E.	180
Beam, Delmer R.	112
Beaumont, Andre G.	160
Bielen, Stanley P.	148
Boggs, Maxine	7
Boggs, Roy and Maxine	8
Boggs, Sr., Roy	6
Bottisham Airfield Museum	282
Bresser, Brigitte	84
Burr, Edward "Ned"	56
Byron, Robert J.	40
Carroll, John E.	135
Charles E. Harold	285
Chittenden, Lawrence L.	228
Clark, Dalton L.	258
Company K/331st - Honor Page	185
Cooper, Marion B.	81
Cowherd, Ernest E.	31
Coyle, Richard J. "Dick"	174
Crews, John C.	102
Curry, David	120
Curry, Thomas D.	121
Curtiss, Franklin P.	94
Davis, Sr., Charles T.	238
Deger, Everett C.	80
Denis, Eugene J.	41
Dickens, Walter	300
Dosch, George E.	216
Dudley, Jess and Winifred	279
Dudley, Jess F. "Jay"	276
Dudley, Winifred "Wee WAC"	280
Ehmet, Joseph E.	43
Enmeier, James M.	18
Faber, James F.	172
Fazzio, Richard	246
Fergusson, Robert C.	237
Foley, David V.	126
Frederickx, Georges	52
Freeman, Vinson and Flo	25
Garrett, James P.	88
Gates, Conrad L.	300
Gates, Myron C.	300
Gates, Rector K.	300
Geppert, Jr., William A. "Bill"	182
Godin, Eugene J.	188
Goff, James E.	24
Halladay, Daniel W.	54
Harmack, Eugene	25
Harmack, Eugene	107
Harold, Charles E.	285
Hauck Brothers	49
Hauck, Millard H.	48
Hickey, James R.	1
Horvath, Frank J.	248
Jenkins, Irvin "Bud"	300
Jenkins, Joseph B.	101
Jones, William G.	76
Kauffman, Robert K.	164
Kesten, Gervis H.	292
Kirby, Harry J.	110
Klepper, Frank A.	157
Kline, Hubert D.	244
Klugiewicz, Aloysius "Al"	163
Letters from My Uncles	170
Long, William I.	51
Malo, Normand R.	72
Martin, Morris W. "Lefty"	44
Mathena, Wilder C.	212
McDonald, Norvel A.	30
McHugh, Thomas L.	77
McNabb, James F. "Mac"	198
McNamara, Anne R. McClure	266
McNamara, John G. "Mac"	264
McNulty, Robert D.	36
Mensing, Roy "Bud"	186
Merrill, Harold L. "Bud"	204
Miller, Boyd H.	300
Miller, Dolores J. Gates	206
Miller, Myron H., Boxing	17
Miller, Myron H., Candy Bar	289
Miller, Myron H., Holocaust	29
Miller, Myron H., My Daddy	196
Miller, Myron H., My Grandpa	169
Miller, Myron H., P47s	137
Miller, Myron H., Patton	70
Miller, Myron H., Raymond Barnes	99
Miller, Myron H., Short Stories	82
Miller, Myron H., Short Stories	232
Miller, Myron H., Short Stories	274
Mills, Frank C.	66
Mitchell, Robert A.	220
Monfort, Alphonse	176
Moore, Kenneth	243
Mulford, Virgil D.	210
Oehmen, Henry C.	34
Op De Beeck, Joannes Jo. "Seppe"	154
Peloquin, Raymond H.	191
Pennebaker, Charles E.	37
Perko, Emil	25
Peterson, Harold D.	299
Port, Jack	10
Ransdall, William R.	47
Rickerson, Ralph M.	20
Riddle, Luther A.	285
Roberts, Claude K.	234
Rounds, Sr., Arlie	5
Rowden, Wilburn C.	58
Rudler, Charles E.	284
Schaeffer, Marvin J.	158
Schneider, Thomas	9
Shely, Jr., Floyd W. "Bill"	119
Shindledecker, Clyde F.	26
Shipley, Sr., Tom, Dragoon Map	92
Shipley, Sr., Tom, Normandy Map	90
Slade, Virgil W.	138
Smith, Everett "Smitty"	286
Smith, Jr., Harry L.	12
Sooter, Robert L.	299
Spriggs, William S. "Bill"	128
St. Clair, John F.	38
Stokes, James W.	259
Studor, George F.	260
Tannenbaum, Henry I.	290
Taylor, Clarence M.	32
Terhanko, George P.	224
Thomason, T.S.	275
Thornton, Orlan J.	22
Tribute Team - Western Europe	108
Turner, Carroll O.	146
West, Alva	62
West, Ethmer	64
Whetton, James J.	296
Wilkinson, Everett E. "Bud"	116
Withers, Ralph E.	256
Wohnhas, Paul	300
Wood, Jr., John A.	14
Young, George R.	2

Photo Credits

Photographs were reprinted with permission by the story submitters and photo credit was given if source was known..
Full page photo credits are as follows:

i	Soldier with Gun	Antony Burch	179	Malempré, Belgium	Myra Miller
1	Colleville-Sur-Mer	Myra Miller	194	Anti-tank	Antony Burch
16	Helmet in the Sand	Reg McHale	201	Following Footsteps	Myra Miller
28	Auschwitz	Liat Roth	223	Memorial	Gilles Billion
42	Chaplain and Medic	Antony Burch	230	Women in War	Antony Burch
97	Omaha Beach	Myra Miller	273	Nurses	Antony Burch
98	St. Malo Street	Myra Miller	293	A Kiss Goodbye	Antony Burch
136	Hedgerows	Reg McHale	296	Sons in the Footsteps	Myra Miller
166	Ghost Flyers	Antony Burch	304	Band of Brothers	Del Miller
168	Grandpa	Dolores Miller	306	Up the Hill	Glyn Nightingale

"Very, very highly recommended as a 'must have' acquisition for any library or individual professing any interest in World War II experiences and their lasting impact on individual lives and the world."
— D. Donovan, Senior Reviewer
Midwest Book Review

www.ingramcontent.com/pod-product-compliance
Lightning Source LLC
Chambersburg PA
CBHW041035020526
44118CB00043BA/2948